SECOND EDITION

SPANISH IS FUN

Lively Lessons for Advancing Students

Book 2

SECOND EDITION

SPANISH IS FUN

Lively Lessons for Advancing Students

Book 2

Heywood Wald, PhD

Former Assistant Principal,
Foreign Language Department
Martin Van Buren High School
New York City

AMSCO SCHOOL PUBLICATIONS, INC.
315 Hudson Street, New York, N.Y. 10013

Audio Program

An audio compact disc program with script to accompany Spanish Is Fun, Book 2, 2nd Edition is available separately from the publisher (ordering code N 325 CD). It is designed to reinforce the skills presented in the textbook and in the accompanying ancillaries. The voices are those of native speakers of Spanish.

Cover and text design by Merrill Haber

Text Illustrations by Ed Malsberg

Please visit our Web site at:
www.amscopub.com

When ordering this book, please specify:
either **R 325 P**
or SPANISH IS FUN, BOOK 2, 2nd Edition (Softbound)
R 325 H
or SPANISH IS FUN, BOOK 2, 2nd Edition (Hardbound)

ISBN: 978-1-56765-485-1 (Softbound)
ISBN: 978-1-56765-486-8 (Hardbound)

Printed in the United States of America

10 12

Preface

SPANISH IS FUN, BOOK 2 offers a program that makes language acquisition a natural, personalized, enjoyable, and rewarding experience. The book provides all the elements for a one-year course.

SPANISH IS FUN, BOOK 2 is designed to help students attain a desirable level of proficiency in the four basic skills—speaking, listening, reading, and writing—developed through simple materials in visually focused topical contexts that students can easily relate to their own experiences. Students are asked questions that require them to speak about their daily lives, express their opinions, and supply real information.

The **SECOND EDITION,** while retaining the proven organization and successful program of previous editions, has been strengthened in several ways:

1. A new introductory chapter serves as a diagnostic test, reviewing material usually covered during the first year of a Spanish-language course.
2. All lesson materials are built on a clearly focused content topic.
3. Each lesson follows a consistent program sequence.
4. Many exercises are presented in a communicative framework, with greater emphasis on personalized communication.
5. Situational conversations and dialog exercises in cartoon-strip fashion are included in every lesson.
6. New and updated Cápsula Cultural sections follow each lesson, with comprehension questions.
7. A new chapter on "La ecología" (ecology) introduces the present-subjunctive tense and contributes to a more varied list of topics.
8. A new Appendix containing "Cosas de la lengua," introduces additional linguistic material that will discuss topics like noun formation, proverbs, onomatopeia, and other interesting topics.
9. A separate **CUADERNO DE EJERCICIOS** provides additional practice.
10. A new audio program to supplement the **SECOND EDITION** is available separately.

SPANISH IS FUN, BOOK 2 consists of five parts. Each part ends with a Repaso (Review), in which each structure is recapitulated and practiced through various Actividades. These include games and puzzles, as well as more conventional exercises.

Each lesson includes a step-by-step sequence of elements designed to make the materials immediately accessible as well as give students the feeling that they can have fun learning and practicing their Spanish.

VOCABULARY

Each lesson begins with topically related sets of drawings that convey the meanings of new words in Spanish without recourse to English. This device enables students to make a direct and vivid association between the Spanish terms and their meanings. The exercises also use pictures to practice Spanish words and expressions.

To facilitate comprehension, the book uses cognates of English words wherever suitable. Beginning a course in this way shows the students that Spanish is not so "foreign" after all and helps them overcome any fears they may have about the difficulty of learning a foreign language.

STRUCTURES

SPANISH IS FUN, BOOK 2 uses a simple, straightforward, guided presentation of new structural elements. These elements are introduced in small learning components at a time—and are directly followed by appropriate Actividades, many of them visually cued, personalized, and communicative. Students thus gain a feeling of accomplishment and success by making their own discoveries and formulating their own conclusions.

DIALOGUES

To encourage students to use Spanish for communication and self-expression, each lesson includes a Diálogo—sometimes practical, sometimes humorous conversations which students complete by filling empty "balloons" with appropriate bits of information. These dialogues serve as springboards for additional personalized conversation.

READING

Each lesson contains a short, entertaining narrative or playlet that features new structural elements and vocabulary and reinforces previously learned grammar and expressions. These passages deal with topics that are related to the everyday experiences of today's student generation. Cognates and near-cognates are used extensively.

CULTURE

Each lesson is followed by a Cápsula Cultural. These twenty-one cultural notes offer students picturesque views and insights into well-known and not so well-known aspects of Hispanic culture.

CUADERNO

SPANISH IS FUN, BOOK 2 has a companion workbook, **CUADERNO DE EJERCICIOS,** which features additional writing practice and stimulating puzzles to supplement the textbook exercises.

TEACHER'S MANUAL AND KEY

A separate Teacher's Manual and Key provides suggestions for teaching all elements in the book, additional oral practice materials, two achievement tests, and a complete Key to all exercises, puzzles, and quizzes.

AUDIO PROGRAM

An audio program on compact discs (CDs), available separately with corresponding script from the publisher, includes for each lesson oral exercises, the narrative or playlet, questions or completions, and the conversation, all with appropriate pauses for response or repetition.

The Author

Contents

TERCERA PARTE

CUARTA PARTE

El mundo hispánico

Spanish America

What is Spanish America? Ask an American to give you an example of a country or place where there are Hispanic people, and the answer is likely to be Mexico, Cuba, or Puerto Rico. That would be a correct and logical answer, of course, because of the more than ten million United States citizens who originally came from those countries.

Spanish America is a lot more, however. In the vast area south of the United States there are eighteen independent Spanish-speaking countries. Together with Spain and Puerto Rico, these countries cover over sixteen percent of the surface of the Earth, with a growing population of over a quarter of a billion people. Spanish is, after English, the most widely used language in the world today.

Let's take a quick bird's-eye view of the Spanish-speaking world. First, there is Mexico, our immediate neighbor to the south, with a population of over eighty million people and an area approximately one-fourth that of the United States.

To the south of Mexico is Central America, with its six Spanish-speaking countries: Guatemala, Costa Rica, El Salvador, Honduras, Nicaragua, and Panama.

East of Mexico and Central America is the Caribbean Sea, with the Spanish-speaking countries of Cuba, the Dominican Republic, and Puerto Rico.

Finally, there is the vast continent of South America, with nine Spanish-speaking countries: Argentina, Bolivia, Colombia, Chile, Ecuador, Peru, Paraguay, Uruguay, and Venezuela. The largest of these countries, Argentina, is one-third the size of the United States.

These countries and their peoples cover a wide spectrum of cultures, climates, races, and human experiences. Together they make up *Hispanoamérica.*

Review Exercises of Level 1

A. Definite Articles (**el, la, los, las**); Indefinite Articles (**un, unos, una, unas**)

Fill in the correct definite and indefinite articles. Form contractions when necessary.

1. Hay ________ vaso en la cocina.
   (*a*)

2. El precio ________ libro no es alto.
   (*of the*)

3. No tenemos ________ dinero de Pedro.
   (*the*)

4. ________ libros están en la biblioteca.
   (*the*)

5. ________ fruta es roja.
   (*the*)

6. Quiero comprar ________ lámpara.
   (*a*)

7. Voy ________ la casa ahora.
   (*to the*)

8. Nueva York es ________ ciudad grande.
   (*a*)

9. El invierno es ________ estación fría.
   (*the*)

10. Deseo comprar ________ zapatos nuevos.
    (*some*)

11. El color ________ flores es bonito.
    (*of the*)

12. ______________ padres de Anita trabajan en la oficina.
(*the*)

13. Son ______________ lecciones más difíciles.
(*the*)

14. Llevo la medicina ______________ hospital.
(*to the*)

15. María va al cine con ______________ amigas.
(*some*)

B. Negative and Interrogative Sentences

Make the following sentences negative.

1. Mi mamá prepara la comida. ______________
2. Carlos es un amigo de la familia. ______________
3. Los abuelos son viejos. ______________
4. Quiero comprar un periódico. ______________
5. El dormitorio tiene dos camas. ______________

Change the following sentences into questions.

1. El alumno contesta bien. ______________
2. Usted habla francés. ______________
3. Tú comprendes la lección. ______________
4. La bandera es azul. ______________
5. Ellos viven en Puerto Rico. ______________

C. Subject Pronouns

Complete the following sentences with the appropriate Spanish subject pronouns.

1. ______________ tengo zapatos negros.
(*I*)

2. ______________ trabajamos en una fábrica.
(*we,* feminine)

3. ______________ estudia todos los días.
(*she*)

4. ______________ son norteamericanas.
(*they,* feminine)

5. ¿Habla ______________ inglés?
(*you,* formal singular)

6. ______________ contestamos correctamente.
(*we,* masculine)

7. ¿Sabemos ______________ bailar?
(*we*)

8. ______________ no desean ir a la escuela.
(*they,* masculine plural)

9. ¿Comprenden ______________ las lecciones?
(*you,* formal plural)

10. ¿No tienes ______________ hambre?
(*you,* informal singular)

D. Present Tense of Regular Verbs

Complete the sentences with the appropriate form of the verb in parentheses.

-AR Verbs

1. Yo ______________ a mis abuelos en la ciudad.
(visitar)

2. ¿Cuándo ______________ tú en la clase?
(entrar)

3. ¿No ______________ Uds. mucha televisión?
(mirar)

4. María ______________ las lecciones.
(practicar)

5. Nosotros no ______________ la radio.
(escuchar)

-ER Verbs

1. ¿ ________________ el niño el ejercicio?
(aprender)

2. Ellos ________________ mucha soda.
(beber)

3. ¿ ________________ Ud. carne o pescado?
(comer)

4. Yo ________________ correctamente.
(responder)

5. ¿ ________________ tú la bicicleta?
(vender)

-IR Verbs

1. ¿ ________________ Uds. en español?
(escribir)

2. La chica ________________ en un apartamento.
(vivir)

3. Nosotras ________________ la puerta del garaje.
(abrir)

4. Mi hermano ________________ buenas notas.
(recibir)

5. Los científicos ________________ cosas importantes.
(descubrir)

E. Preterit Tense of Regular Verbs

Complete the following sentences with the appropriate form of the verbs in the preterit tense.

-AR Verbs

1. Yo ________________ a mis abuelos en la ciudad.
(visitar)

2. ¿Cuándo ________________ tú en la clase?
(entrar)

3. ¿No ________________ Uds. mucha televisión?
(mirar)

4. María ______________ las lecciones.
(practicar)

5. Nosotros no ______________ la radio.
(escuchar)

-ER Verbs

1. ¿ ______________ el niño el ejercicio?
(aprender)

2. Ellos ______________ mucha soda.
(beber)

3. ¿ ______________ Ud. carne o pescado?
(comer)

4. Yo ______________ correctamente.
(responder)

5. ¿ ______________ tú la bicicleta?
(vender)

-IR Verbs

1. ¿ ______________ Uds. en español?
(escribir)

2. La chica ______________ en un apartamento.
(vivir)

3. Nosotras ______________ la puerta del garaje.
(abrir)

4. Mi hermano ______________ buenas notas.
(recibir)

5. Los científicos ______________ cosas importantes.
(descubrir)

F. Present Tense of Irregular Verbs

Complete each sentence with the appropriate form of the verb in parentheses.

1. Yo ______________ pan en casa.
(tener)

2. Nosotros ______________ al aeropuerto.
(ir)

3. ¿__________ Ud. comer ahora?
(querer)

4. Yo siempre __________ la verdad.
(decir)

5. ¿Me __________ Ud. el dinero para la cena?
(dar)

6. ¿Qué __________ Uds. en el verano?
(hacer)

7. Yo __________ la leche en el café.
(poner)

8. Francisco __________ la respuesta.
(saber)

9. ¿Cuándo __________ tú para México?
(salir)

10. Yo __________ la música a la fiesta.
(traer)

11. Mi papá __________ policía.
(ser)

12. Yo __________ contento ahora.
(estar)

13. ¿Cuántos años __________ Ud.?
(tener)

14. Yo __________ a San Juan esta noche.
(ir)

15. ¿Qué __________ Uds.?
(decir)

16. Yo __________ el regalo a mi hermano.
(dar)

17. Él no __________ estudiante.
(ser)

18. ¿Cómo __________ (tú), Pablito?
(estar)

19. Yo ________________ de la escuela a las tres.
(salir)

20. Yo no ________________ la respuesta.
(saber)

G. Uses of **ser** and **estar**

1. María ________________ panameña.
(es / está)

2. Yo ________________ de los Estados Unidos.
(soy / estoy)

3. ¿Cómo ________________ Uds. hoy?
(son / están)

4. Ellos ________________ amigos.
(son / están)

5. Madrid ________________ en España.
(es / está)

6. Tú no ________________ pobre.
(eres / estás)

7. El autor ________________ escribiendo otro libro.
(es / está)

8. Yo ________________ triste.
(soy / estoy)

9. Mis hermanas ________________ altas.
(son / están)

10. Nosotros ________________ estudiantes.
(somos / estamos)

H. Cardinal Numbers

Write out each number in Spanish.

1. Tengo ________________ dólares.
(50)

2. Hay ________________ meses en un año.
(12)

3. Una semana tiene ___Siete___ días.
(7)

4. En un minuto hay ___sesenta___ segundos.
(60)

5. El día tiene ___veinti-cuatro___ horas.
(24)

6. En un siglo hay ___cien___ años.
(100)

7. Quince por dos son ___treinta___.
(30)

8. Ochenta menos diez es ___setenta___.
(70)

9. Una docena es más que ___once___.
(11)

10. Mi padre tiene ___cuarenta___ años.
(40)

I. Telling Time

Complete each of the following time expressions in Spanish.

1. Es la ___una___.
(1:00)

2. Son las ___dos y media___.
(2:30)

3. El tren llega a las ___medianoche___.
(12:00 midnight)

4. Voy a casa a las ___tres y cuarto___.
(3:15 P.M.)

5. Miro la televisión a las ___diez por la noche___.
(10:00 P.M.)

6. Salgo a la ___uno y media___.
(1:30 P.M.)

7. ¿Qué hora es? — Son las siete menos cuarto.
(*6:45 A.M.*)

8. Las clases terminan a las cuatro y veinte.
(*4:20*)

9. Hay una película a las ocho.
(*8:00 P.M.*)

10. Es media día.
(*12:00 noon*)

J. Weather Expressions

Complete all of the following sentences in Spanish.

1. ¿Felipe, ______________________ hoy?
(*how is the weather*)

2. En marzo ______________________ .
(*it's windy*)

3. ¿Cuándo ______________________ ?
(*is it sunny*)

4. ______________________ en el invierno.
(*It's cold*)

5. En el otoño ______________________ .
(*it's cool*)

6. En Miami ______________________ .
(*it's hot*)

7. ______________________ mucho en Alaska.
(*It snows*)

8. Cuando ______________________ voy al cine.
(*it rains*)

9. Generalmente ______________________ en la primavera.
(*it's good weather*)

10. No salgo de la casa cuando ______________________ .
(*it's bad weather*)

K. Descriptive Adjectives

Complete each sentence with the appropriate form of the adjective in parentheses.

EXAMPLE: Las rosas son plantas ______________ .
(bonito)

Las rosas son plantas **bonitas.**

1. Yo conozco muchas canciones ______________ .
(popular)

2. Las lecciones no son ______________ .
(difícil)

3. Hay muchachas ______________ en el equipo de básquetbol.
(alto)

4. Nuestro presidente es ______________ .
(joven)

5. Puerto Rico tienes muchas flores ______________ .
(tropical)

6. La Casa ______________ es un edificio importante.
(Blanco)

7. Los gatos son animales ______________ .
(pequeño)

8. En la universidad hay estudiantes ______________ .
(inteligente)

9. Es una actriz ______________ .
(español)

10. Los abuelos son muy ______________ .
(viejo)

L. Demonstrative Adjectives

Complete the following expressions using **este, esta, estos, estas**, or **ese, esa, esos,** and **esas**.

1. this book ____________ libro
2. that lamp ____________ lámpara
3. these houses ____________ casas
4. those desks ____________ escritorios

5. this kitchen ____________ cocina
6. that shoe ____________ zapato
7. these ties ____________ corbatas
8. those pages ____________ páginas
9. this song ____________ canción
10. that automobile ____________ automóvil

M. Possessive Adjectives

Complete the following expressions using **mi(s), tu(s), su(s),** or **nuestro(-a, -os, -as).**

1. my mistake ____________ falta
2. your (inf. sing.) paper ____________ papel
3. his dentist ____________ dentista
4. her bicycle ____________ bicicleta
5. their teacher ____________ profesor
6. our dog ____________ perro
7. my classes ____________ clases
8. our beaches ____________ playas
9. your (formal) garden ____________ jardín
10. his pants ____________ pantalones

N. **Gustar** (to like)

Express the following English sentences in Spanish, using **me gusta(n), te gusta(n), le gusta(n), nos gusta(n),** or **les gusta(n).**

1. I like the flowers. ______ ________________ las flores.
2. I like the food. ______ ________________ la comida.
3. Do you (inf. sing.) like to sing? ¿ ______ ________________ cantar?
4. She likes the winter. ______ ________________ el invierno.
5. You (formal sing.) like fresh air. ______ ________________ el aire fresco.

6. We like the mountains. ______ ________________ las montañas.

7. We like the country. ______ ________________ el campo.

8. They like the library. ______ ________________ la biblioteca.

9. Do you (plural) like the heat? ¿ ______ ________________ el calor?

10. He likes the furniture. ______ ________________ los muebles.

O. Prepositions

Change the English expression to Spanish, using the appropriate preposition. Use **al** and **del** when necessary.

1. near the house ________________ la casa
2. around the park ________________ el parque
3. under the tree ________________ el árbol
4. in front of the cars ________________ los automóviles
5. behind the garage ________________ el garaje
6. on the table ________________ la mesa
7. above the building ________________ el edificio
8. far from the city ________________ la ciudad
9. opposite the library ________________ la biblioteca
10. through the factory ________________ la fábrica

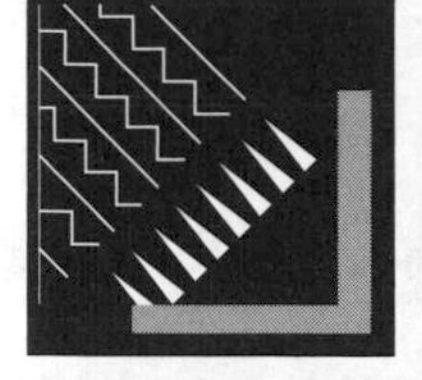

Primera Parte

1

La naturaleza

Interrogative Words: CONOCER and SABER

1 Vocabulario

ACTIVIDAD A

Consult the picture at the beginning of the lesson. Name some of the things found in nature and describe some of the activities that can be done at Villa Hermosa.

En Villa Hermosa la vida es buena. Venga a pasar sus vacaciones aquí, donde disfrutará

____

____

____

____

____

A tour guide is talking to a group of visitors about a trip they're about to take. Read the dialog, paying special attention to the questions.

2 Did you notice the interrogative words **qué** and **cuál(es)** in the dialog between the tour guide and the tourists?

> **¿*Qué* cosas quieren ver?**
>
> **¿*Qué* sitios típicos . . .?**
>
> **¿*Cuáles* son los sitios . . .?**
>
> **¿*Cuáles* son sus intereses?**

Qué and **cuál(es)** both mean *what* or *which.*

Before a form of the verb **ser**, **qué** is used when asking for a definition and **cuál** when asking for a choice.

> NOTE: **Qué** never changes, but **cuál** has a plural form: **cuáles**, when referring to more than one.

Let's look at a few more examples:

¿*Qué* es la Casa Blanca?	*What is the White House?* (definition)
¿*Cuál* es la Casa Blanca?	*Which (one) is the White House?* (choice)

¿Cuál es tu carro?
Este carro, por supuesto

Before verbs other than **ser**, **qué** is used; unless choice (*which one*, *which ones*) is clearly indicated.

¿*Qué* pasa?	*What's going on?*
¿*Qué* dice Ud.?	*What are you saying?*
¿*Qué* quiere?	*What do you want?*
¿*Cuál* quiere?	*Which one do you want?*

Before a noun **qué** is used.

¿*Qué* libro quiere Ud.? *What book do you want?*

3 Un programa de televisión

MC: Buenas noches, amables televidentes. Yo soy su maestro de ceremonias, Baldomero Bocagrande. Bienvenidos a nuestro programa «¿Conoce Ud. a su marido?» Las reglas del concurso son fáciles. Hacemos diez preguntas a una mujer. Ya sabemos las respuestas de su marido. Si las respuestas de los dos son iguales, el matrimonio puede ganar hasta un total de mil dólares, cien dólares por cada respuesta correcta.

Y ahora, vamos a comenzar con nuestra primera concursante, María López. ¿Cómo está, María? Tenemos una serie de preguntas para Ud. La primera pregunta es: ¿Sabe Ud. cuál es la actividad preferida de su marido?

MARÍA: Sí, él prefiere ir al campo.

MC: Muy interesante. ¿Por qué?

MARÍA: Porque le gustan la naturaleza, el sol, el aire fresco, la hierba, los árboles.

MC: ¿Cuáles son algunas de sus cosas favoritas en el campo?

MARÍA: A él le gustan las flores—las rosas y las violetas en particular.

MC: ¿Adónde van Uds. cuando no pueden ir al campo?

el / la televidente *TV viewer*
el maestro de ceremonias *master of ceremonies*
bienvenidos *welcome*
el marido *husband*
el concurso *contest*

los dos *both*
igual(es) *the same*
el matrimonio *married couple*

el / la concursante *contestant*

MARÍA: Vamos al Jardín Botánico o al parque.
MC: ¿Cuál es su parque preferido?
MARÍA: El Parque Bolívar en el centro.
MC: ¿Cuánto cuesta la entrada?
MARÍA: No cuesta nada. Es gratis.
MC: ¿Cuántas veces al año va al campo?
MARÍA: Dos o tres.
MC: Y, ¿cuándo van al parque?
MARÍA: Los fines de semana.
MC: ¿Quiénes van con Uds. generalmente?
MARÍA: Nuestros hijos.
MC: ¿Qué hacen Uds. después?
MARÍA: Vamos a un restaurante a comer, y luego, a casa.
MC: Damas y caballeros, esto es fantástico, sensacional. ¡Un aplauso para María! Sus diez respuestas son exactamente iguales a las de su marido. Felicitaciones, Uds. son un matrimonio perfecto. De veras, María, Ud. conoce muy bien a su marido, Manuel López.
MARÍA: ¿Cómo? Manuel López no es mi marido. Es el marido de la otra concursante.

damas y caballeros *ladies and gentleman*
felicitaciones *congratulations*
de veras *really*
¿cómo? *eh?, what was that?*

ACTIVIDAD B

Answer the questions with complete sentences.

1. ¿Quién es Baldomero Bocagrande?

   ____

2. ¿Qué tipo de programa es «¿Conoce Ud. a su marido?»?

   ____

3. ¿Cuántas preguntas tiene que contestar María?

   ____

4. ¿Cuánto dinero pueden ganar los concursantes?

   ____

5. ¿Por qué le gusta el campo al marido de María?

   ____

6. ¿Cuál es el parque favorito de los López?

____

7. ¿Dónde queda?

____

8. ¿Cuándo salen a comer?

____

9. ¿Adónde van después de comer en el restaurante?

____

10. ¿Quién es Manuel López?

____

ACTIVIDAD C

Work with a partner. One student completes the questions with the word **qué** or **cuál(es)**. The other student answers the guest in a complete Spanish sentence.

1. ¿Cuáles flores le gustan a Ud.?
2. ¿Cuál es su fruta favorita?
3. ¿Qué es un diccionario?
4. ¿Qué es la capital de España?
5. ¿Cuáles son las atracciones de una ciudad?
6. ¿Qué es un insecto beneficioso?
7. ¿Cuál parque prefiere Ud.?
8. ¿En cuál ciudad vive Ud.?
9. ¿Qué son las mariposas?
10. ¿Cuáles son tres bebidas populares?

4 Did you notice all the interrogative expressions in the story in Section 3? What do all question words have in common? __________ If you answered an accent mark, you are correct. **Qué**, **por qué**, **cómo**, **cuándo**, **adónde**, and **dónde** never change. **Quién** has a plural form, **quiénes**, to ask about more than one person. **Cuánto** functions as an adjective and thus agrees in gender and number when a noun follows:

¿Cuánto dinero tienes?	*How much money do you have?*
¿Cuánta carne quieres?	*How much meat do you want?*
¿Cuántos libros lees?	*How many books are you reading?*
¿Cuántas respuestas sabes?	*How many answers do you know?*

ACTIVIDAD D

*

Complete the following questions using the appropriate interrogative word.

1. ¿ Cuántas casas hay en la avenida?
(Cuántas, Cuánto)

2. ¿ Cuál de los dos quiere comprar Ud.?
(Cuál, Qué)

3. ¿ Qué es un circo?
(Cuál, Qué)

4. ¿ Cómo está su papá?
(Cómo, Por qué)

5. ¿ Dónde hace mucho calor?
(Dónde, Cuántos)

6. ¿ Adónde van los autobuses?
(Adónde, Dónde)

7. ¿ Cuántas personas viven en California?
(Cuánta, Cuántas)

8. ¿ Por qué dice Ud. eso?
(Qué, Por qué)

9. ¿ Cuándo vas al cine?
(Cuándo, Cuánto)

10. ¿ Quién quiere mirar el programa?
(Quién, Cuál)

ACTIVIDAD E

Work with a partner. One student completes the question with the proper interrogative word. The other student answers in a complete sentence.

1. ¿ ____________ es el maestro/la maestra de la clase de español? (*who*)

   ____

2. ¿ ____________ quiere ir Ud. después de las clases? (*where*)

   ____

3. ¿ ____________ no come Ud. afuera? (*why*)

   ____

4. ¿ ____________ dinero tiene Ud. en el banco? (*how much*)

   ____

5. ¿ ____________ es un diccionario? (*what*)

   ____

6. ¿ ____________ van a salir de la escuela? (*when*)

   ____

7. ¿ ____________ hijos tienen tus padres? (*how many*)

   ____

8. ¿ ____________ trabajan los sábados? (*who*)

   ____

9. ¿ ____________ es la capital de Puerto Rico? (*what*)

   ____

10. ¿ ____________ queda su restaurante favorito? (*where*)

    ____

5

Two other expressions to obtain information are formed with the word **quién(es)**: **a quién(es)** (whom?) and **de quién(es)** (whose?). Look at the following examples:

***¿A quién* ves?**	*Whom do you see?*
Veo a Juan.	*I see Juan.*

***¿De quién* es el libro?**	*Whose book is it?*
El libro es de Carlos.	*It is Carlos's book.*

Note that if you respond to the question **¿A quién(es) . . .?**, **a** must come after the verb in your answer. If you respond to the question **¿De quién(es) . . .?**, **de** must come after the verb **ser** in your answer.

ACTIVIDAD F

Tell us about yourself by answering the following questions in Spanish.

1. ¿Quién prepara la comida en su casa?

____

2. ¿Quiénes son sus actores favoritos?

____

3. ¿De quién es la casa donde vive Ud.?

____

4. ¿A quién quiere visitar Ud. en las vacaciones?

____

5. ¿A quiénes va a invitar a su fiesta de cumpleaños?

____

6. ¿De quién es Ud. amigo(-a) en su clase?

____

The TV show you read about in Section 3 is called **¿Conoce Ud. a su marido?** (*Do you know your husband?*) One of the questions was **¿Sabe Ud. cuál es su comida favorita?** (*Do you know which is his favorite food?*) Both verbs, **conocer** and **saber**, mean *to know.* Both have an irregular **yo** form in the present tense.

yo	***conozco***	***sé***
tú	**conoces**	**sabes**
Ud., él, ella	**conoce**	**sabe**
nosotros, -as	**conocemos**	**sabemos**
Uds., ellos, ellas	**conocen**	**saben**

When do you use **conocer** and when do you use **saber**? Let's look at some examples:

> ***Conozco* a Miguel, pero no *sé* donde vive.**
>
> *I know (am acquainted with) Miguel,*
> *but I don't know where he lives.*
>
> **¿Conoces ese restaurante? ¿Sabes si es caro?**
>
> *Do you know (are you familiar with) that restaurant?*
> *Do you know if it's expensive?*

Can you see the difference? **Conocer** is always used in the sense of *to be acquainted with, to be familiar with something or somebody*. **Saber** means *to know facts, to have knowledge or information about something*. **Saber** can not be used with nouns that refer to people or places. When **saber** is followed by an infinitive, it means *to know how to*.

> **¿Sabes preparar comida mexicana?**
>
> *Do you know how to prepare Mexican food?*

ACTIVIDAD G

Complete the following sentences with the correct form of **saber** or **conocer**.

1. Yo ______________ que su mamá no está en casa.
2. ¿______________ Uds. A Felipe?
3. ¿______________ Ud. dónde vive el presidente?
4. Yo no ______________ contestar la pregunta.
5. Yo ______________ bien esta ciudad.
6. ¿______________ Ud. al señor Pérez?
7. ¿______________ Uds. a qué hora termina la clase?
8. Yo no ______________ cómo se llama el profesor nuevo.
9. Nosotros no ______________ esa novela.
10. ¿______________ tú si la puerta está cerrada?

Preguntas Personales

1. ¿Cuál es tu programa de televisión favorito? ¿Por qué?

____

2. ¿Cuándo vas al cine?

____

3. ¿Qué tipo de comida te gusta?

____

4. ¿Cuáles son tus restaurantes preferidos?

____

5. ¿Adónde vas generalmente cuando hace calor?

____

Información Personal

You have just been selected to serve as "**maestro de ceremonias**" for your class's TV quiz show. Prepare five questions you would ask one of the contestants.

1. _______________
2. _______________
3. _______________
4. _______________
5. _______________

Composición

You are writing an article for the school paper profiling a "typical" student. What are some of the questions you might ask the students?

Diálogo

You are an investigator getting information from a client. Can you ask the right questions for the answers you are given?

CÁPSULA CULTURAL

Los insectos son buenos para su salud (¡Y son deliciosos!)

¿Comería Ud. insectos? Antes de contestar, considere esto: en muchas partes de Hispanoamérica, y en el mundo entero, los insectos son considerados una golosina.

Por ejemplo, muchos bolivianos comen hormigas tostadas; en el norte del Perú los niños esperan las lluvias, que traen las sisapas, hormigas gigantes de casi dos pulgadas de largo y que se comen crudas. En las calles de la Ciudad de México, si ves a un vendedor con bolsitas de papel, gritando: —«chapulines, chapulines»— ¡él vende saltamontes fritos!

Muchos insectos tienen un alto valor nutritivo. Contienen vitaminas, minerales y pueden contener setenta por ciento de proteína. Muchos especialistas en nutrición dicen que es mejor recibir los nutrientes de un alimento fresco y natural que de un alimento artificial o de una píldora de vitaminas. ¿No está convencido? Pues, ¿le gustan los mariscos? ¿Ha comido langosta, camarones o cangrejos? Estos mariscos populares son crustáceos y pertenecen a la misma clase de animales que los insectos. A veces los llaman «insectos del mar». Entonces, comer una langosta no es muy diferente de comer un grillo o una oruga.

comería *would you eat*
la golosina *delicacy*
la pulgada *inch*
crudo *raw*
la bolsita *small bag*
la píldora *pill*
el camarón *shrimp*
el cangrejo *crab*
pertenecer *to belong*
los llaman *they are called*
la langosta *lobster*
el grillo *cricket*
la oruga *caterpillar*

Para pensar

1. ¿Cuáles son algunos insectos consumidos como alimentos?
2. Describa el valor nutritivo de los insectos.
3. ¿Qué son los crustáceos? Mencione algunos ejemplos.
4. ¿Qué diferencia hay entre un saltamontes y una langosta o un cangrejo?
5. ¿Serán los insectos una fuente de alimento en el futuro? ¿Por qué (no)?

2
En la playa

Stem-Changing Verbs

1 Vocabulario

Actividad: F, G, J, K, L

ACTIVIDAD A

Las seis diferencias The following two pictures were taken at the beach. In the second one, there are six items missing. In Spanish, tell which items are missing.

____

____

____

____

____

____

ACTIVIDAD B

Here's a happy beach scene. But there's been a nasty rumor that *a shark* (**un tiburón**) has been seen in the vicinity. You've been sent by the local newspaper to report on the situation. Describe the scene and tell a story about what you see.

____

____

____

____

____

____

You are at the beach with a group of your friends. Read the dialog and see if you can find all forms of the verbs **querer** (*to want*) and **poder** (*to be able to, can*).

2 Now that you've seen **querer** and **poder** in action, can you fill in the correct forms of the verbs in the box below?

	querer	**poder**
yo	______________	______________
tú	______________	______________
Ud., él, ella	______________	______________
nosotros, -as	______________	______________
Uds., ellos, ellas	______________	______________

What happened to the stem of the verb **querer**? The **e** changed to ______ in all forms except for **nosotros**. What happened to the stem of the verb **poder**? The **o** changed to ______ in all forms except for **nosotros**.

3 There are other verbs that undergo the same changes. We identify them in the vocabulary at the end of the book like this: **empezar (ie)** *(to begin)*, **mover (ue)** *(to move)*. Now let's see some more examples. Can you complete the boxes below?

e to ie	**pensar** (*to think*)	**perder** (*to lose*)	**mentir** (*to lie*)
yo	**p*ie*nso**	______	______
tú	**p*ie*nsas**	______	______
Ud., él, ella	**p*ie*nsa**	______	______
nosotros, -as	**pensamos**	______	______
Uds., ellos, ellas	**p*ie*nsan**	______	______

o to **ue**	**almorzar** (*to have lunch*)	**volver** (*to come back*)	**dormir** (*to sleep*)
yo	**alm*ue*rzo**	______	______
tú	**alm*ue*rzas**	______	______
Ud., él, ella	**alm*ue*rza**	______	______
nosotros, -as	**almorzamos**	______	______
Uds., ellos, ellas	**alm*ue*rzan**	______	______

RULE: Stem changing **-ar** and **-er** verbs change **e** to **ie** and **o** to **ue** in all forms of the present tense, except **nosotros**.

Everyone likes to do something different. What do the students in the class prefer?

EXAMPLE: **Carlos *prefiere* nadar.**

1. Yo ________________ dormir.
2. Tú ________________ ir al cine.
3. Ellos ________________ comer.
4. Miguel y yo ________________ salir.
5. Uds. ________________ cantar.
6. Julia ________________ estudiar.

ACTIVIDAD D

You are observing some children playing on the beach. Using a form of the stem-changing verb **encontrar (ue)**, tell what they find.

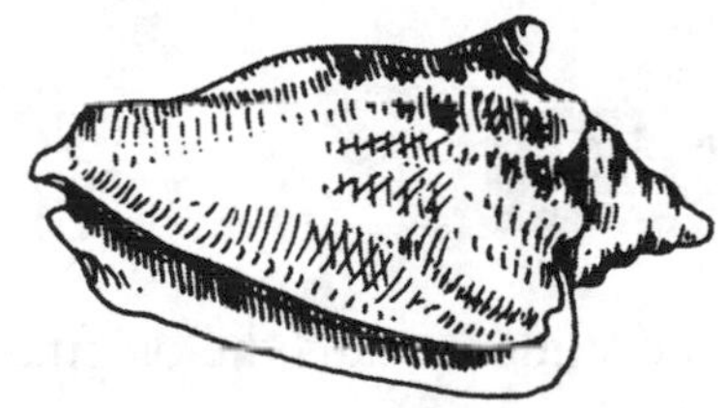

EXAMPLE: **Ellos *encuentran* una concha.**

1. Carlos ____________________.
2. Yo ____________________.

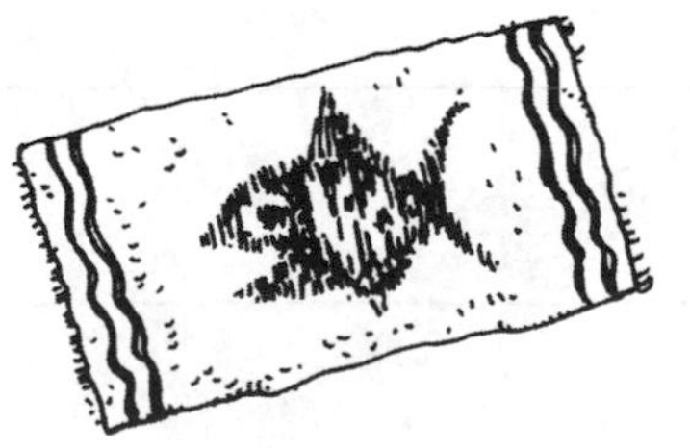

3. Ud. ____________________.
4. Uds. ____________________.

5. Nosotros ____________________.
6. Tú ____________________.

There is one more important verb that has a similar change in the stem: in **jugar**, the **u** changes to **ue** in all forms except for **nosotros**.

yo	**j*ue*go**
tú	**j*ue*gas**
Ud., él, ella	**j*ue*ga**
nosotros, -as	**jugamos**
Uds., ellos, ellas	**j*ue*gan**

ACTIVIDAD E

A difference of opinion Work with a partner. One student reads the original statement. Another student changes the statement to agree with the new subject.

1. Los soldados **defienden** el país.

   Todos nosotros ______________________________ .

2. Mi hermana no **miente**.

   Mis padres ______________________________ .

3. Su gato **duerme** todo el día.

   Los leones ______________________________ .

4. Los niños **juegan** en la playa.

   Yo ______________________________ .

5. ¿No **encuentras** el traje de baño?

   Ud. ______________________________ .

6. ¿**Entiendes** la lección?

   Uds. ______________________________ .

7. Uds. **cierran** la puerta.

   María ______________________________ .

8. ¿Qué **prefiere** Ud.?

   Tú ______________________________ .

9. El pájaro **vuela** por el aire.

   Las mariposas ______________________________ .

ACTIVIDAD F

*

Summer plans Work with a partner. One student asks a question using the correct form of the verb in parentheses. The other student answers in a complete sentence.

1. (jugar) ¿A qué juegan Uds. en el campo?
   Nosotros jugamos futbol.
2. (querer) ¿Adónde quieren ir sus padres?
   Ellos quieren ir a Hawaii.
3. (preferir) ¿Prefiere Ud. ir al Caribe?
   Yo prefiero ir al Caribe.
4. (pensar) ¿Dónde piensas (tú) pasar las vacaciones?
   Yo pienso pasar las vacaiones en las montañas.
5. (almorzar) ¿A qué hora almuerzan las personas en el trópico?
   Ellas almuerzan a las seís.
6. (dormir) ¿Duermo yo mucho?
   No, tú no duermes mucho.
7. (poder) ¿Podemos nosotros viajar a una isla tropical?
   Nosotros podemos viajar a una isla tropical.
8. (encontrar) ¿Encuentra el agente de viajes información sobre excursiones?
   Sí, él encuentra el agente de viajes información sobre excursiones.
9. (costar) ¿Cuánto Cuestan los billetes de avión?
   Un billete Cuestan doscientos.
10. (volver) ¿Cuándo ~~doscientos~~ vuelves tú de Santo Domingo?
    Yo vuelvo mañana.

ACTIVIDAD G

¿Qué hacen estas personas?

Work with a partner. One student poses the question:

¿Qué hace (haces, hacen, etc.)? The other student answers according to the verb clues.

EXAMPLE: (contar) Juan y Pedro Cuentan hasta cien.

¿Qué hacen Juan y Pedro? Juan y Pedro *cuentan* hasta cien.

1. (almorzar) Los estudiantes almuerzan en la cafetería.
2. (empezar) Yo empiezo a trabajar.
3. (volver) Nosotros volvemos a casa.
4. (dormir) Mi abuelo duerme la siesta.
5. (encontrar) María y yo encontramos el libro.
6. (perder) Uds. pierden la paciencia.
7. (cerrar) Ellas cierran la tienda.

En la playa de una isla tropical

Now let's read a story about an adventure at the beach. Look for the stem-changing verbs of another type.

Es un día de sol brillante. Estamos en una playa casi desierta de una isla tropical. Vemos las olas del mar y la arena blanca. Una brisa suave **mueve** las palmeras.

En la distancia, vemos a dos personas. **Siguen** las huellas de su perro, caminando lentamente por la orilla del mar, y **sonríen** mientras hablan. ¿Qué dicen?

seguir (i) *to follow*

LA CHICA: Oh, Fernando. ¡Que contenta estoy! Esta isla es un paraíso. Ahora, el mundo no existe.

EL CHICO: Sí, tienes razón. Estamos lejos de los problemas del mundo. Pero, ¿quieres saber una cosa? Esta isla pacífica tiene una historia trágica, de violencia y de piratas.

LA CHICA: Oh, sí. ¡Qué romántico! Entonces, es seguro que hay tesoros debajo de la arena — perlas, diamantes, rubíes, monedas de oro . . .

EL CHICO: Quizás. Pero, ¿quién sabe dónde están?

La chica ve una cosa que brilla en la arena. Es una botella con un papel viejo adentro.

LA CHICA: (**ríe** alegremente) Mira, aquí hay un mapa. ¿Crees que **sirve**?

reír (í) *to laugh*
servir (i) *to serve, be useful*

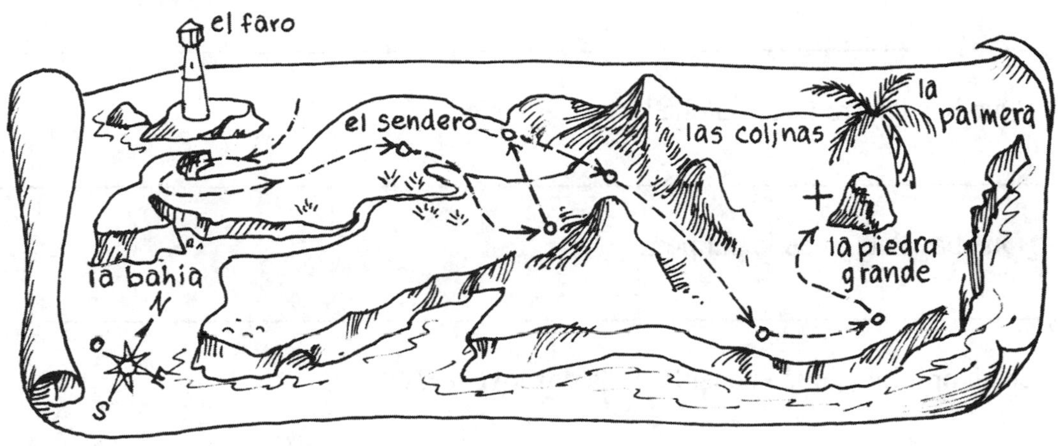

EL CHICO: Sí, es un mapa de un tesoro. Pero eso es imposible. ¡Es ridículo!

LA CHICA: No es imposible, Fernando. Allí hay una piedra grande debajo de una palmera, como **muestra** el mapa. ¿Qué piensas? ¿Buscamos el tesoro allí?

Los dos empiezan a **cavar** con las manos. Después de veinte minutos, Fernando grita, ¡Mira, Juanita! ¡Hay algo aquí! ¿Que encuentran los dos jóvenes en la arena?

mostrar (ue) *to show*
cavar *to dig*

ACTIVIDAD H

Answer the following questions about the story.

1. ¿Cómo es la isla?

____

2. ¿Quiénes están en la playa?

____

3. ¿Qué hacen en la playa?

____

4. ¿Qué piensa la chica sobre la isla?

____

5. ¿Cuál es la opinión del chico?

____

6. Según la chica, ¿qué hay debajo de la arena?

____

7. ¿Qué encuentra la chica en la arena?

____

8. ¿Qué hay dentro de la botella?

____

9. ¿Qué hay debajo de la palmera?

____

10. En su opinión, ¿qué encuentran los dos jóvenes?

____

There were four verbs in the story that belong to a third class of stem-changing verbs:

reír **sonreír** **seguir** **servir**

How are they different from the verbs we've already learned? These verbs are all -IR verbs. Let's see how they change:

	re*ír*	**sonre*ír***	**segu*ir***	**serv*ir***
yo	**r*í*o**	**sonr*í*o**	**s*i*go**	**s*i*rvo**
tú	**r*í*es**	**sonr*í*es**	**s*i*gues**	**s*i*rves**
Ud., él, ella	**r*í*e**	**sonr*í*e**	**s*i*gue**	**s*i*rve**
nosotros, -as	**reímos**	**sonreímos**	**seguimos**	**servimos**
Uds., ellos, ellas	**r*í*en**	**sonr*í*en**	**s*i*guen**	**s*i*rven**

Now you know. Some -IR verbs change the **e** in the stem to **i** in all forms of the present tense except for **nosotros**. This change is indicated in the end vocabulary as follows: **reír(í)**. Other common verbs in this category are **pedir(i)** and **repetir(i)**.

ACTIVIDAD I

You overhear several individuals in a Spanish restaurant. Each orders something different. Complete their orders with the correct form of the verb **pedir(i)**.

1. Yo ________________ arroz con pollo.
2. Fernando ________________ sopa.
3. Roberto y Carlos ________________ una tortilla.
4. Doris y yo ________________ una ensalada mixta.
5. Tú ________________ bistec.
6. El mesero pregunta: —«¿Qué ________________ Uds.?»

ACTIVIDAD J

Now, let's try all the new verbs we've just learned.

1. (reír) Carlos ________________ en el cine.
2. (sonreír) ¿Por qué ________________ (tú), ahora?
3. (servir) Yo ________________ la comida a mi familia.
4. (seguir) Nosotros ________________ las huellas del perro.
5. (repetir) Uds. siempre ________________ lo que decimos.
6. (pedir) Manuel y Jorge ________________ un café.

ACTIVIDAD K

At the beach. Let's see what these people are doing.

1. (querer) Un niño ________________ aprender a nadar.
2. (dormir) La madre ________________ bajo la sombrilla.
3. (encender) El padre ________________ el fuego para la barbacoa.
4. (pedir) Yo ________________ una soda en el quiosco.

5. (preferir) Mi hermanito prefiere jugar en la arena.
6. (perder) Tú pierdes la pelota de playa.
7. (encontrar) Mario y José encuentran un caracol muy bonito.
8. (entender) Yo no entiendo lo que grita mi madre.
9. (repetir) Ella repite sus palabras.
10. (pensar, nevar) Yo pienso : —«¡Qué bien que no nieve en el verano!»
11. (sonreír) El salvavidas sonríe .
12. (seguir) Dos perros siguen a mi hermanito.

ACTIVIDAD L ✱

You are in a hotel in San Juan and want to say or ask the following in Spanish:

1. (entender) Yo no entiendo español muy bien.
2. (costar) ¿Cuánto cuesta un cuarto?
3. (dormir) Generalmente nosotros dormimos en cuartos diferentes.
4. (querer) Mi familia quiere el cuarto para una semana.
5. (servir) ¿A qué hora sirven Uds. el desayuno?
6. (pedir) ¿Dónde pedimos nosotros direcciones?
7. (cerrar) ¿A qué hora cierran Uds. la cafetería?
8. (llover) ¿ Llueve mucho en el verano?
9. (preferir) Mis hermanos prefieren ir a la playa ahora.
10. (volver) Mi mamá vuelve al hotel a la una.

Diálogo

José is calling Carmen on the phone. What is Carmen saying?

Preguntas Personales

1. ¿Qué haces en la playa?

____

2. ¿Vives cerca de una playa? ¿De cuál?

____

3. ¿Lees libros sobre piratas? ¿Por qué (no)?

____

4. ¿Dónde puedes encontrar tesoros?

____

5. ¿En qué islas del Caribe hablan español?

____

Información Personal

Draw a treasure map. Write five sentences giving the clues necessary to find the treasure:

EXAMPLE: **Hay una piedra grande debajo de una palmera.**

1. ______________________________
2. ______________________________
3. ______________________________
4. ______________________________
5. ______________________________

CÁPSULA CULTURAL

Una playa diferente todos los días

¿Le gustaría pasar sus vacaciones en una playa en España? Pero, ¿cuál? ¡Hay más de dos mil! El país de España forma parte de la Península Ibérica, que tiene una costa de 1,698 (mil seiscientas noventa y ocho) millas con más de 2,000 playas y 200 balnearios.

Para identificar con precisión la localidad de cada área en el mapa, los españoles han dividido todo el territorio en siete secciones o costas. La Costa Brava es un área montañosa de la costa mediterránea que se extiende hasta la frontera de Francia.

Después viene la Costa Dorada, que pasa por Barcelona con sus playas de arena de color de oro. Después viene la Costa del Azahar, con sus grandes playas que pasan por Valencia. Sigue la Costa Blanca, que ofrece un invierno muy suave. Por fin, la última costa en el Mediterráneo es la popular Costa del Sol, que da a África.

Hay dos costas más en el Atlántico: En el sur está la Costa de la Luz, que se extiende hasta la frontera portuguesa. La costa al norte del Atlántico se llama la Costa Verde, a causa de su abundante vegetación verde.

A causa del gran volumen de turismo y construcción en la costa, voluntarios de la *Coastwatch* europea examinan cada año los desperdicios dejados en las playas españolas para inspeccionar el daño ambiental y preparar actividades de rehabilitación necesarias.

el balneario *beach resort*

bravo *wild*

dorado *golden*
la arena *sand*
el azahar *orange blossom*

por fin *finally*
dar a *to face*

a causa de *because of*

los desperdicios *waste, garbage*
dejado *left*
el daño ambiental *environmental damage*

Para pensar

1. Describa la costa de la Península Ibérica.
2. ¿Qué son las costas? ¿Por qué las han creado los españoles?
3. ¿Cuántas costas hay en España? ¿Cómo se llaman?
4. ¿Qué trabajo hace la *Coastwatch*?
5. ¿Cuáles son algunos problemas causados por el exceso de turismo? ¿Qué podemos hacer para remediarlos?

3

En la joyería

Negative and Affirmative Expressions

1 Vocabulario

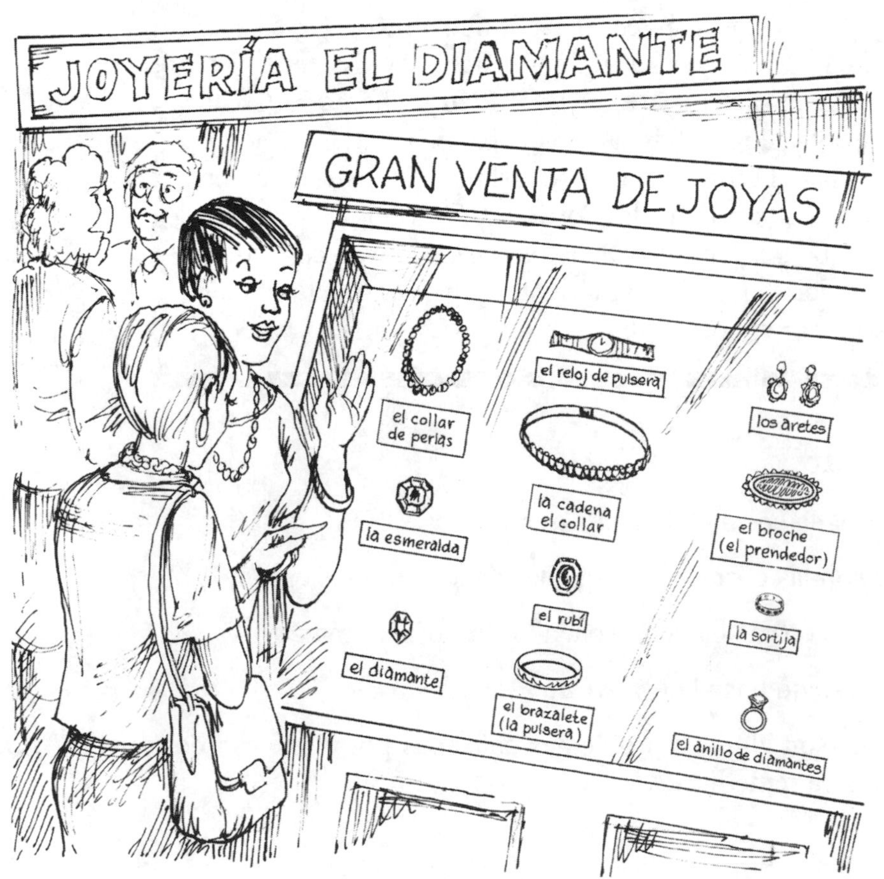

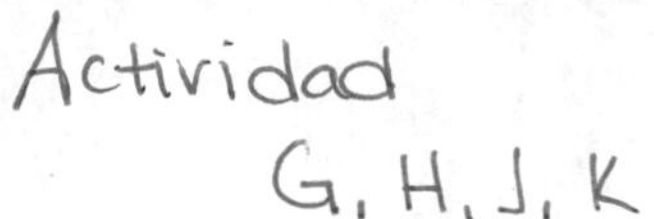

ACTIVIDAD A

Juan has a job in a jewelry store. The manager has told him to place labels on all the articles in the showcase for the big sale. Can you help him?

cadena de oro $100	**collar de esmeraldas $900**
brazalete de plata $150	**aretes de perlas $55**
anillo de diamantes $500	**broche de rubíes $300**

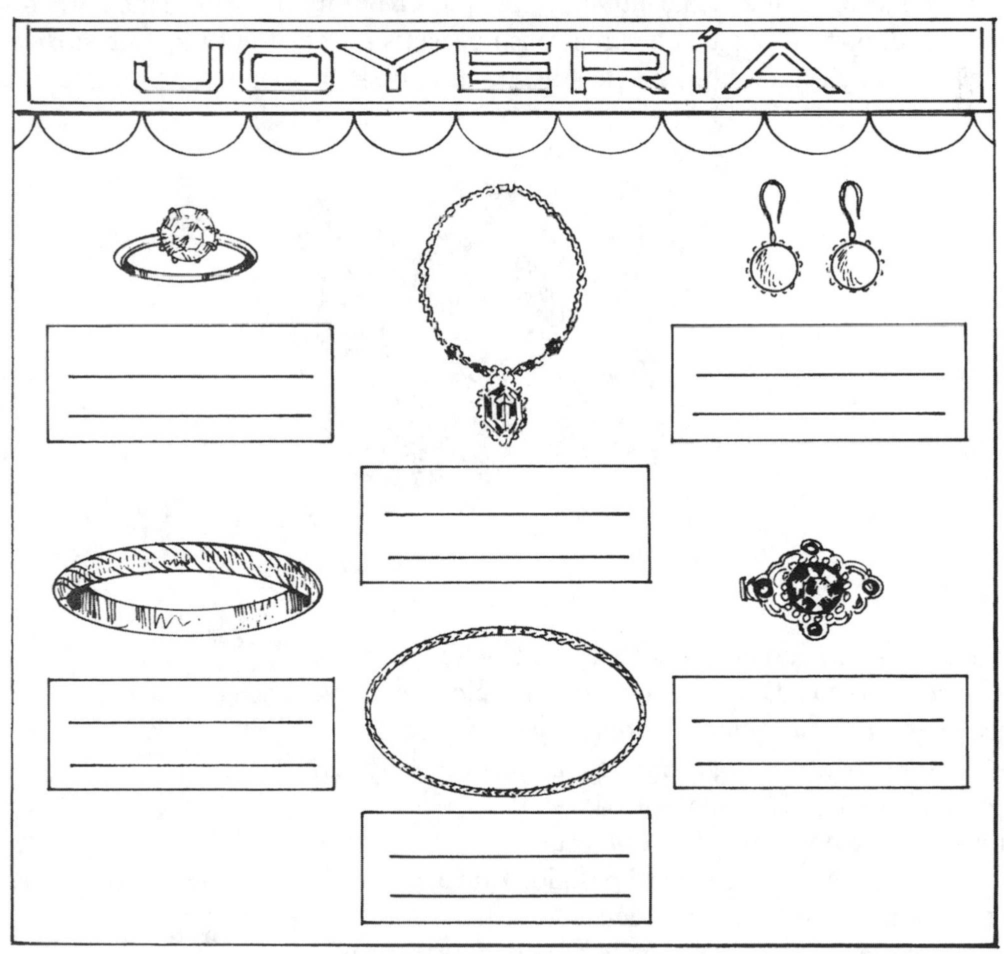

ACTIVIDAD B

You are buying holiday presents in the jewelry department of a department store. What should you buy for these people on your list?

EXAMPLE: Tu padre: **Compro un reloj de pulsera para mi padre.**

1. Tu amigo Juan: ______________________________
2. Tu amiga Carla: ______________________________
3. Tu mamá: ______________________________
4. Tu hermana Clarita: ______________________________
5. Tu hermano Miguel: ______________________________

You already know the most common negative word in the Spanish language: **no**. To make any sentence negative, simply put **no** before the verb. There are, however, other important negative expressions in Spanish. Read the following story and pay careful attention to the new negatives and to their corresponding affirmatives.

La magia

Un hombre está sentado en una silla delante de un grupo de personas, con las espalda hacia ellos. Tiene los ojos cubiertos. **No** puede ver **nada**. Su ayudante toma una cosa y dice:

—Maestro. Ahora tengo algo en la mano. ¿Qué es? Necesito saber. Dígame. Ahora, ¿sabe?

El hombre piensa un momento y contesta:

—Veo algo. **No** es **ni** grande **ni** pesado. **Tampoco** es pequeño. Es . . . es . . . una cadena.

—Estupendo, sensacional—grita el ayudante.—El maestro **nunca** comete un error, **no** falla **jamás**. Siempre tiene razón. Un aplauso, por favor.

¿Pero, qué pasa aquí? ¿Es la magia de veras? ¿Es un mago el hombre? ¿Puede él ver cosas que **nadie** ve? ¿O es una simple ilusión? Si Ud. tiene buena memoria puede hacer lo mismo. Primero necesita una clave. Por ejemplo, en la clave del maestro, cada letra del alfabeto tiene una palabra equivalente. El maestro sabe de memoria esta tabla de equivalentes.

hacia *towards*
nada *nothing, anything*
algo *something*
ni . . . ni *neither . . . nor*
tampoco *either, neither*
nunca *never*
fallar *to fail*
jamás *never*
el mago *magician*
nadie *nobody*
la clave *key (to code)*
saber de memoria *to know by heart*

TABLA DE EQUIVALENTES	
ahora = a	**seguramente = h**
vamos = b	**nombre Ud. = i**
maestro = c	**rápido = j**
¿qué? = d	**bueno = l**
necesito = e	**mire = m**
haga el favor = f	**dígame = n**
muy bien = g	

Entonces, para descifrar el mensaje secreto, el mago toma simplemente la primera palabra de cada frase que dice el ayudante:

primero/a *first*

—Maestro. Ahora tengo algo en la mano. ¿Qué es? Necesito saber. Dígame. Ahora, ¿sabe?

PRIMERA PALABRA	LETRA EQUIVALENTE
maestro	**C**
ahora	**A**
qué	**D**
necesito	**E**
dígame	**N**
ahora	**A**

¿Comprende ahora cómo el mago hace su magia? Ahora Ud. también puede sorprender a sus amigos con su «poder mental».

poder *power*

Answer the following questions about the store.

1. ¿Dónde está sentado el mago?

____

2. ¿Por qué no puede ver nada?

____

3. ¿Qué dice primero el ayudante del mago?

____

4. ¿Qué hace el mago antes de contestar?

____

5. ¿Qué tiene el ayudante en la mano?

____

6. ¿En qué consiste la clave del mago?

____

7. ¿Qué sabe de memoria el maestro?

____

8. ¿Qué palabra de cada frase es importante?

____

9. ¿Cuántas letras tiene la palabra «cadena»?

____

10. ¿Cuántas frases usa el ayudante del mago?

____

2

Notice the following negative expressions in the preceding story.

***Nadie* ve.**	*No one sees.*
***Tampoco* es pequeño.**	*He is not small either.*
No puede ver *nada*.	*He/She can't see anything.*
***Nunca* comete un error.**	*He/She never makes a mistake.*
No es *ni* grande *ni* pesado.	*He is neither big nor heavy.*
No falla jamás.	*He is never wrong.*

Now read the following expressions.

No puede ver *nada*. ***Nada* puede ver.**	*He can't see anything.*
No comete *nunca* un error. ***Nunca* comete un error.**	*He never makes a mistake.*

No es pequeño *tampoco*. ***Tampoco* es pequeño.**	*He is not small either.*
cosas que no ve *nadie* **cosas que *nadie* ve**	*things that no one sees*
No falla jamás. ***Jamás* falla.**	*He never fails.*

Look at the first sentence in each pair. Where is the negative word placed? Directly before the verb. Now look at second sentence in each pair. What word is placed directly before the verb? ________________ Where is the negative word placed? ________________

RULE: There are two ways of negating a sentence in Spanish:

(a) **no** + verb + negative word

(b) negative word + verb

ACTIVIDAD D

Work with a partner. One student reads a negative expression from the ones above. The partner then changes the expression to the positive using one of the sentences that follow. Then switch roles.

EXAMPLE: ***Nadie* ve.** ***Alguien* ve.**

1. También es pequeño. ________________
2. Siempre comete un error. ________________
3. Puede ver algo. ________________
4. Siempre falla. ________________
5. Es grande y pesado. ________________

ACTIVIDAD E

María likes to do what her older sister, Rosa, does. What does María say?

EXAMPLE: **Yo no compro joyas. ¿Y tú?**
Yo *tampoco* compro joyas. OR **Yo *no* compro joyas *tampoco*.**

1. Yo no quiero el collar. ¿Y tú?

____

2. Yo no uso aretes. ¿Y tú?

____

3. Yo no encuentro el reloj. ¿Y tú?

____

4. Yo no sé hacer magia. ¿Y tú?

____

5. Yo no puedo ir a la joyería. ¿Y tú?

____

ACTIVIDAD F

Say that you don't ever do the following things:

EXAMPLE: **comer chocolate**
Yo *nunca* (*jamás*) como chocolate.
Yo no como *nunca* (*jamás*) chocolate.

1. trabajar los domingos

____

2. comprar joyas

____

3. tomar el sol

____

4. decir mentiras

____

5. comer afuera

____

Fernando doesn't like certain foods. What does he tell his mother?

EXAMPLE: **las frutas . . . las legumbres**
No me gustan ni las frutas ni las legumbres.

1. el maíz . . . el arroz
   No me gustan ni el mais ni el arros.
2. la leche . . . el jugo
   No me gusta ningún beber.
3. el pollo . . . el rosbif
   No me gusta ni el pollo ni el rosbif.
4. los tacos . . . las enchiladas
   No me gustan ni los tacos ni las enchiladas.
5. las naranjas . . . las manzanas
   No me gustan ni las naranjas ni las manzanas.

NOTE: When the object of a verb is a negative or an affirmative word referring to a person, the personal **a** is used:

Veo *a* alguien.	*I see someone.*
No veo *a* nadie.	*I don't see anyone.*

ACTIVIDAD H

Miguel takes great pleasure in saying the opposite of what his twin brother Marcos says. Give Miguel's negative statements. Work with a partner.

EXAMPLE: **Yo oigo *algo*. ¿Y tú?** **Yo no oigo *nada*.**

1. Yo veo a alguien. ¿Y tú? Yo no veo a nadie .
2. Yo escribo algo. ¿Y tú? Yo no escribo nada.
3. Yo busco a alguien. ¿Y tú? Yo no busco a nadie.
4. Yo tomo algo. ¿Y tú? Yo no tomo nada
5. Yo quiero a alguien. ¿Y tú? Yo no quiero a nadie.

ACTIVIDAD I

Your mother is asking you some questions. Answer them negatively.

1. ¿Haces algo ahora?

____

2. ¿Conoces a alguien en México?

____

3. ¿Dices siempre la verdad?

____

4. ¿Quieres comer algo?

____

5. ¿Vas al cine con tus amigos?

____

6. ¿Llamas a alguien por teléfono?

____

3

There is one more negative word (**ninguno, -a, -os, -as** *none, not any, no*) and one more affirmative word (**alguno, -a, -os, -as** *any, some*) that need your special attention. Look at the following examples:

¿Quieres hacer *alguna* pregunta?	*Do you want to ask any question?*
No, no quiero hacer *ninguna* pregunta.	*No, I don't want to ask any question.*
¿Necesitas *algún* consejo?	*Do you need some advice?*
No, no necesito *ningún* consejo.	*No, I don't need any advice.*
¿Ves *algunos* libros aquí?	*Do you see some books here?*
No, no veo *ningunos* libros aquí.	*No, I don't see any books here.*
¿Puedes comprar *algunas* cosas?	*Can you buy some things?*
No, no puedo comprar *ningunas* cosas.	*No, I can't buy any things.*

Did you observe that both **alguno** and **ninguno** agree in gender and number with nouns they accompany? What's more, they become **algún** and **ningún** before a masculine singular noun:

¿Tienes *algún* amigo español?	*Do you have any Spanish friend?*
No, no tengo *ningún* amigo español.	*No, I don't have any Spanish friend.*

ACTIVIDAD J

Your friend is offering you different things. Say that you don't want any:

EXAMPLE: **¿Quieres *algún* postre? No, gracias. No quiero *ningún* postre.**

1. ¿Quieres alguna torta? No quiero ningún a torta

2. ¿Quieres algunos discos? No quiero ningunos discos
3. ¿Quieres alguna fruta? No quiero ninguna fruta
4. ¿Quieres algún libro? No quiero ningún libro
5. ¿Quieres algún plato típico? No quiero ningún plato típico

ACTIVIDAD K

You are in a contrary mood today. Answer the following questions negatively.

1. Carlos va a la fiesta. ¿Y tú?

   Yo no voy ninguna la fiesta

2. ¿Sabes algo sobre el Paraguay?

   Yo no se nada sobre el Paraguay

3. ¿Va tu hermana siempre al cine por la noche?

   Mi hermana no va nunca al cine

4. ¿Conocen tus padres a alguien en España?

   Mis padres no conocen nadie

5. ¿Vale algún libro mil dólares?

   No vale libro ningún

6. ¿Qué exámenes tienes los sábados?

   Nunca tengo un exámene los sábados

7. ¿Está abierta alguna tienda hoy?

   No está abierta ninguna tienda hoy

8. ¿Tienes algún trabajo para mañana?

   No tengo ningún trabajo para mañana

9. ¿Quieres comer un pastel o un sándwich?

   No quiero comer ningún ni

10. ¿Ves algo interesante en la joyería?

    No veo nada interesante

Diálogo

In this conversation, you have the role of Javier Jalapeño, an assistant to a great magician.

Preguntas Personales

1. ¿Por qué le gusta ver a mucha gente las ilusiones?

____

2. ¿Qué significa la expresión «la mano es más rápida que el ojo»?

____

3. ¿Qué regalos prefieres dar (o recibir)?

____

4. ¿Generalmente, quiénes usan joyas?

____

5. ¿Qué clase de joyas usa una chica (un chico)?

____

Información Personal

Tell us about yourself by completing the following paragraph.

Los fines de semana yo prefiero ______________ (*1.*) pero no me gusta ______________ (*2.*). Mis platos favoritos son ______________ (*3.*) y ______________ (*4.*). Nunca como ni ______________ (*5.*) ni ______________ (*6.*). Generalmente paso mis ratos libres ______________ (*7.*), pero nunca ______________ (*8.*).

Composición

You want to put on a comedy skit as *El Gran Fandango*, the world's greatest mind reader, before your Spanish class. To demonstrate your abilities, think of an object. Make up a key and write the sentences that your assistant will use to enable you to "read minds." Then get into pairs and try it with your partner.

CÁPSULA CULTURAL

El oro: el metal deseado

A través de los siglos, la gente ha viajado a tierras desconocidas y peligrosas en busca de oro. La mayoría de los exploradores europeos que vinieron a Las Américas buscaban oro en los territorios de los aztecas de México y los incas del Perú. Siglos después, durante las famosas «fiebres del oro», miles de personas fueron a California y a Alaska con la esperanza de encontrar oro y hacerse ricos. Muchos de ellos murieron en el esfuerzo.

¿Por qué existe este deseo tan fuerte de poseer este metal? El oro siempre ha sido valioso, parcialmente a causa de su escasez. Pero el oro es también un metal hermoso y lustroso. Además es blando y fácil de moldear en muchas formas. Se ha usado para hacer monedas y joyas por su propiedad de no oxidarse. El oro está medido en quilates: 24 quilates es el oro puro.

En Bogotá, Colombia, está el Museo del Oro, donde se exhiben más de 30,000 piezas de oro, incluso máscaras, pendientes y adornos de toda clase. Para los indígenas que fabricaban estas obras de arte, el oro era «el sudor del sol».

a través de *through*
la fiebre del oro *gold rush*
el esfuerzo *attempt, effort*
la escasez *shortage*
oxidarse *to rust*
el quilate *carat*
donde *where*
incluso *including*
el indígena *native*
sudor *sweat*

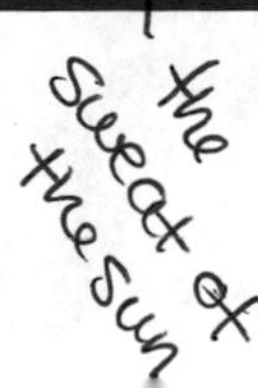

Para pensar

1. ¿Qué ha hecho mucha gente para adquirir el oro?
2. ¿Qué pasó durante la «fiebre del oro»?
3. ¿Por qué ha sido valioso el oro?
4. ¿Qué es El Museo del Oro y dónde está?
5. ¿Cuáles son algunos problemas causados por la extracción de minerales de la tierra?

4

El fin de semana

Formal and Informal Commands

1 Vocabulario

What can we do for fun on a weekend?

ir de compras

Ir a un concierto de rock

ver una película

hacer ejercicio

jugar a los bolos

patinar

ir al teatro

patinar en el hielo

ver una exhibición en el museo

nadar en la piscina

montar a caballo

2

Do you enjoy any of the activities at the beginning of this lesson? How about inviting one or more of your friends to join you? It's very simple. Look at the following examples.

¡*Vamos* a la fiesta!	*Let's go to the party!*
¡*Vamos a* jugar al monopolio!	*Let's play monopoly!*

Vamos is used to express *let's go*. **Vamos a** + infinitive is used to express *let's*.

NOTE: Did you notice the inverted exclamation mark (¡) before each sentence starting with **vamos**? In Spanish, sentences that have a normal exclamation mark at the end also have an inverted exclamation mark at the beginning.

ACTIVIDAD A

Tell your friend to do the following activities with you.

EXAMPLE: dance **Vamos a bailar.**

1. skate ____________________
2. see a horror movie ____________________
3. play soccer ____________________
4. go bowling ____________________
5. visit the museum ____________________
6. swim in the swimming pool ____________________

ACTIVIDAD B

A friend of the family is flying in this weekend. Tell him/her to join you in five different activities.

EXAMPLE: **¡*Vamos a* un concierto de rock!**

1. ______________________________

2. ______________________________

3. ______________________________

4. ______________________________

5. ______________________________

El hipnotismo

Read the following story about a hypnotist to find out how to command people to do things.

Es sábado por la noche y la familia Colón da un paseo por la avenida, mientras decide cómo pasar el tiempo.

dar un paseo *to take a walk*

SR. COLÓN: Vamos al centro. Así podemos ir al cine y después tomar algo en uno de los cafés.

el centro *downtown*

CHITO (un niño de 14 años): ¿Por qué no vamos al estadio para ver si hay un partido de fútbol esta noche?

MARILUZ (su hermana de 15 años): No me gusta el fútbol. Yo prefiero ir a la plaza. Siempre hay conciertos de rock los fines de semana.

En ese momento pasan por delante del Teatro Real, famoso por sus programas de variedades.

CHITO: ¡**Mira**, mamá! ¿Qué dice ese letrero?

el letrero *sign*

MARILUZ: Tonto, ¿no sabes leer? Anuncian al hipnotista Mandrako, el Maravilloso.

CHITO: Pero, ¿qué es un hipnotista?

SR. COLÓN: Es un hombre que vive de la ignorancia de la gente.

SRA. COLÓN: ¡Carlos, no **digas** eso! El hipnotismo, hijo, es el arte de crear en una persona un estado similar al sueño, y así la persona acepta órdenes sin resistir.

SR. COLÓN: Sí, especialmente si la persona es un individuo débil.

MARILUZ: ¡**Miren**! La función empieza a las siete y son las siete en punto. ¡Vamos a verla!

la función *show*

TODOS: ¡Buena idea!

Compran las entradas y entran en el teatro oscuro y toman asiento. Mandrako, un hombre alto y flaco, vestido todo de negro, está en el escenario. Ve al Sr. Colón y dice:

la entrada *ticket*
oscuro *dark*
tomar asiento *to have a sit*
el escenario *stage*

MANDRAKO: ¡Ud., señor! **Suba** por favor.

SR. COLÓN (a su familia): Voy a participar sólo para demostrar que todo esto es una estupidez.

MANDRAKO: **Tome** asiento, por favor. Ahora **mire** mi reloj. Ud. tiene sueño, mucho sueño. **Cierre** los ojos. Ahora, **abra** la boca y **ladre** como un perro. **Meta** su dedo en el oído y **salte** como un mono, **corra** como un gato. Muy bien. Ahora voy a contar hasta diez y puede abrir los ojos. No va a recordar nada.

ladrar *to bark*
saltar *to jump*
recordar (ue) *to remember*

Cuando el Sr. Colón vuelve a su asiento, dice:

SR. COLÓN: ¡Qué estupidez! ¿No ves que un hombre inteligente como yo no es susceptible.

SRA. COLÓN: Claro, mi amor. ¿Pero, por qué no sacas el dedo de tu oído ahora?

sacar *to take out*

ACTIVIDAD C

Answer the following questions about the story.

1. ¿Qué hace la familia Colón?

____

2. ¿Quién es Mandrako?

____

3. ¿Qué es el hipnotismo?

____

4. ¿Qué dice el Sr. Colón sobre el hipnotismo?

____

5. ¿Qué dice Mandrako para hipnotizar al Sr. Colón?

____

6. ¿Qué hace el Sr. Colón bajo la influencia de Mandrako?

____

7. ¿Qué dice el Sr. Colón cuando vuelve a su asiento?

____

8. ¿Qué dice la Sra. Colón?

____

3

Mandrako gave a number of commands to Mr. Colón. In some he used the pronoun **Ud.** and in others he didn't. That's because the use of the pronoun is optional. Let's list some of Mandrako's commands.

-AR VERBS	**-ER** VERBS	**-IR** VERBS
Tome **Ud. asiento.** ***Mire*** **mi reloj.**	***Meta*** **su dedo en el oído.** ***Corra*** **como un gato.**	***Suba*** **ahora.** ***Abra*** **la boca.**

These are called formal commands. They are used when addressing people as **Ud.** or **Uds.** In the formal command forms, **-AR** verbs end in **-e**, **-ER** and **-IR** verbs end in **-a**. To give a formal command, drop the **-o** of the **yo**-form of the present tense and add the appropriate endings.

INFINITIVE	PRESENT TENSE YO-FORM	FORMAL COMMAND	MEANING
habl*ar* **com*er*** **dorm*ir***	**habl-** **com-** **duerm-**	**Habl*e*** **Com*a*** **Duerm*a***	***Speak*** ***Eat*** ***Sleep***

To make a formal command plural, add the letter **n** to the singular command.

SINGULAR	PLURAL
Cierre **(Ud.) la ventana.** **No** ***sirva*** **(Ud.) el café ahora.** ***Repita*** **(Ud.) la lección.**	***Cierren*** **(Uds.) la ventana.** **No** ***sirvan*** **(Uds.) el café ahora.** ***Repitan*** **(Uds.) la lección.**

ACTIVIDAD D

Work with a partner. One student makes up a command. The other student acts it out.

EXAMPLE: STUDENT 1 STUDENT 2

mirar la televisión **Mire la televisión.**

Tú:

1. leer el periódico ______________________
2. comprar una revista ______________________
3. subir al autobús ______________________
4. entrar en la clase ______________________
5. beber un café ______________________
6. estudiar la lección ______________________
7. montar a caballo ______________________
8. dormir la siesta ______________________
9. comer un pedazo de pizza ______________________
10. nadar en la piscina ______________________

ACTIVIDAD E

Now you be the teacher for the day. Tell your students to do the following.

EXAMPLE: entrar en la clase ***Entren*** **en la clase.**

1. cerrar las ventanas ______________________
2. abrir el libro de español ______________________

3. no dormir en clase ______________________

4. repetir las palabras ______________________

5. aprender un poema ______________________

Some verbs in Spanish have an irregular **yo** form. These verbs also follow the same rule to form the formal command.

INFINITIVE	PRESENT TENSE YO-FORM	FORMAL COMMAND	
		SINGULAR	PLURAL
decir (*to say*)	**digo**	**Dig*a***	**Dig*an***
hacer (*to do*)	**hago**	**Hag*a***	**Hag*an***
oír (*to hear*)	**oigo**	**Oig*a***	**Oig*an***
poner (*to put*)	**pongo**	**Pong*a***	**Pong*an***
salir (*to go out*)	**salgo**	**Salg*a***	**Salg*an***
tener (*to have*)	**tengo**	**Teng*a***	**Teng*an***
traer (*to bring*)	**traigo**	**Traig*a***	**Traig*an***
venir (*to come*)	**vengo**	**Veng*a***	**Veng*an***

NOTE: There are three important verbs that do not follow the rule for formal commands: **dar, ir,** and **ser**. You will have to memorize the following forms:

(dar) ***Dé*** **(Ud.) un ejemplo.**
Den (Uds.) un ejemplo. } *Give an example.*

(ir) ***Vaya*** **(Ud.) a casa.**
Vayan **(Uds.) a casa.** } *Go home.*

(ser) **No *sea* (Ud.) tonto.**
No sean (Uds.) tontos. } *Don't be foolish.*

ACTIVIDAD F

Give a formal command using the following phrases.

EXAMPLE: decir la verdad (Ud.) ***Diga* la verdad.**

1. dar la información (Ud.) ______________________

2. oír la explosión (Uds.) ______________________

3. poner el libro sobre la mesa (Ud.) ______________________

4. no salir (Uds.) ______________________

5. tener mucho cuidado (Ud.) ______________________

6. venir mañana (Ud.) ______________________

7. ser bueno con su hermanita (Ud.) ______________________

8. decir la verdad (Uds.) ______________________

9. no ir al centro (Uds.) ______________________

10. hacer el trabajo (Ud.) ______________________

ACTIVIDAD G

Express the following formal commands in Spanish.

EXAMPLE: Write the answer. ***Escriba* la respuesta.**

1. Give an example. (Ud.) ______________________

2. Bring a Spanish film. (Ud.) ______________________

3. Don't leave now. (Uds.) ______________________

4. Say something. (Ud.) ______________________

5. Go to the cafeteria now. (Uds.) ______________________

5

You now know how to give formal commands (Ud., Uds.). But what happens if you want to tell a friend or somebody you address as **tú** to do something? You must use the INFORMAL COMMAND. To form an informal command, use the **Ud./él/ella** form of the present tense.

PRESENT TENSE UD./ÉL/ELLA	INFORMAL COMMAND	MEANING
Ud./él/ella *lee* el libro. **Ud./él/ella *compra* los discos.** **Ud./él/ella *abre* la ventana.**	**¡*Lee* el libro!** **¡*Compra* los discos!** **¡*Abre* la ventana!**	*Read the book!* *Buy the records!* *Open the window!*

NOTE: To make the informal command plural, use the **Uds.**-form of the formal command.

(Tú)	***Habla* despacio.**	*Speak slowly.*
(Uds.)	***Hablen* despacio.**	

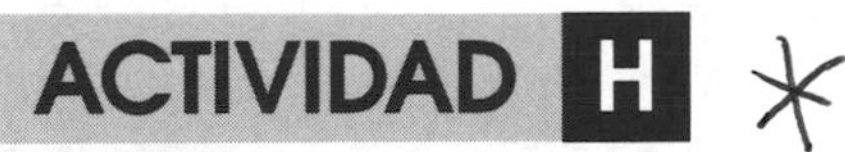

Tell one of your friends to do the following activities.

1. visitar el museo conmigo

____

2. escribir la tarea en español

____

3. comprar entradas para nosotros

____

4. jugar a los bolos este sábado

____

5. patinar en el parque el fin de semana

____

6. almorzar en mi casa

____

7. hablar conmigo después de la clase

____

8. comer en la cafetería conmigo

____

9. ayudar a tus amigos

____

10. volver a mi casa temprano

____

If you want to tell a friend *not* to do something, you must go back to the *formal* command form and add an **-s.**

¡*Salga* (Ud.)!	**¡No *salgas* (tú)!**
¡*Abra* (Ud.) la ventana!	**¡No *abras* (tú) la ventana!**
¡*Mire* (Ud.) ese programa!	**¡No *mires* (tú) ese programa!**

Express the following commands in the **tú**-form in Spanish.

EXAMPLE: Write all the words. Don't write only the first word.

Escribe todas las palabras. _No escribas_ solo la primera palabra.

1. Eat all your lunch. Don't eat only the dessert.

   ____

2. Speak with your father. Don't speak with your mother.

   ____

3. Study the lesson. Don't study only the vocabulary.

   ____

4. Listen to the teacher. Don't listen to your friend.

   ____

5. Call Monday. Don't call Tuesday.

   ____

7

Many verbs have irregular familiar command forms. Here are some of the most common:

decir: *di*	**salir: *sal***
hacer: *haz*	**ser: *sé***
ir: *ve*	**tener: *ten***
poner: *pon*	**venir: *ven***

The negative forms of those commands are regular:

No *digas*	**No *salgas***
No *hagas*	**No *seas***
No *vayas*	**No *tengas***
No *pongas*	**No *vengas***

ACTIVIDAD J

Complete the following informal commands to your friend with the correct form of the verb in parentheses.

1. (poner) ¡No ____________________ la mesa allí!
2. (ir) ¡No ____________________ a la tienda ahora!
3. (comprar) ¡____________________ las entradas hoy!
4. (comer) ¡____________________ temprano para salir después!
5. (hacer) ¡____________________ las tareas esta noche!
6. (decir) ¡____________________ siempre la verdad!
7. (venir) ¡____________________ temprano! ¡No ____________________ tarde!
8. (salir) ¡____________________ del cuarto!
9. (vender) ¡____________________ tu carro!
10. (ir) ¡____________________ a ver la película!

ACTIVIDAD K

Your mother tells you to do certain things and not do others. Express her commands in the informal form in Spanish.

1. Go to school. Don't go to the movies.

   ____

2. Do your homework. Don't watch television.

   ____

3. Be good. Don't tell lies.

4. Be careful. Don't run.

5. Close the door, go to your room, and put your coat there.

6. Read a good book. Don't listen to records.

Preguntas Personales

1. ¿Generalmente qué haces el sábado por la noche?

2. En el invierno, ¿qué haces para pasar el tiempo?

3. ¿Qué tipo de películas te gusta ver?

4. ¿Vas al teatro? ¿Te gustan las comedias o los dramas? ¿Por qué?

5. ¿Sabes montar a caballo? ¿Si no, quieres aprender?

6. ¿Asistes a conciertos de música clásica? Si no, ¿qué tipo de música prefieres?

7. ¿Son los bolos una actividad atlética? ¿Por qué sí o no?

8. ¿Qué deportes practicas?

Diálogo

You are talking with a friend about plans for the weekend.

Información Personal

You have been selected to play the part of "El Gran Fandango," the world's greatest hypnotist. Using some of the commands you have just learned, tell a subject what you wish him/her to do.

1. ______________________________

2. ______________________________

3. ______________________________

4. ______________________________

5. ______________________________

6. ______________________________

CÁPSULA CULTURAL

«¿Papá, me das mi domingo?»

En la mayoría de los países hispanoamericanos el domingo es el día de la familia, cuando todos se reúnen y comparten juntos. Pero el domingo es también un día importante para los niños. ¿Por qué? Porque los domingos los niños les preguntan a sus padres: —«¿Me das mi domingo?» Así es como piden su dinero.

compartir *to share*

El domingo es el día cuando los adultos dan dinero a los niños. Los chicos pueden comprar lo que quieran o necesiten o lo pueden ahorrar. Ellos deciden qué comprarán, no sus padres. Realmente es el día cuando los adultos les dedican tiempo a los hijos, llevándolos al parque, a la feria, o a otros lugares divertidos e interesantes. Y es el día en que los niños se divierten comprándose cosas que quizás los adultos no les comprarían.

Para pensar

1. ¿Cómo pasan los domingos las familias en los países hispanoamericanos?
2. ¿Por qué es importante el domingo para los niños en México?
3. ¿Qué significa «¿me das mi domingo?»?
4. ¿Qué pueden hacer los niños con el dinero que reciben?
5. ¿Por qué es importante para los miembros de una familia pasar tiempo juntos?

1 Cora mucho
2 Coma comida buena
3 Duerma cuando Ud. necesita dormir
4 Ame muchas personas y animales
5

Pañales

Consejos – advice

El príncipe Guillermo
la princesa Kate
Visiten otros países

Arnold – No vuelva
- Venga a mi casa pero cuente a María primero
- quedese (keep)

Esfuersase → Try harder
Esforzarse
↳ put in the effort

Tratar → to try new things

5
Cartas al periódico

Adjectives and Adverbs

1 Vocabulario

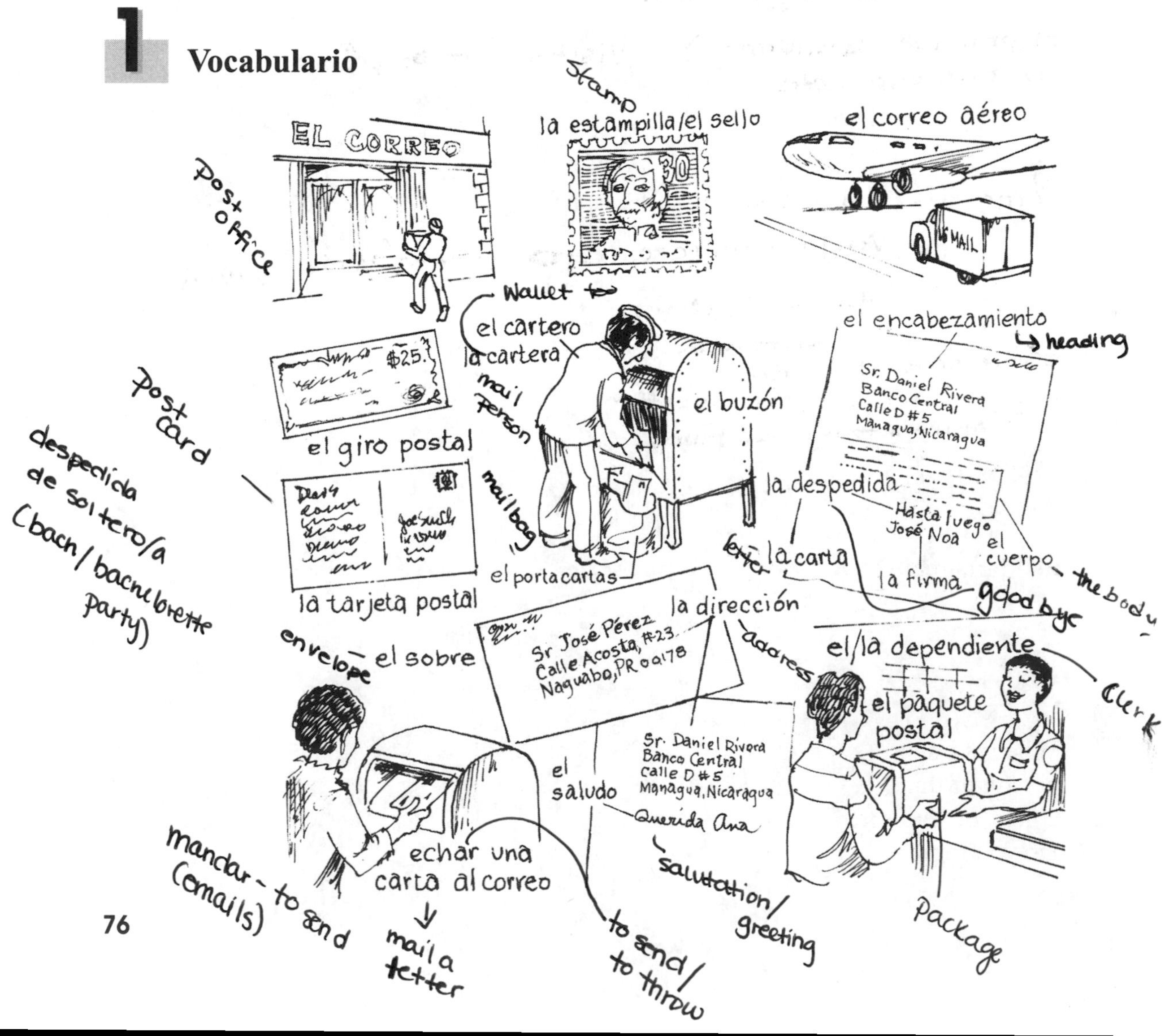

ACTIVIDAD A

Picture story. Mario is sending a letter to his friend Marta in Ponce, Puerto Rico. These are the steps he takes.

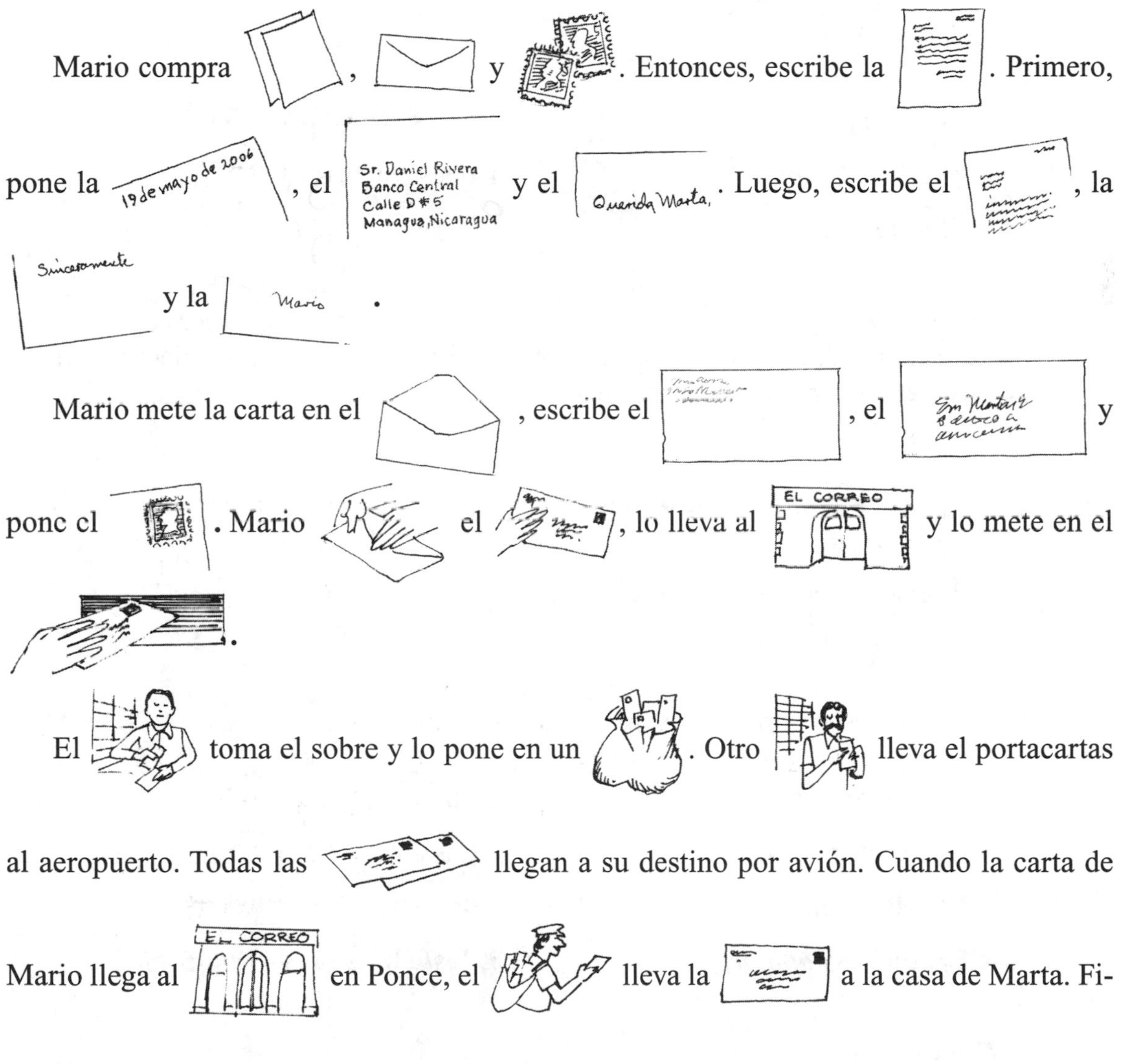

Mario compra ______, ______ y ______. Entonces, escribe la ______. Primero, pone la ______, el ______ y el ______. Luego, escribe el ______, la ______ y la ______.

Mario mete la carta en el ______, escribe el ______, el ______ y pone el ______. Mario ______ el ______, lo lleva al ______ y lo mete en el ______.

El ______ toma el sobre y lo pone en un ______. Otro ______ lleva el portacartas al aeropuerto. Todas las ______ llegan a su destino por avión. Cuando la carta de Mario llega al ______ en Ponce, el ______ lleva la ______ a la casa de Marta. Finalmente Marta recibe su carta. ¡Está contentísima!

2 When we speak about someone or something, we use adjectives to describe that person or thing. You already know that adjectives in Spanish agree in gender (masculine or feminine) and number (singular or plural) with the noun they describe. Do you remember how to make an adjective feminine?

Él es *simpático*. — **Ella es** simpática.

Él es *inteligente*. — **Ella es** inteligente.

Él es *joven*. — **Ella es** joven.

Adjectives ending in **o** change the **o** to **a** in the feminine form. Other adjectives remain unchanged. Remember, however, that there is an exception: adjectives of nationality ending in a consonant add an **a** for the feminine form. Look at the following examples.

Carlos es *español* y María es *española*. — *Carlos is Spanish and María is Spanish.*

Paul es *francés* y Monique es *francesa*. — *Paul is French and Monique is French.*

How do we describe more than one person or thing?

Él es *pequeño*. — **Ellos son** pequeños.

Ella es *pequeña*. — **Ellas son** pequeñas.

Él / ella es *fuerte*. — **Ellos/ellas son** fuertes.

Él / ella es *popular*. — **Ellos/ellas son** populares.

The rules are very simple:

RULES: If the singular adjective ends in a vowel, add **s** to form the plural. If the singular adjective ends in a consonant, add **es** to form the plural.

You also know that descriptive adjectives usually follow the noun:

Compro un sobre *azul*. — *I buy a blue envelope.*

Leo un periódico *argentino*. — *I read an Argentinean newspaper.*

ACTIVIDAD B

One of your classmates describes some people or objects to you. You want to know about other people or things.

EXAMPLE: YOUR CLASSMATE: **Miguel es mexicano. (Isabel)**
YOU: **¿Es *Isabel mexicana* también?**

1. YOUR CLASSMATE: La nueva profesora es española. (el director)
   YOU: Es el director español también

2. YOUR CLASSMATE: El español es fácil. (la biología)
   YOU: Es la biología fácil también?

3. YOUR CLASSMATE: El carro de Eduardo es amarillo. (su casa)
   YOU: Es su casa amarilla también?

4. YOUR CLASSMATE: Mi perro es grande y gordo. (tus gatos)
   YOU: Son tus gatos grandes y gordos también?

5. YOUR CLASSMATE: El padre de Raúl es alto y rubio. (la madre)
   YOU: Es la madre de Raúl alta y rubia también

6. YOUR CLASSMATE: Mis hermanas son simpáticas. (tus hermanos)
   YOU: Son tus hermanos simpáticos también?

3

Do you remember **alguno** and **ninguno**? They stand before the noun and drop the final **o** before a masculine singular noun:

¿Conoces a *algún* periodista?	*Do you know any newspaperman?*
No, no conozco a *ningún* periodista.	*No, I don't know any newspaperman.*

There is a special group of adjectives that may stand before or after the noun. Look at the following examples:

Luis es un chico *bueno*.	**Luis es un *buen* chico.**	*Louis is a good boy.*
José es un alumno *malo*.	**José es un *mal* alumno.**	*Joe is a bad student.*

Leo el capítulo *primero*.	**Leo el *primer* capítulo.**	*I read the first chapter.*
Vivo en el piso *tercero*.	**Vivo en el *tercer* piso.**	*I live on the third floor.*

The sentences in both Spanish columns mean the same thing. What happened to the adjectives in the right column? ________________ . They dropped the final **o**. The adjective was shortened. What is the gender of the nouns described by those adjectives? ________________ . Are they singular or plural? ________________ .

4

Now look at these sentences:

El español es mi *tercera* clase.	*Spanish is my third class.*
Ellas son *malas* alumnas.	*They are bad students.*
Los *primeros* capítulos son largos.	*The first chapters are long.*
Luis y Carlos son *buenos* chicos.	*Luis and Carlos are good boys.*

Were the adjectives shortened in the above sentences? ________ . Here's the easy rule:

RULE: **Bueno, malo, primero,** and **tercero** are shortened only before a masculine singular noun.

ACTIVIDAD C

Complete the following sentences with the correct form of the adjective in parentheses.

1. Siempre saco __malas__ notas en álgebra. (malo)
2. ¿Tienes __algunas__ preguntas? (alguno)
3. Cuando hace __mal__ tiempo, leo un __buen__ libro. (malo, bueno)
4. Es la __tercera__ vez que repito la palabra. (tercero)
5. Me gustan las __primeras__ semanas del verano. (primero)
6. El __tercer__ mes del año es marzo. (tercero)
7. La __primera__ página de la lección es fácil. (primero)

8. ____________ día voy a hablar bien el español. (alguno)

9. Yo no tengo ____________ examen. (ninguno)

10. Quiero comer un ____________ desayuno. (bueno)

ACTIVIDAD D

Francisco is always saying the opposite of his twin brother Fernando:

EXAMPLE: **Carlos es un buen amigo.** **No, Carlos es un *mal* amigo.**

1. María es una mala estudiante. ____________________
2. Hoy hace buen tiempo. ____________________
3. El hijo del Sr. Pérez es un mal chico. ____________________
4. Ella saca buenas notas en español. ____________________
5. Leer es un mal hábito. ____________________

5

The adjective **grande** can also stand before or after the noun. But look what happens:

Buenos Aires es una ciudad *grande*.	*Buenos Aires is a large city.*
Buenos Aires es una *gran* ciudad.	*Buenos Aires is a great city.*
El general es un soldado *grande*.	*The general is a large soldier.*
El general es un *gran* soldado.	*The general is a great soldier.*
Nueva York tiene edificios grandes.	*New York has large buildings.*
Nueva York tiene grandes edificios.	*New York has great buildings.*

How do you express great before a singular noun (masculine or feminine)? ____________ . Before a plural noun (masculine or feminine)? __________ . What does the adjective **grande(s)** mean when placed after a noun?

RULES: After a noun, **grande(-s)** means *large* or *big*.
Before a noun, **gran (grandes)** means great.

ACTIVIDAD E

Describe five large or great people, places, things, using a form of **grande.**

EXAMPLE: Simón Bolívar: **un gran general**

1. ______________________________
2. ______________________________
3. ______________________________
4. ______________________________
5. ______________________________

ACTIVIDAD F

Here are some statements taken from a newspaper. Look at the following index and tell in what section they would be found.

EXAMPLE: un nocaut en el último round *la sección deportiva*

1. ¡Gran venta de ropa de verano! ______________
2. Hombre roba varias tiendas. ______________

3. Necesitamos más policías para combatir el crimen. ______________

4. Tienes que tener más confianza en tus relaciones. ______________

5. Carro negro, en buenas condiciones, precio bajo. ______________

6. Anotación final: Yanquis 7, Atléticos 3 ______________

7. Pérez-Carvajal anuncian matrimonio. ______________

8. *Ataque de los Monstruos del Espacio* estrena en el Teatro Capri. ______________

9. Mundo Latino (Variedades) Canal 7 ______________

10. Joven de 25 años busca persona atractiva para una relación seria ______________

Problemas de amor

Let's read now about a special section of a newspaper — **el consultorio sentimental**.

Todos los días millones de personas por todo el mundo compran periódicos. ¿Qué leen estas personas? ¿Las noticias, los anuncios, los artículos? Claro que sí. Pero también leen una sección importante para ellos: «El consultorio sentimental».

¿Estás triste y solo? ¿Tienes problemas personales que no puedes resolver? Quizás necesitas la ayuda profesional de Doña Lupita. Todos los días miles de personas escriben cartas a su «Consultorio Sentimental» del periódico para pedir consejo. ¿Estás de acuerdo con los consejos que da la gran Lupita?

el consejo *advice*
estar de acuerdo *to agree*

Querida Lupita:

Tengo trece años y estoy enamorada seriamente por primera vez. Él tiene catorce años y está en mi tercera clase del día. Es amable, inteligente, simpático y alegre. Baila divinamente y participa activamente en muchos deportes. Yo soy seria, estudiosa, cuida-

enamorado *in love*

cuidadoso *careful*

dosa y sincera. Tengo un gran sentido del humor y muchas personas dicen que soy atractiva. Mi problema es que quiero salir con él, pero soy tímida y no puedo iniciar una conversación con él. ¿Qué debo hacer? Ayúdeme, por favor.

deber *should*

Desesperada

Querida Desesperada:

¡Eres una gran chica! Debes tener confianza. Los chicos prefieren una chica como tú, bonita, seria y simpática. Tienes que darle una oportunidad al chico de conocerte como eres realmente. ¿Por qué no lo llamas por teléfono? ¿O le escribes una nota? Si tienes miedo, ¿por qué no organizas una fiesta en casa y lo invitas? Buena suerte.

confianza *confidence*

Doña Lupita

ACTIVIDAD G

Answer the following questions about the story.

1. ¿Quiénes escriben cartas a Doña Lupita?

2. ¿Cómo se llama la sección del periódico para personas con problemas personales?

3. ¿Quién es «Desesperada»?

4. ¿Cuál es el problema de «Desesperada»?

5. ¿Cómo es «Desesperada»?

6. ¿Cómo es el chico que ella describe?

____

7. ¿Qué consejos da Doña Lupita?

____

8. ¿Estás de acuerdo con sus consejos? ¿Por qué (no)?

____

There are some new words in the story ending in **-mente**. Do you recall them? **Activamente**, **divinamente**, **seriamente**, and so on. These are called adverbs—expressions that describe another adverb, and adjective, or a verb. How are they formed? Very simply, **muy facílmente**: just add the ending **-mente** to the feminine singular form of the adjective. (**-mente** is usually the equivalent to the English *-ly*.) Let's look at some examples:

FEMININE FORM OF ADJECTIVE	ADVERB
rápida **seria** **fácil**	**rápida*mente*** quickly **seria*mente*** - seriously **fácil*mente*** - easily

"-ly"

Can you continue giving the adverbs formed from the following adjectives?

atento	*attentive; polite*	atentamente
ciego	*blind*	ciegamente
loco	*crazy*	locamente
popular	*popular*	popularmente
útil	*useful*	útilmente
hábil	*skillful*	hábilmente

Your friend Julia was chosen for the lead in the school play. Tell why.

EXAMPLE: **Ella es hábil. Ella actúa *hábilmente*.**

1. Ella es seria. Ella actúa Seriamente.

2. Ella es natural. Ella actúa naturalmente.

3. Ella es inteligente. Ella actúa inteligentamente.

4. Ella es magnífica. Ella actúa magnificamente.

5. Ella es dulce. Ella actúa dulcemente.

ACTIVIDAD I

You are asked to describe how some of your friends do certain things.

EXAMPLE: **Víctor participa *activamente* en los deportes.**

1. Rosa habla perfectamente el francés. (perfectly)

2. Fernando estudia seriamente las matemáticas. (seriously)

3. Carlos siempre entra rapidamente en la clase. (quickly)

4. Tomás habla inteligentemente. (intelligently)

5. Miguel come ~~fácilmente~~ Cuidadosamente. (carefully)

6. Simón aprende facílmente el español. (easily)

7. Juanita es muy inteligente. (really)

8. Susana siempre actúa locamente. (crazily)

7 There are other common adverbs that are not formed from adjectives. Here is a list of the most important ones:

ahora *now*	**hoy** *today*	**muy** *very*
bastante *enough*	**lejos** *far, far away*	**poco** *little*
bien *well*	**mal** *badly, poorly*	**pronto** *soon*
casi *almost*	**mañana** *tomorrow*	**siempre** *always*
cerca *near, nearby*	**más** *more*	**tarde** *late*
demasiado *too (much)*	**menos** *less*	**temprano** *early*
despacio *slowly*	**mucho** *a lot, much*	**ya** *already*
después *later, afterwards*		

ACTIVIDAD J

Margarita always says the opposite of what her mother says. What does Margarita say?

EXAMPLE: **Tu padre baila bien.** **No, mi padre baila *mal.***

1. Tu hermanito come poco. mucho
2. Tú vas a llegar tarde. temprano
3. Tu hermana debe trabajar menos. más
4. Tus abuelos viven cerca. lejos
5. Tú debes salir ahora. después

ACTIVIDAD K

Work with a partner. One student asks the question: **¿Cuándo vas a . . . ?** The other student answers using a Spanish adverb.

EXAMPLE: **hacer la tarea de español** (tomorrow)
¿Cuándo vas a hacer la tarea de español?
Voy a hacer la tarea de español *mañana.*

1. ir al cine (today) Voy al cine hoy
2. escribir una carta (afterwards) Voy a escribir una carta después
3. salir de la clase (soon) Voy a salir de la clase pronto
4. leer el periódico (now) Voy a leer el periódico ahora
5. dormir (early) Voy a dormir temprano

8 **Bien** and **bueno; mal** and **malo**

Remember that **bien** and **mal** are adverbs. They describe actions and don't change their form. **Bueno** and **malo** are adjectives. They describe nouns and agree with them in gender and number.

As with other descriptive adjectives, **bueno** and **malo** agree with the noun and usually follow it.

María es *buena*.	**Pablo es *malo*.**
Jorge es *bueno*.	**Rosa es *mala*.**
María y Jorge son buenos.	**Pablo y Rosa son *malos*.**
But:	
María escribe *bien*.	**Pablo escribe *mal*.**
María y Jorge escriben *bien*.	**Pablo y Rosa escriben *mal*.**

Complete with the correct word: **bien** or **bueno (buena, buenos, buenas)**.

1. La película es buena .

2. Roberto es un amigo bueno.

3. Yo estoy bien, gracias.

4. Tú cantas y bailas muy bien.

5. Leo una novela buena.

6. Dan películas buenas en el Teatro Colón.

7. Ricardo es un niño bueno.

8. El bebé duerme bien.

ACTIVIDAD M

Repeat **Actividad L**, using **mal** or **malo (mala, malos, malas)**.

1. La película es mala.

2. Roberto es un amigo malo.

3. Yo estoy mal.

4. Tú cantas y bailas muy mal.

5. Leo una novela mala.

6. Dan películas malas en el Teatro Colón.

7. El bebé duerme mal.

Preguntas Personales

1. ¿Qué periódico lees?

____

2. ¿Qué sección del periódico prefieres?

____

3. ¿Te gusta escribir cartas? ¿Por qué o por qué no?

____

4. ¿Por qué colecciona la gente estampillas?

____

5. ¿Qué tipo de novela te gusta leer? ¿Por qué?

____

6. ¿Qué clase de correo reciben en tu casa?

____

7. ¿Publica tu escuela algún periódico? ¿Cómo se llama? ¿Qué piensas de él? ¿Es bueno?

____

8. ¿Crees que es posible recibir consejos útiles del «consultorio sentimental» de un periódico? ¿Por qué sí o no?

____

Información Personal

Tell how you do the following activities.

1. Yo aprendo español ______________________ .

2. Yo hablo ______________________ .

3. Yo como ______________________ .

4. Yo contesto ______________________ en clase.

5. Yo camino ______________________ .

Composición

You are writing to the "Consultorio Sentimental" of a newspaper. Tell them your name and age, describe yourself, and ask advice to solve a real or imaginary problem.

___________ de ___________ de 20___

Querido (-a) ______________:

____

____

____

____

____

____

____

____

____

____

Un cordial saludo de

____

CÁPSULA CULTURAL

¡Noticias de última hora!

Hay miles de periódicos y revistas publicados diariamente en el mundo de habla española. Estas publicaciones tratan de una variedad de asuntos: noticias internacionales y locales, deportes, cine, comida, moda, automóviles, televisión, salud, negocios, dinero, etc.

En España e Hispanoamérica hay kioscos o puestos de periódicos y revistas en casi cada esquina importante. Estos kioscos ofrecen una gran selección de periódicos, revistas, libros de bolsillo y otros materiales de lectura. Algunas de las publicaciones más populares son para los adolescentes y jóvenes.

Si echamos una mirada al índice de una de estas revistas, vemos secciones de «gente», «belleza», «moda», «chismes», «salud», «consultorio sentimental» y «humor».

A veces, hay una tira cómica con dibujos o una «fotonovela». Las fotonovelas son muy populares entre los jóvenes. Son cuentos cortos románticos, ilustrados con fotografías.

De esta manera, el lector puede leer un cuento mientras mira las fotos de las personas. ¡Es como mirar una telenovela!

el asunto *matter*

casi *almost*

el bolsillo *pocket*

el índice *table of contents*

el chisme *gossip*

Para pensar

1. ¿Dónde se venden los periódicos y las revistas?
2. ¿De qué materias tratan?
3. ¿Qué se lee en la sección del horóscopo?
4. ¿Si necesitas consejo sobre relaciones románticas, qué sección consultas?
5. Algunos creen que el Internet va a reemplazar los periódicos y las revistas. ¿Qué opinas?

Repaso I

(Lecciones 1–5)

LECCIÓN 1

a. Spanish interrogatives

¿a quién(-es)? *whom?*

¿adónde? *where (to)?*

¿cómo? *how?*

¿cuál(-es)? *what? which one(s)?*

¿cuándo? *when?*

¿cuánto (-a, -os, -as)? *how much (many)?*

¿de quién(-es)? *whose?*

¿dónde? *where?*

¿por qué? *why*

¿qué? *what?, which?*

¿quién(-es)? *who?*

b. **Conocer** and **saber** mean *to know.* **Conocer** is used in the sense of *to be acquainted, to be familiar with*; **saber** means *to know facts, to have information about something*:

Conozco **ese libro.**	*I know (I am familiar with) that book.*
Sé **que ella viene mañana.**	*I know that she's coming tomorrow.*

Saber followed by an infinitive means *to know how to.*

El ***sabe hablar*** **español.**	*He knows how to speak Spanish.*

LECCIÓN 2

Some Spanish verbs have stem changes in all forms of the present tense, except for **nosotros**. There are three types of changes:

(1) **-AR, -ER**, and **-IR** verbs that change **e** to **ie**.

pensar	**p*ie*nso, p*ie*nsas, p*ie*nsa, pensamos, p*ie*nsan**
perder	**p*ie*rdo, p*ie*rdes, p*ie*rde, perdemos, p*ie*rden**
mentir	**m*ie*nto, m*ie*ntes, m*ie*nte, mentimos, m*ie*nten**

(2) **-AR, -ER**, and **-IR** verbs that change **o** to **ue**.

almorzar	**alm*ue*rzo, alm*ue*rzas, alm*ue*rza, almorzamos, alm*ue*rzan**
volver	**v*ue*lvo, v*ue*lves, v*ue*lve, volvemos, v*ue*lven**
dormir	**d*ue*rmo, d*ue*rmes, d*ue*rme, dormimos, d*ue*rmen**

NOTE: **Jugar** changes **u** to **ue**: **j*ue*go, j*ue*gas, j*ue*ga, jugamos, j*ue*gan**

(3) **-IR** verbs that change **e** to **i**.

repetir	**repito, repites, repite, repetimos, repiten**

LECCIÓN 3

a. Spanish negatives and their corresponding affirmative expressions:

NEGATIVE	AFFIRMATIVE
nada *nothing*	**algo** *something*
nadie *no one, nobody*	**alguien** *someone, somebody*
ni . . . ni *neither . . . nor*	**o** *or*
nunca / **jamás** } *never*	**siempre** *always*
tampoco *neither*	**también** *also, too*
ninguno (-a, -os, -as) *no, none*	**alguno (-a, -os, -as)** *any, some*

b. There are two ways of negating a sentence in Spanish.

no + verb + negative word:	***No*** **quiero** ***nada***.	*I don't want anything.*
negative word + verb:	***Nada*** **quiero**.	

c. When the object of a verb is a negative or an affirmative word referring to a person, the personal **a** is used.

Llamo a alguien. *I call someone.*

No llamo a nadie. *I don't call anyone.*
A nadie llamo. *I call no one.*

LECCIÓN 4

a. **Vamos a** + infinitive is used in Spanish to express *let us*.

Vamos a jugar **al tenis**. *Let's play tennis.*

Vamos is used to express *let's go*:

Vamos a **la fiesta**. *Let's go to the party.*

b. Singular formal commands are formed by changing the ending **-o** of the **yo**-form of the present tense to **-e** for **-AR** verbs and to **-a** for **-ER** and **-IR** verbs. Plural formal commands are formed by adding **-n** to the singular command.

	REGULAR COMMANDS		
INFINITIVE	PRESENT TENSE YO-FORM	FORMAL COMMAND	
		SINGULAR	PLURAL
hablar	**habl*o***	**habl*e***	**habl*en***
comer	**com*o***	**com*a***	**com*an***
dormir	**duerm*o***	**duerm*a***	**duerm*an***

	IRREGULAR COMMANDS	
INFINITIVE	SINGULAR	PLURAL
dar	**dé**	**den**
ir	**vaya**	**vayan**
ser	**sea**	**sean**

c. Informal commands in the singular (**tú**-form) are identical with the **Ud./él/ella**-form of the present tense.

INFINITIVE	UD./ÉL/ELLA-FORM	INFORMAL COMMAND
hablar	**habl*a***	**habl*a***
comer	**com*e***	**com*e***
dormir	**duerm*e***	**duerm*e***

d. Negative informal commands in the singular (**tú**-form) are formed by adding **s** to the singular formal command.

FORMAL COMMAND	NEGATIVE INFORMAL COMMAND
salga	**no salga*s***

e. Many verbs have irregular informal command forms:

decir: di	**ir: ve**	**salir: sal**	**tener: ten**
hacer: haz	**poner: pon**	**ser: sé**	**venir: ven**

LECCIÓN 5

a. Adjectives agree in gender and number with the nouns they describe. Adjectives that end in **o** change the **o** to **a** in the feminine form. Other adjectives remain unchanged, except for adjectives of nationality, which have feminine forms in **-a: el alumno español, la alumna española**.

To form the plural of adjectives, add **s** to an adjective ending in a vowel and **es** to an adjective ending in a consonant.

inteligent*e* **inteligente*s***

azu*l* **azul*es***

Descriptive adjectives in Spanish usually follow the noun.

una mujer *fuerte*

b. The adjectives **alguno** and **ninguno** stand before the noun and drop the final **o** before a masculine singular noun.

¿Tienes *algún* periódico?

No, no tengo *ningún* periódico.

c. **Bueno, malo, primero,** and **tercero** may stand before or after the noun. They are shortened before a masculine singular noun.

Voy a un *buen* hotel. / Voy a un hotel *bueno*.

Es un *mal* consejo. / Es un consejo *malo*.

Lean el *primer* capítulo. / Lean el capítulo *primero*.

Vivo en el *tercer* piso. / Vivo en el piso *tercero*.

d. **Grande** means *large* when it stands after the noun. It means *great* when it stands before the noun. **Grande** becomes **gran** before a singular noun.

Madrid es una gran ciudad.	*Madrid is a great city.*
Mi abuelo es un hombre grande.	*My grandfather is a large man.*

e. Adverbs describe another adverb, an adjective, or a verb. Adverbs are usually formed by adding **-mente** to the singular feminine form of the adjective.

rápida **rápida*mente***

Some common adverbs are not formed from adjectives.

f. The adverbs **bien** and **mal** do not charge form. The adjectives **bueno** and **malo** agree in gender and number with the noun they describe.

Ella habla *bien* (*mal*). / Ellas hablan *bien* (*mal*).

Ella es *buena* (*mala*). / Ellas son *buenas* (*malas*).

Here are ten pictures of people doing various activities. Complete the description below each picture by using the correct for of one of the following verbs.

almorzar	**costar**	**jugar**	**preferir**	**servir**
comenzar	**dormir**	**pensar**	**querer**	**sonreír**

1. El bebé __________ la siesta.

2. Los alumnos __________ en la cafetería.

3. La Sra. Gómez __________ empanadas.

4. Anita y Juanita __________ .

5. La mamá pregunta: «¿Qué traje de baño __________ ?»

6. Jorge __________ en Rosita.

7. ¿Cuánto __________ esta cadena?

8. Los muchachos __________ a los bolos.

9. Carlitos __________ las gafas de sol.

10. La película __________ pronto.

ACTIVIDAD B

¿Quién es Mandrako el mago? Read the following sentences and then decide which one of the five men they describe. Put an X in the correct circle.

No lleva nunca sombrero.
No lleva corbata tampoco.
Lleva gafas muy grandes.
Sonríe siempre.
Usa un arete en una oreja.
También lleva una cadena de oro.
Jamás lleva traje.
No tiene mucho pelo pero tiene barba.

ACTIVIDAD C

How many of these words do you remember? Fill in the Spanish words, then read down the boxed column of letters. What do Miguel and Rosa see at the beach?

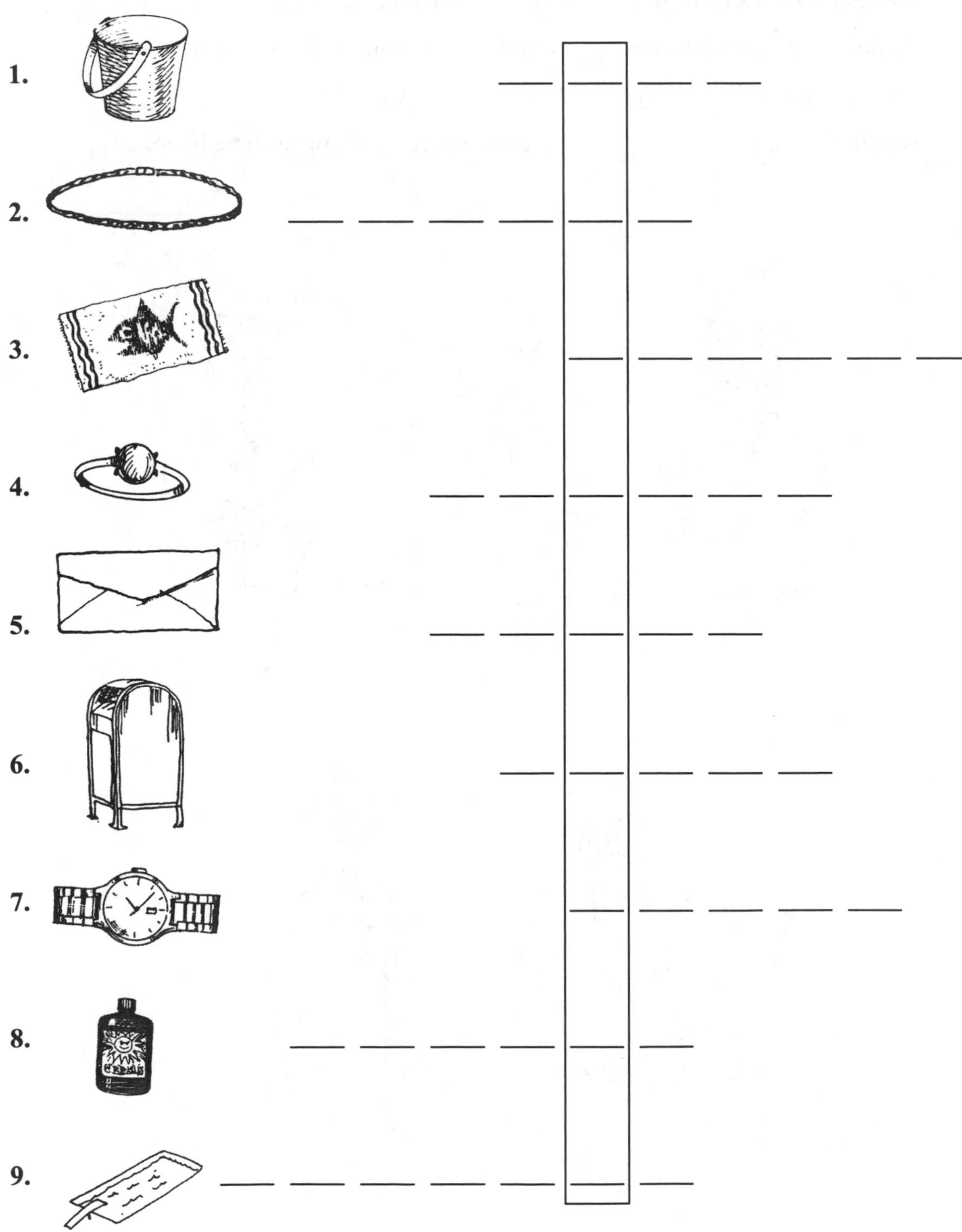

ACTIVIDAD D

Hidden in the puzzle below are

8 ADJECTIVES 16 ADVERBS

______	______	______
______	______	______
______	______	______
______	______	______
______	______	______
______	______	______
______	______	______
______	______	______

Find the hidden words, circle them in the puzzle, and then write them in the space above. The words may read from left to right, right or left, up or down, or diagonally.

C	A	S	I	E	M	P	R	E	E
H	F	S	O	N	E	M	R	T	L
U	O	C	Á	Ñ	B	U	E	N	A
O	I	Y	U	M	I	C	E	I	M
G	R	A	N	D	E	H	D	S	N
E	E	S	U	O	N	O	R	G	O
I	S	L	C	E	R	C	A	U	J
C	C	O	D	I	M	Í	T	N	E
E	P	R	O	N	T	O	C	O	L
H	Á	B	I	L	M	E	N	T	E

ACTIVIDAD E

Here are eight pictures. Write an appropriate command under each of the pictures, using the following verbs.

cerrar	**ir**	**poner**	**traer**	**volver**
comprar	**mirar**	**salir**	**venir**	

1. ¡No ________ la televisión ahora!

2. ¡Manuela, ____________ Ud. a la pizarra!

3. ¡________ Ud. el televisor allí!

4. ¡No ____________ el vestido rojo,

____________ el azul!

5. ¡____________ a jugar afuera!

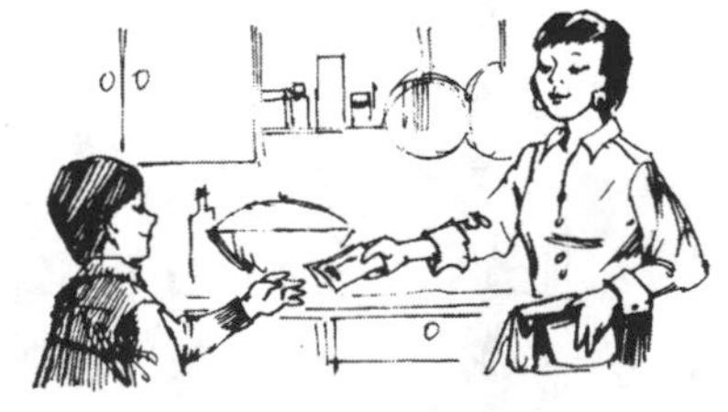

6. ¡________ a la tienda y ________ pan!

7. ¡No ____________ a casa tarde!

8. ¡________ Ud. la ventana, por favor!

ACTIVIDAD F

Unscramble the words. Then unscramble the letters in the circles to find out the message you received by mail after responding to an ad in a newspaper.

EROCOR ◯ ☐ ☐ ☐ ☐ ◯

ATACR ☐ ◯ ☐ ◯ ☐

DIERÓCIPO ☐ ☐ ☐ ◯ ☐ ☐ ◯ ☐ ☐

NUACISON ☐ ◯ ☐ ☐ ☐ ☐ ☐ ◯

Recibimos buenas ______________________.

ACTIVIDAD G

Let's do something special this weekend. What? To find the answer, write the letters in the blanks below:

1. Podemos ir al museo para ver la ___ ___ ___ (1) ___ ___ ___ ___ ___ (2) ___ (3) ___ de arte.

2. Hay un ___ ___ ___ (4) ___ ___ ___ (5) ___ (6) ___ ___ de música clásica.

3. En el cine dan una ___ (7) ___ (11) ___ ___ ___ ___ ___ (8) ___ (9) de ciencia ficción.

4. ¿Quieres ir a ___ ___ ___ ___ ___ (12) ___ esta noche?

5. En el estadio hay un ___ ___ ___ ___ (13) ___ (10) ___ ___ ___ ___ (14)

___ ___ ___ ___ ___ (15) ___ (16)

¡Vamos a ___ (7) ___ (12) ___ (13) ___ (10) ___ (4) ___ (9) ___ (6) ___ (11) ___ (3) ___ (5) ___ (8)

___ (1) ___ (2) ___ (14) ___ (16) ___ (15) **!**

ACTIVIDAD H

Crucigrama

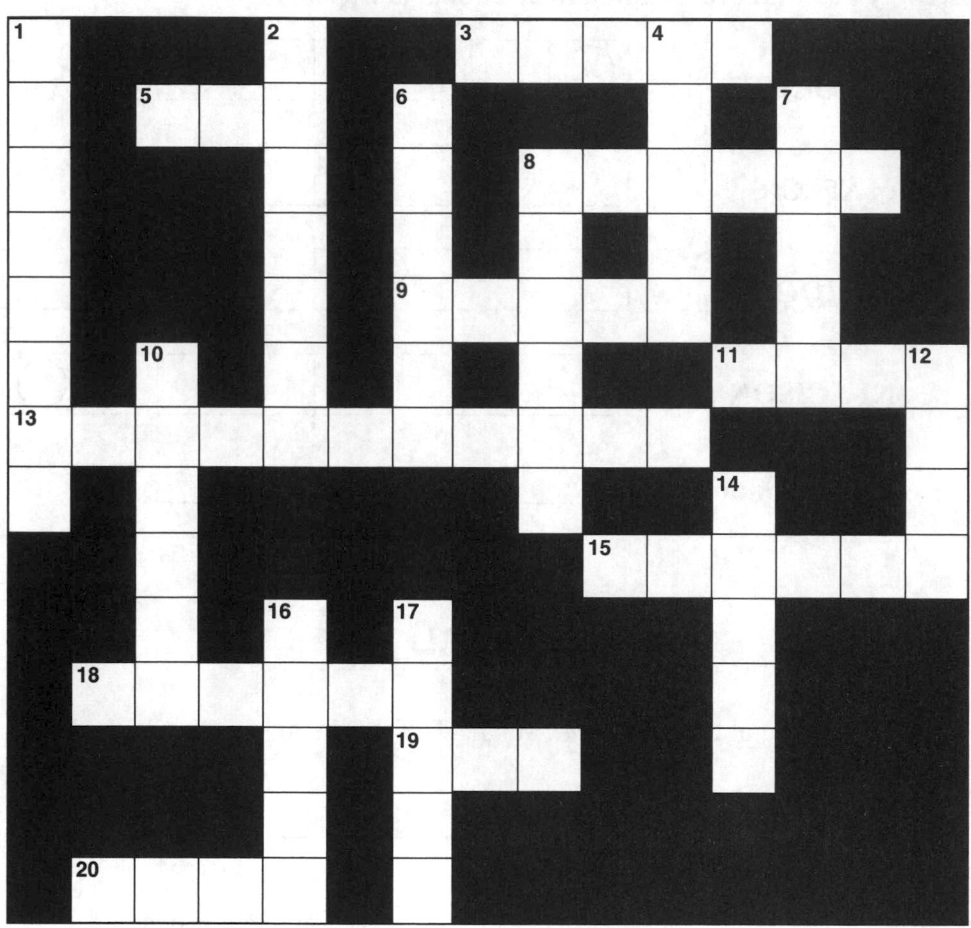

HORIZONTALES

3. leaves
5. river
8. rock, stone
9. spider
11. flower
13. grasshopper
15. earth, soil
18. bird
19. sun
20. lake

VERTICALES

1. butterfly
2. ant
4. bee
6. worm
7. tree
8. plant
10. rain
12. frog
14. grass
16. field
17. fly

ACTIVIDAD I

Picture Story Can you read this story? Whenever you come to a picture, read it as if it were a Spanish word.

Jorge Luis Pérez tiene 13 años. Hoy es  y está en la  con sus . Su le pone  en todo el  porque hace mucho . A Jorge Luis le gustan la , el 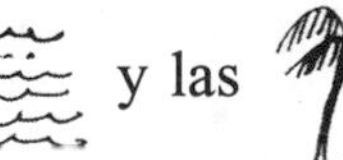 y las . Él quiere vivir en una  tropical, tener un  y pasar los días en . La Sra. Pérez se pone las , extiende su  sobre la  al lado de una  y toma el . El Sr. Pérez prepara la para la . Mientras tanto, Jorge Luis juega con sus , por la  con su , en el , busca  y hace un  con su  y su . Un  perfecto.

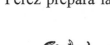

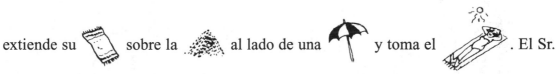

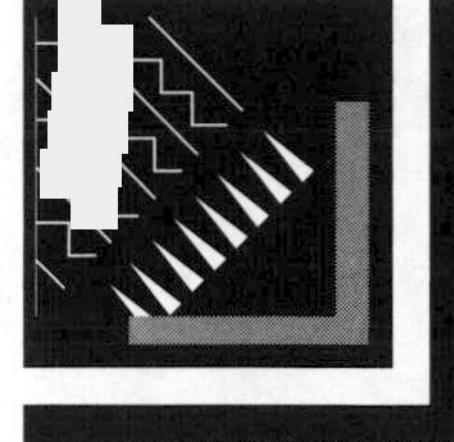

Segunda Parte

6

Por la mañana / Por la noche

Reflexive Verbs; Passive SE

1 Vocabulario

The new words that follow are all verbs. They belong to a special family of verbs called REFLEXIVE VERBS. See if you can guess their meanings.

Match the descriptions with the pictures:

Él se peina.	**Nosotras nos acostamos.**
Ellas se visten.	**Uds. se cepillan los dientes.**
Tú te despiertas.	**Carlos se levanta.**
Yo me lavo.	**Mi papá se afeita.**

1. ______________________

2. ______________________

3. ______________________

4. ______________________

5. ______________________ 6. ______________________

7. ______________________ 8. ______________________

2 A verb is reflexive when the subject does something to itself. To use a verb "reflexively," we add a special pronoun, called a *reflexive pronoun*, to indicate that the subject and object of the verb refer to the same person or thing. You probably noticed, however, that some English verbs do not seem to be reflexive while their Spanish equivalents are.

For example, *to get up* is **levantarse**. The verb **levantar** by itself, without the reflexive pronoun, means simply *to raise or to lift*:

Él *levanta* la mesa. *He lifts the table.*

But:

Él *se levanta*. *He gets up.* (literally, *He lifts himself.*)

Let's look at some more reflexive verbs in Spanish that are not reflexive in English. Just remember that the reflexive pronoun in Spanish REFLECTS the action expressed by the verb on the subject:

La abuela *divierte* a los niños. *The grandmother amuses the children.*

La abuela *se divierte*. *The grandmother has fun (amuses herself).*

El papá *acuesta* al bebé. *The father puts the baby to bed.*

El papá *se acuesta*. *The father goes to bed (puts himself to bed).*

Llamo **a Luis.**	*I call Luis.*
Me llamo **Luis.**	*My name is Luis (I call myself Luis).*

ACTIVIDAD B

In each group, select the sentence with a reflexive verb:

1. (a) Se lava con agua fría.
(b) Lava el carro con agua fría.

2. (a) La muchacha mira la televisión.
(b) La muchacha se mira en el espejo.

3. (a) Mi madre viste a mi hermana.
(b) Mi madre se viste.

4. (a) Ud. se despierta temprano.
(b) Ud. despierta a su mamá temprano.

5. (a) José pone el abrigo en la silla.
(b) José se pone el abrigo.

El ciclismo

Let's read a story about a very popular sport— bicycle racing. How many reflexive verbs can you identify?

En España y en muchos países hispanoamericanos, el ciclismo es más que un deporte—es una pasión. En Colombia, por ejemplo, cada año más de sesenta ciclistas participan en una carrera de varios días. El ganador es un héroe nacional y recibe mucho dinero y regalos.

la carrera *race*
el ganador *winner*

Escuchemos una entrevista con el joven Víctor Veloz, un ciclista muy popular.

PERIODISTA: Buenos días, Víctor. Queremos saber cómo vive un campeón. ¿Puedes describir un día típico de tu vida?

VÍCTOR: Bueno. Por lo general, me despierto muy temprano, a las cinco de la mañana. Me gusta practicar cuando no hace mucho calor.

PERIODISTA: Sí, claro. ¿Qué haces para comenzar el día?

VÍCTOR: Después de levantarme, me lavo la cara y las manos, me afeito y me cepillo los dientes.

PERIODISTA: Sí, sí, comprendo. Eso hacemos todos. ¿Pero, haces algo especial para hacerte campeón?

hacerse *to become*

VÍCTOR: Tomo un desayuno ligero. Me visto, me pongo los zapatos, me peino y salgo a practicar dos o tres horas. Luego vuelvo a casa, me baño y almuerzo. Después del almuerzo, que es bastante grande, me acuesto.

ligero *light*

PERIODISTA: ¿Y después, qué haces por la tarde?

VÍCTOR: Hago ejercicios y monto en bicicleta dos o tres horas más. Me siento a comer a las siete y media y me acuesto antes de las diez. Necesito mucho descanso y no tengo tiempo para divertirme.

sentarse (ie) *to sit down*

PERIODISTA: Muy interesante. Veo que no haces nada excepcional. Todos los jóvenes tienen la misma oportunidad de hacerse campeones. Todos son iguales. A propósito, tienes una bicicleta bonita. ¿Cuánto vale?

valer *to be worth, to cost*

VÍCTOR: Diez mil dólares.

Answer each question using complete sentences.

1. ¿Qué es el ciclismo para muchos hispanoamericanos?

____

2. ¿Qué recibe generalmente el ganador?

____

3. ¿Qué quiere saber el periodista sobre Víctor Veloz?

____

4. ¿Por qué se levanta Víctor tan temprano?

____

5. ¿Qué hace Víctor después de levantarse?

____

6. ¿Qué clase de desayuno toma Víctor?

____

7. ¿Qué hace Víctor después del almuerzo? ¿Por qué?

____

8. Según el periodista, ¿qué oportunidades tienen todos los jóvenes?

____

9. ¿Cómo es la bicicleta de Víctor?

____

10. ¿Qué necesita Ud. para hacerse campeón en un deporte?

____

ACTIVIDAD D

Sí o no. Víctor Veloz is talking about himself. If a statement is incorrect, change it to make it correct. Work with a partner.

EXAMPLE: **Me desvisto después de acostarme.**
No. Ud. ***se desviste antes de acostarse.***

1. Me despierto a las siete de la mañana.

____

2. Me lavo antes de levantarme.

____

3. Me visto antes del desayuno.

____

4. Me siento a descansar después del almuerzo.

____

5. Me baño cuando me levanto por la mañana.

____

6. Me afeito después del desayuno.

____

7. Me acuesto a medianoche.

____

8. Necesito acostarme tarde.

____

ACTIVIDAD E

You are the person in the picture. What do you do in the morning?

EXAMPLE:

Me despierto.

1. ____________________ 2. ____________________

3. ____________________ 4. ____________________

5. ______________________ 6. ______________________

ACTIVIDAD F

What do you do in the evening?

1. ______________________ 2. ______________________

3. ______________________ 4. ______________________

5. ______________________ 6. ______________________

3 Look at the following sentence: **Yo me lavo.** Whom am I washing? _________ Is the action being performed on the subject or on someone else? _____________ Do the subject (**yo**) and the reflexive pronoun (**me**) refer to the same person or to two different people?

NOTE: Different subjects require different reflexive pronouns.

yo *me* lavo	**nosotros *nos* lavamos**
tú *te* lavas	
Ud. *se* lava	**Uds. *se* lavan**
él *se* lava	**ellos *se* lavan**
ella *se* lava	**ellas *se* lavan**

RULE: In a sentence using a reflexive verb, the subject is also the object of the action. The reflexive pronoun is placed before the conjugated verb.

ACTIVIDAD G

What is Gerardo's routine? Look at the picture and say what Gerardo does at the time indicated.

EXAMPLE:

Gerardo se despierta a las seis y media de la mañana.

1. ____

2. ______________________________

3. ______________________________

4. ______________________________

5. ______________________________

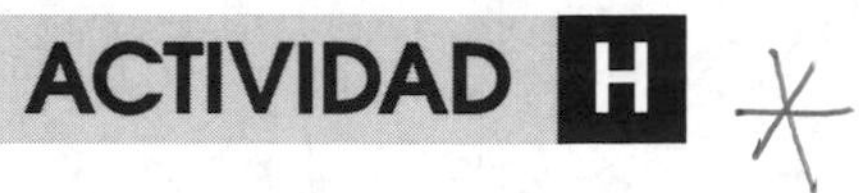

Complete each sentence with the correct reflexive pronoun.

1. Yo ___me___ despierto a las seis.

2. Ellos siempre ______________ levantan tarde.

3. ¿A qué hora ______________ acuestan Uds.?

4. Nosotros ______________ vestimos antes de salir.

5. ¿Cuándo ______________ baña Ud.?

6. Tú ______________ lavas las manos antes de comer.

7. Marta ______________ peina tres veces al día.

8. Nosotras ______________ cepillamos el pelo todas las noches.

ACTIVIDAD I

What are all these people doing? Complete the sentences with the correct form of the verb in parentheses:

1. (acostarse) Yo ____________ ______________________ temprano.
2. (bañarse) Ella ____________ ______________________ con agua fría.
3. (sentarse) Tú ____________ ______________________ cuando estás cansado.
4. (peinarse) Rosa ____________ ______________________ antes de ir a la fiesta.
5. (dormirse) Los niños ____________ ______________________ después de mirar la televisión.
6. (ponerse) Ud. ____________ ______________________ el suéter que compró.
7. (despertarse) Nosotros ____________ ______________________ tarde los domingos.
8. (vestirse) Uds. ____________ ______________________ rápido.

9. (quitarse) Yo me quito los zapatos cuando llego a casa.

10. (afeitarse) Mis hermanos se afeitan dos veces al día.

4

In Spanish reflexive constructions, we do not use the possessive adjective (**mi**, **tu**, **su**, etc.) with parts of the body or wearing apparel, since the reflexive pronoun obviously refers to the subject. The definite article is used instead.

Tú te lavas *el* pelo.	*You wash your hair.* (literally; *You wash yourself the hair)*
El se pone *los* zapatos.	*He puts on his shoes.*
Yo me cepillo *los* dientes.	*I brush my teeth.*
Ud. se quita *el* abrigo.	*You take off your coat.*

ACTIVIDAD J

Work with a partner. One student asks: **¿Qué haces ahora?** The other student describes what he/she is doing.

EXAMPLE: get up **¿Qué haces ahora?** ***Yo me levanto.***

1. wash face Yo me lavo la cara
2. brush teeth Me cepillo los dientes
3. brush hair Me cepillo el pelo
4. take off pajamas Me quito los pijamas
5. put on shoes and socks Me visto pongo los zapatos y los calcetínes.

5

In all the sentences up to this point, the reflexive pronoun came directly before the conjugated verb: **Yo me lavo con agua fría**. In a negative sentence, the reflexive pronoun is not separated from the verb. The word **no** stands before the reflexive pronoun.

Yo *no me lavo* con agua y jabón.	*I don't wash myself with water and soap.*
Tú *no te acuestas* a las seis.	*You don't go to bed at six o'clock.*

ACTIVIDAD K

Say that one of the persons listed doesn't do any activity at a certain time.

EXAMPLE: tú / no peinarse / a medianoche
Tú *no te peinas* a medianoche.

Carlos	no acostarse	las siete de la mañana
Yo	no despertarse	las once de la noche
Mis padres	no peinarse	las doce de la noche
Tú	no dormirse	medianoche
Uds.	no levantarse	las cuatro de la tarde
Ud.	no sentarse	las dos de la tarde
Mi madre	no cepillarse los dientes	mediodía

1. Carlos no se acuesta a las siete de la manana
2. Yo no me despierto a las once de la noche
3. Mis padres no se peinan a las doce de la noche
4. Tú no te duermes a medianoche
5. Uds. no se levantan a las cuatro de la tarde
6. Mi madre no se cepilla los dientes a mediodía

How are reflexive verbs used to give a command? Look at this short game of **Simón dice** and then answer the questions that follow.

Simón dice (al Sr. López):	**¡Levánte*se* (Ud.)!**	**¡No *se* levante (Ud.)!**
	¡Láve*se* (Ud.)!	**¡No *se* lave (Ud.)!**
	¡Vísta*se* (Ud.)!	**¡No *se* vista (Ud.)!**
Simón dice (a sus amigos):	**¡Levánten*se* (Uds.)!**	**¡No *se* levanten (Uds.)!**
	¡Láven*se* (Uds.)!	**¡No *se* laven (Uds.)!**
	¡Vístan*se* (Uds.)!	**¡No *se* vistan (Uds.)!**
Simón dice (a Josefina):	**¡Levánta*te*!**	**¡No *te* levantes!**
	¡Láva*te*!	**¡No *te* laves!**
	¡Víste*te*!	**¡No *te* vistas!**

Where is the reflexive pronoun in relationship to the verb? In the affirmative (yes) command, the reflexive pronoun is AFTER the verb and attached to it. Note also that all the affirmative commands of reflexive verbs have an accent mark to retain the original stress. In a negative (no) command, the reflexive pronoun is BEFORE the verb; **no** is placed BEFORE the reflexive pronoun.

ACTIVIDAD L

Tell a friend to do the following.

1. Wake up! ____________________
2. Take a bath! ____________________
3. Brush your teeth! ____________________
4. Have fun! ____________________
5. Go to bed! ____________________
6. Comb your hair! ____________________

ACTIVIDAD M

Make the commands in Actividad L negative.

1. ____________________
2. ____________________
3. ____________________
4. ____________________
5. ____________________
6. ____________________

ACTIVIDAD N

Tell the students (**Uds.**) in the class to do the following.

1. Wake up early! ______________________
2. Take off your coat(s)! ______________________
3. Wash your hands! ______________________
4. Sit down now! ______________________
5. Have fun! ______________________
6. Comb your hair! ______________________

ACTIVIDAD O

Make the commands in Actividad N negative.

1. ______________________
2. ______________________
3. ______________________
4. ______________________
5. ______________________
6. ______________________

ACTIVIDAD P

You be the teacher. Tell a student to do or not to do the following.

1. Don't take off your hat! ______________________
2. Put on your coat! ______________________
3. Get up from the chair! ______________________
4. Don't wash your face! ______________________

5. Don't sit down! ______________________

6. Don't fall asleep! ______________________

7

What happens when the reflexive verb is used as an infinitive? Look at the following examples:

Voy a *bañarme* ahora.	*I'm going to take a bath now.*
El bebé no quiere *acostarse*.	*The baby doesn't want to go to bed.*
No debes *dormirte* en clase.	*You shouldn't fall asleep in class.*

Where is the reflexive pronoun placed? It is placed after the infinitive and attached to it.

ACTIVIDAD Q

Complete the following sentences, using the correct Spanish form of the verb in parentheses.

1. Él no quiere ______________ las manos con jabón. (*to wash*)
2. Felipe y yo queremos ______________ allí. (*to sit down*)
3. ¡______________ Ud. ahora mismo! (*to bed*)
4. El niño no puede ______________ . (*to fall asleep*)
5. Nosotros vamos a ______________ en las vacaciones. (*to have fun*)
6. No tengo tiempo de ______________ ahora. (*to take a bath*)
7. El ciclista debe ______________ temprano. (*to get up*)
8. ¡______________ (tú) el pelo bien! (*brush*)
9. ¡______________ Ud. aquí, por favor! (*sit down*)
10. Cuando hace frío tengo que ______________ un suéter. (*to put on*)

ACTIVIDAD R

You are writing a letter to a pen pal in Mexico. Include some of the following information: When you get up on weekends, your usual routine to get ready for school, what you do on weekends, what you do for fun, etc.

Querida Lupe:

¿Qué haces generalmente durante la semana? En una semana típica, yo ______________________

____

____

____

____

Mi madre me dice ______________________

____

____

____

Tu amigo de siempre,

Eduardo

8 Passive or impersonal **se**

The pronoun **se** has another important use in Spanish. It is used when there is no particular person doing the action. (There is no specific subject mentioned.) In English we can say a variety of things: one, you, we, people, it is etc.
In Spanish we just use **se**. Here are some examples:

SPANISH	ENGLISH EQUIVALENT
Aquí *se* habla español.	*Spanish is spoken here.* *One speaks Spanish here.* *You, we, they, people (*in general) *speak Spanish here.*
***Se* dice que hace calor en el trópico.**	*They say that it's hot in the tropics.* *It is said that it's hot in the tropics.*

SPANISH	ENGLISH EQUIVALENT
¿Cómo *se* va al centro?	*How do you get downtown?* *How does one get downtown?*
***Se* come bien en París.**	*You eat well in Paris.* *One eats well in Paris.*
***Se* prohibe fumar.**	*No smoking.* *It is forbidden to smoke.*

NOTE: The verb following se is usually in the singular. However, if there is a plural noun immediately following the verb, the verb is used in the third-person plural form:

Se habl*an muchas lenguas* en Sudamérica.

No se permit*en coches* en la avenida.

Se cierr*an los bancos* a las dos.

¿Por dónde se sale? Everything is new to you in Madrid and you are asking for information. Follow the example.

EXAMPLE: **por dónde / salir del museo**
¿Por dónde se sale del museo?

1. cuándo / abrir las tiendas ______________________
2. qué / poder comprar en esta tienda ______________________
3. por dónde / entrar en el teatro ______________________
4. cómo / subir al autobús ______________________
5. cuándo / permitir visitas ______________________
6. en qué / ir al jardín botánico ______________________
7. qué / hacer para divertirse ______________________
8. cómo / llegar a la estación ______________________

ACTIVIDAD T

The construction **se** is very often seen on signs. See if you can match the expressions with the corresponding sign.

1. SE PROHÍBE FUMAR
2. SE VENDE CASA
3. SE NECESITA SECRETARIA
4. SE CAMBIA DINERO
5. SE SIRVE COMIDA CRIOLLA
6. SE ABRE A LA UNA
7. NO SE PERMITE APARCAR
8. SE ALQUILAN CUARTOS
9. SE INSTALAN TELEVISORES
10. NO SE ACEPTAN CHEQUES

(a) we open at 1:00
(b) rooms for rent
(c) no parking
(d) we do not accept checks
(e) TVs installed
(f) currency exchange
(g) house for sale
(h) home style cooking
(i) secretary wanted
(j) no smoking

Diálogo

Ud. es un(a) ciclista famoso(a). Un periodista quiere escribir un artículo para un periódico y le hace varias preguntas.

Preguntas Personales

1. ¿Cómo te diviertes en las vacaciones?

____

2. ¿Cómo te vistes durante el verano?

____

3. ¿A qué hora te despiertas los domingos?

____

4. ¿Cuántas veces al día te cepillas los dientes?

____

5. ¿Qué deportes se practican en tu escuela?

____

Información Personal

List five things you do in the morning before leaving for school.

1. ______________________________

____

2. ______________________________

____

3. ______________________________

____

4. ______________________________

____

5. ______________________________

____

CÁPSULA CULTURAL

La bicicleta: el automóvil de los niños

El automóvil en Hispanoamérica es todavía un artículo de lujo para muchos. Debido a su alto costo, las familias con autos por lo general tienen sólo uno. Con ese único auto se hace todo: llevar a los niños a la escuela, hacer las compras semanales, ir al trabajo y pasear los fines de semana.

No es como en los Estados Unidos, donde muchas veces cada miembro mayor de edad tiene su propio automóvil. Los jóvenes adolescentes norteamericanos esperan comprarse y conducir su propio auto. En Hispanoamérica los jóvenes pueden sacar la licencia de conducir, pero en general no obtienen un automóvil hasta muchos años después.

Como nota curiosa, en Hispanoamérica se dice que el primer automóvil que uno tiene es un triciclo, que luego se convierte en una bicicleta. Cuando los niños reciben por primera vez una bicicleta con ruedas de entrenamiento, dicen: "Ahora yo también tengo mi carro".

lujo *luxury*
debido a *due to*

sacar la licencia *to get a license*

las ruedas de entrenamiento *training wheels*

Para pensar

1. ¿Por qué muchas de las familias de Hispanoamérica tienen sólo un carro?
2. ¿Qué cosas hacen con el automóvil?
3. ¿Qué esperan los adolescentes de los Estados Unidos?
4. Para un niño hispano, ¿cómo es su bicicleta?
5. ¿Cuáles son algunos de los problemas de una sociedad que depende del automóvil?

Do activities in Chapter 7 for next week!

7
Una historia policíaca

Preterit Tense

1 Vocabulario

ACTIVIDAD A

¿Qué pasa? Write about what's going on in the picture.

1. ______________________________

2. ______________________________

3. ______________________________

4. ______________________________

5. ______________________________

ACTIVIDAD B

Las cinco diferencias There are two crimes scenes illustrated below. They look similar, but there are five differences between them. Find out what they are.

2

Up to now we have talked about things happening **ahora** (now), **hoy** (today), and even **mañana** (tomorrow). How do you express actions or events that took place **anoche** (last night), **ayer** (yesterday), **las semana pasada** (last week), or **el año pasado** (last year)? Of course, you need to use verbs in a past tense. One such past tense in Spanish is the preterit.

Las joyas robadas

Here's a story about a theft and a smart detective. Pay special attention to the verbs in bold type. They are in the preterit (past) tense.

Dejó de llover a las dos de la tarde. El inspector Delgado **abrió** la ventana de su oficina y **miró** hacia la calle. En ese momento **sonó** el teléfono. La señora Laura Moreno, muy nerviosa, **preguntó:**

dejar de *to stop*
sonar *to sound, to ring*

—¿Puede Ud. venir a mi casa inmediatamente?

El inspector salió y **llegó** veinte minutos más tarde a la casa de la señora Moreno. **Tocó** a la puerta. Laura **abrió** y **dijo**:

—Pase, pase, Inspector Delgado. ¡**Ocurrió** algo terrible! **Salí** temprano esta mañana para visitar a mi amiga Fernanda y cuando **regresé** una hora después, **encontré** la puerta de la casa abierta. **Entré** y **vi** la sombra de un hombre en el estudio de mi marido. En ese momento el hombre me **vio** y **saltó** por la ventana. **Corrió** por el jardín y yo **corrí** detrás de él, pero él **entró** rápidamente en un carro y **se escapó**. En el estudio **encontré** abierta la caja fuerte y **descubrí** que el ladrón **robó** mis joyas. Valen una fortuna, casi un millón dólares. Afortunadamente están aseguradas».

la sombra *shadow*
la caja fuerte *safe*
asegurado *insured*

—¿**Reconoció** Ud. al hombre, señora?

—No estoy completamente segura porque no **vi** su cara, pero creo que el ladrón puede ser Juan, un empleado que **despedimos** la semana pasada. Él sabe dónde tengo mis joyas. Además, **encontré** esta gorra en el jardín. Es de Juan.

despedir *to dismiss, to fire*

El inspector **escuchó** todo con mucha atención, **examinó**, los muebles en desorden, y **salió** al jardín. **Vio** las huellas de unos zapatos de hombre en la tierra mojada.

mojado *wet*

—Inspector Delgado, ¿quiere más información sobre Juan? Puedo darle toda la ayuda necesaria para atrapar al ladrón.

—¡Señora, quiero saber la verdad y no las mentiras que **contó** Ud.!

¿Cómo sabe el inspector que la historia de Laura es falsa?

¿Qué creen Uds. que **pasó** realmente? ¿Quién **robó** las joyas?

* * *

SOLUCIÓN: Según Laura, ella **corrió** detrás del ladrón por el jardín. Pero en el jardín el inspector encontró solamente las huellas de un hombre.

ACTIVIDAD C

Answer the questions based on the story.

1. ¿Quién llamó al inspector Delgado?

2. ¿A qué hora llegó el inspector a casa de la Sra. Moreno?

3. ¿Qué vio Laura en el estudio de su marido?

4. ¿Cómo reaccionó el hombre cuando vio a Laura?

5. Según Laura, ¿cómo se escapó el ladrón?

6. ¿Qué encontró Laura en el jardín?

7. ¿Qué examinó el inspector?

8. ¿Qué vio el inspector en el jardín?

9. ¿Según el inspector, que contó Laura?

10. ¿Cómo resolvió el misterio el inspector?

3

To form the preterit tense of regular verbs, simply remove the **-ar, -er**, or **-ir** ending of the verb and substitute another ending:

	rob*ar* *to steal*	**corr*er*** *to run*	**descubr*ir*** *to discover*
yo	**rob*é***	**corr*í***	**descubr*í***
tú	**rob*aste***	**corr*iste***	**descubr*iste***
Ud., él, ella	**rob*ó***	**corr*ió***	**descubr*ió***
nosotros, -as	**rob*amos***	**corr*imos***	**descubr*imos***
Uds., ellos, ellas	**rob*aron***	**corr*ieron***	**descubr*ieron***

There is one **-AR** verb (**dar**) that takes the **-ER** endings in the preterit tense instead of the regular **-AR** endings.

d*ar* *to give*			
yo	***di***	**nosotros, -as**	***dimos***
tú	***diste***		
Ud., él, ella	***dio***	**Uds., ellos, ellas**	***dieron***

ACTIVIDAD D

You were a witness to a bank robbery and are testifying in court. Complete the sentences with the preterit form of the verb in parentheses.

1. Yo entré (entrar) en el banco a las once de la mañana.

2. Dos hombres entraron (entrar) detrás de mí y cerraron (cerrar) la puerta.

3. Una señora y yo Comenzamos (comenzar) a gritar.

4. El director del banco escuchó (escuchar) los gritos y llamó (llamar) a la policía.

5. La policía llegaron (llegar) pronto.

6. Los ladrones no robaron nada.
(robar)

7. El director del banco dio las gracias a la policía.
(dar)

ACTIVIDAD E

On Monday morning, your teacher wants to know what the students did on Sunday. Complete the sentences with the preterit form of the verb in parentheses.

1. Yo dormí hasta las diez.
(dormir)

2. Manuel comí en casa de sus abuelos.
(comer)

3. Jorge y Raúl vemos una película de horror.
(ver)

4. Tú saliste de compras con tus padres.
(salir)

5. Mis hermanos y yo recibimos amigos en el aeropuerto.
(recibir)

6. Uds. _______________ un paseo por el parque.
(dar)

7. Rosario _______________ tres millas.
(correr)

8. Pablo y María _______________ cartas.
(escribir)

ACTIVIDAD F

You have just returned from a weekend at a friend's house and your little brother wants to know what you did. Answer the questions.

1. ¿Saliste a comer a un restaurante?

Sí, salí a comer a un restaurante

2. ¿Qué comiste?

Comí frijoles

3. ¿Viste alguna película buena?

____

4. ¿Compraste el regalo para mamá?

____

5. ¿A qué hora te despertaste el domingo?

____

6. ¿Nadaste en la piscina?

____

7. ¿Diste un paseo por el centro de la ciudad?

____

8. ¿Te divertiste mucho?

____

9. ¿Conociste a los padres de tu amigo?

____

10. ¿Invitaste a tu amigo a venir a nuestra casa?

____

-AR and -ER verbs with stem changes in the present tense have regular forms in the preterit. -IR verbs with stem changes in the present tense (**e** to **ie, o** to **ue,** and **e** to **i**) change **e** to **i** and **o** to **u** in the third-person singular and plural of the preterit. Let's look at some examples.

	PRESENT TENSE YO-FORM	PRETERIT
encontrar (ue)	**enc*ue*ntro**	**encontré, encontraste, encontró, encontramos, encontraron**
pensar (ie)	**p*ie*nso**	**pensé, pensaste, pensó, pensamos, pensaron**
perder (ie)	**p*ie*rdo**	**perdí, perdiste, perdió, perdimos, perdieron**
volver (ue)	**v*ue*lvo**	**volví, volviste, volvió, volvimos, volvieron**
But:		
mentir (ie)	**m*ie*nto**	**mentí, mentiste, *mintió,* mentimos, *mintieron***
dormir (ue)	**d*ue*rmo**	**dormí, dormiste, *durmió,* dormimos, *durmieron***
pedir (i)	**p*i*do**	**pedí, pediste, *pidió,* pedimos, *pidieron***
servir (i)	**s*i*rvo**	**serví, serviste, *sirvió,* servimos, *sirvieron***

ACTIVIDAD G

You went with some friends to a restaurant last night. Using the verb **pedir**, say what each of you ordered.

1. Yo pedí un bistec con papas fritas.

2. Manuel pidió el pollo frito.

3. Rosa y yo pedimos una limonada.

4. Tú pediste la sopa del día.

5. Los hermanos Gómez pidieron hamburguesas.

6. María pidió sopa y una hamburguesa.

5

There are many verbs in Spanish with irregular preterit forms that change their stem completely.

tener *to have*			
yo	**tuve**	**nosotros**	**tuvimos**
tú	**tuviste**		
Ud., él, ella	**tuvo**	**Uds., ellos, ellas**	**tuvieron**

The following verbs also have stem changes.

estar **est*uv*e**

poder **p*u*de**

poner **p*u*se**

querer **qu*is*e**

venir **v*i*ne**

hacer **h*i*ce**

Yo dije buenas noches a mi novio y mi gato.

Yo dije buenos dias a mi gato (mi novio dormía)

Yo quise correr, pero no pude.

NOTE: The stem of the verb **hacer** changes from **hac** to **hiz** in the third-person singular to keep the **c** sound: **hizo**

Read the following dialog that contains many stem changes in the preterit tense.

The common endings of these verbs are:

e
iste
o
imos
ieron

Complete the table below:

	estar *to be*	**hacer** *to do, make*	**poder** *to be able*	**poner** *to put*	**querer** *to want*	**tener** *to have*	**venir** *to come*
	est-	**hic-**	**pud-**	**pus-**	**quis-**	**tuv-**	**vin-**
yo	**estuve**	**hice**	pude	puse	quise	tuve	vine
tú	**estuviste**	**hiciste**	pudiste	pusiste	quisiste	tuviste	viniste
Ud., él, ella	**estuvo**	**hizo**	pudo	puso	quiso	tuvo	vino
nosotros -as	**estuvimos**	**hicimos**	pudimos	pusimos	quisimos	tuvimos	vinimos
Uds., ellos, ellas	**estuvieron**	**hicieron**	pudieron	pusieron	quisieron	tuvieron	vinieron

ACTIVIDAD H

*

Complete each sentence with the correct form of the verb in parentheses.

1. El sábado pasado yo no _quesimos_ ir a la fiesta.
(querer)

2. Mis abuelos _vin ieron_ a visitarnos ayer.
(venir)

3. Esta mañana Ud. se _puso_ los jeans nuevos.
(ponerse)

4. ¿Dónde _est uvistes_ tú el verano pasado?
(estar)

5. Nosotros no ______________ terminar las tareas anoche.
(poder)

6. El verano pasado ellas ______________ que trabajar.
(tener)

7. ¿Qué ______________ Uds. el fin de semana pasado?
(hacer)

8. ¿Quién ______________ ausente el lunes pasado?
(estar)

9. ¿Donde ______________ tú los periódicos que compré?
(poner)

ACTIVIDAD I

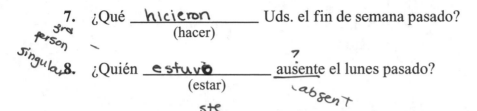

The following things are happening today. How would you say they happened yesterday? Work with a partner.

EXAMPLE: **Mis primos vienen a visitarme.**
Mis primos *vinieron* a visitarme.

1. Yo no puedo ver esa película. ______________
2. Ellos hacen todo el trabajo. ______________
3. Mi mamá pone la comida en las mesa. ______________
4. Los ladrones pueden escaparse. ______________
5. Nosotros tenemos que ir a la escuela. ______________
6. Tú no quieres comer afuera. ______________
7. María hace un viaje a México. ______________
8. Yo no tengo tiempo. ______________
9. ¿Dónde ponen Uds. los periódicos? ______________
10. Ud. viene por la mañana. ______________

6 There are two verbs that share the same irregular forms in the preterit, **ser** and **ir**. Only the context makes clear what the meaning is.

	ser *to be*	**ir** *to go*
yo	**fui**	**fui**
tú	**fuiste**	**fuiste**
Ud., él, ella	**fue**	**fue**
nosotros, -as	**fuimos**	**fuimos**
Uds., ellos, ellas	**fueron**	**fueron**

Mi hermano *fue* testigo del robo. — *My brother was a witness to the robbery.*

Él *fue* a declarar al cuartel de policía. — *He went to testify at the police station.*

After the summer vacation, you and your friends ask each other where you went.

1. ¿Adónde ______________ tú, Javier?

2. ¿Y Uds., Margarita y Rosario, adónde ______________ ?

3. ¿Adónde ______________ Roberto?

ACTIVIDAD K

You are on a school trip to Madrid and are keeping a diary. Complete the following entries with the correct form of the verb in parentheses.

Ayer nosotros ______________ (hacer) muchas cosas. Por la mañana nosotros ______________ (ir) al Museo del Prado y ______________ (ver) varias exhibiciones. Jorge y Darío no ______________ (querer) ir con nosotros y ______________ (ir) de compras. Por la tarde yo __________ (salir) a dar un paseo con María por el Parque del Retiro. Ella __________ (ponerse) zapatos nuevos y no __________ (poder) caminar mucho. Nosotros __________ (tener) que tomar un taxi para regresar al hotel. Por la noche un amigo español __________ (venir) al hotel y nosotros dos __________ (salir) a comer afuera. En el restaurante mi amigo __________ (pedir) una comida típica española. El mesero __________ (servir) muy despacio. Nosotros __________ (estar) en el restaurante hasta muy tarde y yo __________ (acostarse) después de medianoche.

7 Verbs with roots ending in a vowel + **-ER** or **-IR** share some common irregularities in the preterit. Let's look at two of them.

	creer	**oír**
yo	**cre*í***	**o*í***
tú	**cre*í*ste**	**o*í*ste**
Ud., él, ella	**crey*ó***	**oy*ó***
nosotros, -as	**cre*í*mos**	**o*í*mos**
Uds., ellos, ellas	**cre*y*eron**	**o*y*eron**

Note that the **i** has an accent mark in the **yo, tú,** and **nosotros** forms. In the other two forms, the **i** changes to **y**. Can you complete the table below?

	leer	**caerse**
yo	**leí**	**me caí**
tú	__________	**te** __________
Ud., él, ella	__________	**se** __________
nosotros, -as	__________	**nos** __________
Uds., ellos, ellas	__________	**se** __________

ACTIVIDAD L

You have heard rumors about a trip to Mexico during the holiday break. Complete the sentences with the correct preterit tense form of the verb **oír**.

1. Yo ______________ que la escuela planea un viaje a México.

2. ¿______________ tú lo mismo?

3. Yo no, pero Juan ______________ eso también.

4. Y Julia y Mercedes ______________ que no va a costar mucho.

5. ¿Qué ______________ Uds.?

6. Nosotros ______________ que el viaje va a ser en diciembre.

8

Remember the endings shared by some irregular verbs? **-e, -iste, -o, -imos, -ieron**. There are two verbs (**decir** [to say] and **traer** [to bring]) with similar irregular stems that have the same endings except for the third-person plural (**-eron** instead of **-ieron**).

	decir	traer
yo	**dij*e***	**traj*e***
tú	**dij*iste***	**traj*iste***
Ud., él, ella	**dij*o***	**traj*o***
nosotros, -as	**dij*imos***	**traj*imos***
Uds., ellos, ellas	**dij*eron***	**traj*eron***

ACTIVIDAD M

Somebody organized a surprise party for you and you want to know who brought the different foods. Complete the sentences with the correct preterit form of **traer**.

1. ¿Qué ______________ tú, Daniel?

2. Yo ______________ los sándwiches.

3. Y Ud., Srta. López, ¿qué ______________ ?

Leyó un

4. Margarita y yo trajimos las sodas.

5. Rosa trajo la torta.

6. José y su hermano trajeron los globos (balloons).

ACTIVIDAD N

Answer the following questions in complete Spanish sentences. Work with a partner who will ask you the question.

1. ¿Leyó Ud. el periódico ayer?

____

2. ¿Quién fue el primer presidente de los Estados Unidos?

____

3. ¿Dónde estuvo Ud. el domingo pasado?

____

4. ¿Qué tiempo hizo el fin de semana pasado?

____

5. ¿Quién vino tarde a la clase hoy?

____

6. ¿Quién oyó las noticias en su casa anoche?

____

7. ¿Para qué clase tuvo Ud. que hacer tareas anoche?

____

8. ¿Qué dijo la professora a la clase de matemáticas?

____

Preguntas Personales

1. ¿Adónde fuiste el sábado pasado por la noche?

____

2. ¿Qué hiciste anoche?

____

3. ¿A qué hora saliste de casa esta mañana?

____

4. ¿A qué hora te acostaste anoche?

____

5. ¿Trabajaste la semana pasada?

____

Diálogo

You were found at night near the scene of a crime, and the next day a policeman wants to question you. Here are your answers. What are the questions?

Información Personal

Make a list of five things you did yesterday:

1. ______________________________

2. ______________________________

3. ______________________________

4. ______________________________

5. ______________________________

Composición

You witnessed a robbery. Fill out the following police report.

INFORME DEL TESTIGO

Apellido: ____________ **Nombre:** ____________ **Edad:** ____________

Dirección: ________________ **Teléfono:** ________________

____

1. ¿Qué vio Ud.?

____

____

2. ¿Dónde tuvo lugar el incidente?

____

____

3. ¿Qué hicieron los ladrones?

____

____

4. ¿Pudo ver la cara de los ladrones?

____

____

5. ¿Adónde fueron los ladrones después?

____

____

CÁPSULA CULTURAL

¡Auxilio, policía!

Si estás en un apuro en un país extranjero, ¿adónde vas por ayuda? A un policía, por supuesto. Pero, ¿a qué tipo? En España, por ejemplo hay tres tipos diferentes de policía:

La *Policía Nacional* se encuentra en las ciudades. Llevan uniforme marrón, están armados y guardan los edificios oficiales. Otro grupo que se emplea por todo el país es la *Guardia Civil*. Sus miembros patrullan en autos o motocicletas y se encuentran generalmente en las áreas rurales. Llevan uniforme verde y un sombrero distinto llamado el *tricornio*. Un tercer grupo es la *Policía Municipal* (los Urbanos). Estos oficiales trabajan para los varios gobiernos municipales y son, básicamente, policías de tránsito, aunque tienen jurisdicción en asuntos de orden pública. Generalmente, llevan uniformes azules en el invierno y blancos en el verano.

Una nota curiosa: Costa Rica es el sólo país de habla hispana sin fuerzas armadas. El presidente abolió el ejército y hoy este país de Centroamérica es el único país que tiene sólo su policía para defenderse.

estar en un apuro *to be in trouble*

encontrarse *to be found*

marrón *brown*

patrullar *to patrol*

jurisdicción *jurisdiction*

Para pensar

1. ¿Cuáles son los diferentes tipos de policía de España?
2. ¿Cómos se llama el sombrero de los miembros de la Guardia Civil?
3. ¿Qué trabajo hacen básicamente los Urbanos?
4. ¿Cómo es diferente Costa Rica de los otros países hispanoamericanos?
5. ¿Qué piensas de la idea de abolir las fuerzas armadas de un país?

8

Las vacaciones

Imperfect Tense

1 Vocabulario

ACTIVIDAD A

Here's a picture of a wonderful resort place. Can you describe some of the things people are doing?

ACTIVIDAD B

Sometimes you need the right equipment to be able to enjoy an activity. Can you name the activities in which you would use these pieces of equipment?

1.  ____________________

2. ____________________

3. ____________________

4. ____________________

5. ____________________

6. ____________________

7. ____________________

8. ____________________

9. ____________________

10. ____________________

Doctor, tengo muchos problemas

Let's read a one-act play about a man with a lot of problems. Pay attention to the verbs in bold type. These verbs are in the imperfect, another past tense in Spanish.

Escena: El consultorio del famoso psiquiatra Salvador Sesohueco. La enfermera está en el despacho. El paciente está acostado en el sofá mientras el doctor toma notas.

el consultorio *doctor's office*

DOCTOR: Dígame, Sr. Comequeso, ¿desde cuándo tiene esos sentimientos de inseguridad?

desde *since*

PACIENTE: Toda mi vida, doctor.

DOCTOR: ¿De veras? Pero, ¿qué relación **tenía** con sus amiguitos cuando **era** niño?

PACIENTE: Casi no **tenía** amigos. No **veía** a nadie. **Estaba** en casa todos los días con mi mamá.

DOCTOR: ¿Pero cuando Ud. tenía dieciséis o diecisiete años, con quién **salía** Ud.?

PACIENTE: Con mi mamá.

DOCTOR: Ajá. ¿Cuántos años tiene Ud. ahora?

PACIENTE: Tengo treinta y cinco años.

DOCTOR: ¿Es casado?

PACIENTE: Sí, señor.

DOCTOR: ¿Adónde **iba** Ud. de vacaciones cuando **era** soltero?

soltero *single*

PACIENTE: Mi mamá y yo **íbamos** al campo a descansar. Ahora voy con mi mujer a casa de mi suegra.

suegra *mother-in-law*

DOCTOR: Pero, ¿no tiene Ud. deseos de divertirse, de jugar al golf o al tenis, de hacer un viaje?

PACIENTE: Sí, doctor, pero mi mujer no me da permiso.

DOCTOR: Señor Comequeso, no necesito oír más. Veo bien su problema. Ud. necesita más confianza. Antes Ud. **dependía** de su mamá y ahora depende de su mujer. Voy a hacer un programa para convertirlo en un hombre libre e independiente como yo.

PACIENTE: Gracias, doctor. Yo **quería** ser independiente cuando **era** joven y ahora quiero ser como Ud. Yo lo admiro mucho.

La enfermera entra y dice: «Hay una llamada telefónica para Ud., doctor. Es su esposa».

DOCTOR: (en el teléfono) Hola, Silvia. ¿Cómo estás, mi vida? No, claro que no estoy ocupado para ti. ¿Cómo? ¿Quieres llevar a tu mamá esta noche con nosotros? Claro que sí, no hay problema. Tú sabes que siempre tienes razón.

ACTIVIDAD C

Answer the questions based on the dialog.

1. ¿Dónde está el Sr. Comequeso?

 ____

2. ¿Qué hace el doctor mientras el paciente habla?

 ____

3. ¿Cuántos amigos tenía el paciente cuando era niño?

 ____

4. ¿Con quién salía cuando tenía 17 años?

 ____

5. ¿Adónde iba el paciente a pasar las vacaciones con su mamá?

 ____

6. ¿Por qué no hace un viaje el Sr. Comequeso?

 ____

7. Según el psiquiatra, ¿cuál es el problema del paciente?

 ____

8. ¿Qué va a hacer el psiquiatra?

 ____

9. ¿Quién llama por teléfono?

____

10. En su opinión, ¿qué tipo de hombre es el doctor?

____

2

In Spanish, there are different ways to express actions in the past. You have already learned one tense, the preterit. Now let's learn another, the imperfect. Later on, we'll see the differences in use between the two. Look at the following examples:

Yo *jugaba* al tenis todos los días.	*I played, was playing, I used to play tennis every day.*
Tú *descansabas* en el campo.	*You used to rest, etc. in the country.*
Ud. *remaba* en el lago.	*You used to row, etc. in the lake.*
Ella *nadaba* en la piscina.	*She used to swim, etc. in the swimming pool.*
Nosotros *montábamos* a caballo.	*We used to go, etc. horseback riding.*
Uds. *sacaban* muchas fotos.	*You used to take, etc. a lot of pictures.*
Ellos *pescaban* en el río.	*They used to fish, etc. in the river.*

All the above verbs are -AR verbs. What endings were added to the stem to form the imperfect?

yo	***-aba***
tú	***-abas***
Ud., él, ella	***-aba***
nosotros, -as	***-ábamos***
Uds., ellos, ellas	***-aban***

ACTIVIDAD D

You are reminiscing with a friend about your childhood. Complete the sentences with the correct form of the imperfect of the verb in parentheses.

1. Yo ________________ todos los días en el parque.
(jugar)

2. Mi madre ________________ por las mañanas.
(trabajar)

3. Mi hermanito y yo ________________ a los abuelos los domingos.
(visitar)

4. Mis padres ________________ las vacaciones en la playa.
(pasar)

5. Nuestros abuelos nos ________________ muchos dulces.
(comprar)

6. Yo ________________ muy temprano.
(despertarse)

7. Por las tardes tú y yo ________________ la televisión.
(mira)

8. Mi hermana ________________ por teléfono todo el tiempo.
(hablar)

9. Tú ________________ el almuerzo en mi casa.
(tomar)

10. En el invierno ________________ mucho.
(nevar)

3

Now let's look at these examples of -ER and -IR verbs.

-ER	-IR
Yo *comía* en la cafetería. **Tú *corrías* rápido.** **Ud. *quería* ser dentista.** **Él *hacía* bien las tareas.** **Nosotros *teníamos* mucho dinero.** **Uds. leían en español.** **Ellas *sabían* la lección.**	**Yo *salía* temprano.** **Tú nunca *mentías*.** **Ud. *dormía* mucho.** **Ella *vivía* en Nueva York.** **Nosotras *decíamos* siempre la verdad.** **Uds. se *reían* mucho.** **Ellos *servían* la comida**

Note that the endings are the same for both -ER and -IR verbs. Write them in the space provided.

yo	____________	**nosotros**	____________
tú	____________		____________
Ud. / él / ella	____________	**Uds. / ellos / ellas**	____________

ACTIVIDAD E

Here's a description of what's going on in the classroom now. Say that the same thing used to happen last year by changing the sentences to the correct form of the imperfect. Work with a partner who will read these sentences in the present tense:

EXAMPLE: La maestra dice: «Buenos días».
El año pasado la maestra decía: «Buenos días».

1. Un alumno abre las ventanas.

____

2. Yo quiero hablar en español.

____

3. Los alumnos saben contestar bien.

____

4. Nosotros tenemos muchas tareas.

____

5. Tú lees y escribes en español.

____

6. El director viene a nuestra clase.

____

7. Uds. se duermen en clase.

____

8. Yo entiendo la lección.

____

9. Ud. cree todo lo que dice la maestra.

____

10. Los alumnos conocen a todos los profesores.

____

ACTIVIDAD F

Using the construction **hace** + time expression + imperfect tense, write five things you used to do two years ago. You may use the following verbs:

dormir	**leer**	**trabajar**	**escribir**
vivir	**hacer**	**pasar**	**nadar**

EXAMPLE: **Hace dos años yo vivía en otra ciudad.**

1. ____________________

2. ____________________

3. ____________________

4. ____________________

5. ____________________

There are only three verbs with irregular forms in the imperfect tense. One of them, **ver,** keeps the **e** of the **-ER** ending in all forms; **ser** and **ir** are irregular. Memorize their forms.

	ser	**ir**
yo	*era*	*iba*
tú	*eras*	*ibas*
Ud., él, ella	*era*	*iba*
nosotros, -as	*éramos*	*íbamos*
Uds., ellos, ellas	*eran*	*iban*

ver			
yo	**v*e*ía**	**nosotros, -as**	**v*e*íamos**
tú	**v*e*ías**		
Ud., él, ella	**v*e*ía**	**Uds., ellos, ellas**	**v*e*ían**

ACTIVIDAD G

You are talking with some friends about the past. Complete the sentences with the correct forms of the imperfect of **ser**.

1. Tú ______________ bueno en matemáticas.
2. Javier ______________ mi mejor amigo.
3. Yo ______________ capitán del equipo de fútbol.
4. La maestra ______________ muy estricta.
5. Tú y yo ______________ los campeones de tenis.
6. María y Rosa ______________ las muchachas más bonitas de la clase.
7. Uds. ______________ malos estudiantes.

ACTIVIDAD H

Where did the following people go when you were little?

EXAMPLE: mi hermana / a la universidad
Cuando yo era niño, mi hermana iba a la universidad.

1. mis padres / al campo ______________________________
2. yo / a la escuela ______________________________
3. mi abuelo / a la plaza ______________________________
4. Ud. / al cine ______________________________
5. tú / al parque ______________________________
6. Uds. / al supermercado ______________________________

ACTIVIDAD I

You want to ask your mother questions about her life when she was a child. Here are the answers. Make up your questions. Work with a partner.

EXAMPLE: Yo jugaba en el parque.
Mami, ¿dónde jugabas cuando eras niña?

1. Yo vivía en una ciudad muy grande.

¿Dónde ____?

2. En las vacaciones mis padres y yo íbamos a las montañas.

¿Adónde ____?

3. Yo tenía muchos amigos.

¿Cuántos ____?

4. Yo veía a mis abuelos todos los domingos.

¿Cuándo ____?

5. Yo iba a la escuela en bicicleta.

¿Cómo ____?

6. Los fines de semana yo salía al parque con Luisa.

¿Con quién ____?

Preguntas Personales

1. ¿Qué hacías cuando eras niño(a)?

____

2. ¿Dónde vivías hace cinco años?

____

3. ¿A qué escuela ibas entonces?

____

4. ¿Qué tipo de alumno(a) eras?

____

5. ¿Quién era tu mejor amigo(a)?

____

Información Personal

You are a psychiatrist who just opened a new office. Your first client is lying on the couch. Think of five questions you want to ask about his or her childhood. You may want to use some of the following verbs:

vivir	**jugar**	**hacer**	**saber**
ir	**ser**	**tener**	**querer**

1. ______________________________
2. ______________________________
3. ______________________________
4. ______________________________
5. ______________________________

Composición

The school nurse is trying to set up a summer program and needs some information from the students about how they spent their vacations as children. Tell the following:

1. where you used to go
2. how you traveled there
3. what the weather was like
4. what usually did there
5. why you liked or disliked the vacation

EXAMPLE: **Yo siempre viajaba con mis padres a Puerto Plata.**

Diálogo

Because of the problems he's been having lately, Mr. Moreno is undergoing psychoanalysis. What does he tell the psychiatrist?

CÁPSULA CULTURAL

Las vacaciones en Hispanoamérica

El concepto de vacaciones en Hispanoamérica es diferente al de los Estados Unidos o los países europeos. En realidad, los días de fiesta son las vacaciones para la mayoría de la gente en Hispanoamérica. Debido a las condiciones sociales y económicas, en la mayoría de los países del mundo hispano los beneficios laborales, por ejemplo las vacaciones pagadas, no son tan buenos como en otros países del mundo. Y en los casos en donde ofrecen vacaciones, la gente no gana lo suficiente como para viajar al extranjero. Quizás es por eso que los hispanoamericanos generalmente no posponen sus vacaciones, como es común en los Estados Unidos.

La recreación es parte de la vida diaria. Y si se ha trabajado toda la semana, entonces se toma el fin de semana para descansar y divertirse. Familias enteras van en excursiones a balnearios o a la playa, con comida, juegos y baile.

debido a *due to*

los beneficios laborales *employment benefits*

ganar *to earn*

diario *daily*

Para pensar

1. ¿Cómo compara el concepto de vacaciones en Hispanoamérica y en los Estados Unidos?
2. ¿Cómo son los beneficios laborales en Hispanoamérica, comparados con otros países?
3. ¿Por qué los hispanoamericanos no viajan generalmente al extranjero?
4. ¿Qué hacen las familias hispanoamericanas durante los fines de semana?
5. ¿Por qué es importante tener la oportunidad de divertirse?

9

¿Cuándo?

Imperfect and Preterit Tenses Compared

1 Vocabulario

Note how the following vocabulary words (**mañana**, **ayer**, etc.) relate to each other.

ANTEAYER
HOY
PASADO MAÑANA
LA SEMANA PASADA
AYER
MAÑANA

LUNES	MARTES	MIÉRCOLES	JUEVES	VIERNES	SÁBADO	DOMINGO
		1	2	3	4	5
6	7	8	9	10	11	12
13	14	15	**16**	17	18	19
20	21	22	23	24	25	26
27	28	29	30			

LA SEMANA PRÓXIMA (QUE VIENE)
DE HOY EN QUINCE DÍAS
DE HOY EN OCHO DÍAS

MEDIDAS DE TIEMPO

un minuto = 60 segundos	un mes = 30/31 días (4 semanas)
una hora = 60 minutos	un año = 12 meses
un día = 24 horas	un siglo = 100 años
una semana = 7 días	la eternidad

ACTIVIDAD A

¿Si hoy es el primero de enero, cuando

(1) fue el 31 de diciembre? ______________________

(2) fue el 30 de diciembre? ______________________

(3) va a ser el 2 de enero? ______________________

(4) va a ser el 3 de enero? ______________________

(5) va a ser el 8 de enero? ______________________

(6) va a ser el 15 de enero? ______________________

ACTIVIDAD B

Match the expressions in the left column with their definitions in the right column. Write the matching letter in the space provided.

1. 60 minutos ______

2. 60 segundos ______

3. 12 meses ______

4. en dos semanas ______

5. el día antes de ayer ______

6. el día después de hoy ______

7. cien años ______

a. un minuto
b. de hoy en ocho
c. de hoy en quince
d. una hora
e. pasado mañana
f. ayer
g. la eternidad
h. anteayer
i. mañana
j. un siglo
k. un año

8. en una semana ______

9. el día después de mañana ______

10. el tiempo infinito ______

La adivina

Since we are learning about time expressions and the past, let's read a story about a fortune teller (**una adivina**).

ROSANA: Josefina, ¿quieres venir conmigo a consultar a la vieja adivina, doña Matilde? Todas nuestras amigas dicen que ella puede ver el pasado y predecir el futuro.

JOSEFINA: ¡Me sorprendes! Tú eres inteligente y racional. Y sin embargo crees en esas cosas. Yo no voy a gastar mi dinero así. Pero, si insistes, como eres mi mejor amiga, te acompaño.

sin embargo *nevertheless*

ROSANA: Bien. Vamos pasado mañana, el viernes por la tarde.

Llega el viernes y las dos amigas están sentadas alrededor de una mesa. En el centro de la mesa hay una bola de cristal. La adivina habla.

MATILDE: Voy a comenzar con el pasado de la Srta. Rosana. Cuando Ud. era niña, Ud. contaba con los dedos de las manos y de los pies. Sólamente hace poco aprendió Ud. a calcular.

hace poco *a little while ago*

ROSANA: Al contrario. Yo era muy buena en matemáticas. Gané mi primer premio en matemáticas cuando tenía diez años.

MATILDE: Cuando Ud. tenía 16 años decía mentiras de sus amigas.

ROSANA: ¡Jamás!

MATILDE: Finalmente, en su clase de español, Ud. escribía notas anónimas a los muchachos guapos.

ROSANA: Todos esto es ridículo. No quiero escuchar más. Vamos, Josefina. Tú tenías razón. ¡Qué estúpida soy! ¡Ella no sabe nada!

MATILDE: Un momento. Veo algo interesante sobre su amiga Josefina en la bola de cristal.

JOSEFINA: ¿Oh? ¿Qué ve Ud.?

MATILDE: Veo a una muchacha tímida y nerviosa.

JOSEFINA: Cierto.

MATILDE: Estaba enamorada secretamente de Antonio, el atleta más popular de la escuela.

JOSEFINA: Sí, sí, es verdad. Siga, siga. Es increíble, Ud. sabe muchísimo.

MATILDE: Eso es todo por hoy. Si quieren saber más, vengan la semana que viene.

Las dos jóvenes salen a la calle.

JOSEFINA: No comprendo cómo ella sabía esas cosas de mi pasado.¡Es realmente una maravilla!

ROSANA: ¡Qué va! Tu hermana la visitó la semana pasada y tú sabes la boca grande que ella tiene.

¡qué va! *no way!*

ACTIVIDAD C

Answer each question with a complete sentence.

1. ¿Quién es y cómo se llama la adivina?

____

2. Según Rosana, ¿qué puede hacer doña Matilde?

____

3. ¿Qué cree Josefina de esas cosas y qué dice?

____

4. ¿Qué tiene la adivina en el centro de la mesa?

____

5. ¿Qué sabía la adivina del pasado de Rosana?

____

6. ¿Qué dijo del pasado de Josefina?

____

7. ¿Qué opinión tiene Rosana de doña Matilde?

____

8. ¿Qué piensa Josefina?

____

9. Según Rosana, ¿por qué sabe doña Matilda cosas del pasado de Josefina?

____

10. En su opinión, ¿por qué creen algunas personas en los adivinos?

____

2 You have now learned the two most important past tenses in Spanish. Let's look at them:

Siempre ***llegaba*** tarde, pero un domingo ***llegó*** temprano.

Iba a la escuela en carro, pero un día ***tuve*** que ir en bus.

Todos los sábados ***venía*** mi tío, pero el sábado pasado **no *vino***.

What time expressions are used in the clauses on the left? What do they tell us about the actions described?

RULE: In Spanish we use the imperfect to express what used to happen or happened over and over again — that is, repeated or habitual actions in the past. That's why the imperfect is often used with expressions like **por lo general** (*in general*), **a menudo** (*often*), **siempre** (*always*), **todos los días** (*every day*).

What time expressions are used in the clauses on the right?

Un día, un domingo, or **el sábado pasado** imply that the action happened at a specific time.

In Spanish, we use the preterit to express specific events that are not habitual, that started and ended within a specific time frame. That's why the preterit is often used with expressions that determine a specific time, like **anoche** *(last night)*, **ayer** *(yesterday)*, **esta mañana** *(this morning)*, **el lunes pasado** *(last Monday)*, and others.

ACTIVIDAD D

The preterit and imperfect forms of the verb are given in each of the following sentences. Select the correct choice.

1. ____________________ al cine a menudo.
(Iban, Fueron)

2. ¿Quién _________________ las tareas anoche?
(hizo, hacía)

3. Me _________________ a las ocho el lunes pasado.
(desperté, despertaba)

4. Ella _________________ de casa temprano esta mañana.
(salía, salió)

5. ¿Dónde _________________ siempre el autobús?
(tomabas, tomaste)

6. ¿Dónde _________________ el autobús ayer?
(tomabas, tomaste)

7. Por lo general, yo _________________ en el parque.
(corría, corrí)

8. Los domingos Juan _________________ a sus abuelos.
(visitaba, visitó)

9. Todos los viernes _________________ temprano a casa.
(llegábamos, llegamos)

10. El viernes pasado _________________ tarde.
(llegábamos, llegamos)

ACTIVIDAD E

You are at a party where everyone is talking about the past. Using the cues provided, make statements about the way it was. Be careful, some verbs have to be used in the preterit and some in the perfect.

1. yo / ir todos los sábados al cine

____

2. nosotros / estar una vez en Nueva York

____

3. yo / salir a dar un paseo todas las noches

____

4. Juan / leer dos novelas el verano pasado

____

5. nosotros / nadar a menudo en la piscina

____

6. mis padres / viajar a Europa hace un año

____

7. Uds. / ir a la playa todos los veranos

____

8. tu hermana / trabajar por lo general hasta tarde

____

9. mi tío / venir de España hace cinco años

____

10. tú / llegar siempre tarde a la escuela

____

3

There is still more to learn about the past. Look carefully at these sentences:

Yo *dormía* cuando *sonó* el teléfono.	*I was sleeping when the telephone rang.*
Ud. *estaba* en casa cuando *llamé.*	*You were at home when I called.*
Rosa *escribía* una carta cuando *llegó* su amiga.	*Rose was writing a letter when her friend arrived.*
Hacía* sol cuando *salimos.	*The sun was shining when we left.*

How many actions are described in each sentence? ______________ How many verb tenses are used in each sentence? ______________ Which tenses are they? ______________ and ______________ . Which word combines the two clauses describing the two actions? ______________ .

Let's summarize: The IMPERFECT describes an ongoing or continuous past action lasting an unspecified amount of time. In English, we can say *was* (*were*) + . . . ing, or *used to* . . . The PRETERIT expresses a specific past action that happened at one point while the other action was in progress. Imagine two cameras—an instant and a video camera. Which one would represent the imperfect? ______________ the preterit? ______________ .

ACTIVIDAD F

Complete the sentence with the correct form of the preterit or the imperfect of the verb in parentheses.

1. Eran las cuatro de la tarde cuando tú ____________ (llegar) a casa.

2. El sábado pasado Juan ____________ (jugar) al fútbol con sus hermanos.

3. Yo siempre ____________ (levantarse) temprano.

4. Mi padre ____________ (leer) cuando mi madre ____________ (llamar).

5. El año pasado ellas ____________ (ir) a Colombia.

6. Cuando yo ____________ (ver) a Luis, él ____________ (llevar) un traje muy elegante.

7. Por lo general, ellos ____________ (hacer) las tareas juntos.

8. Tú siempre ____________ (recibir) muchas cartas.

9. Yo ____________ (lavarse) cuando alguien ____________ (tocar) a la puerta.

10. Cuando mi hermano ____________ (nacer), nosotros ____________ (vivir) en Miami.

ACTIVIDAD G

Your neighbor's window was broken in a ball game, and she complained to your father. Answer his questions.

1. ¿Dónde estabas esta tarde cuando yo entré en casa?

____

2. ¿Con quién jugabas cuando te llamé?

____

3. ¿A qué jugaban Uds.?

____

4. ¿Qué hiciste al ver que la pelota caía en otra casa?

____

5. ¿Qué hacía la vecina (neighbor) cuando la pelota cayó en su casa?

____

6. ¿Dónde estaba tu madre cuando Uds. terminaron de jugar?

____

7. ¿Qué le dijiste a tu mamá sobre la ventana?

____

Read this short description of a little girl's holiday:

> **Era** el diez de junio y **eran** las siete de la mañana. El sol **brillaba** y **hacía** un tiempo precioso. **Estábamos** en un hotel al lado de la playa y por la ventana se **veía** el mar. En la playa **había** otra muchacha. **Era** alta y **llevaba** un traje de baño rojo. Yo **quería** jugar con ella, pero **tenía** que esperar a mis padres porque yo **tenía** solamente ocho años. Mis padres **dormían** . . .

Which tense did the girl use? _______________ She used the IMPERFECT to describe circumstances and conditions in the past. The circumstances and conditions may refer to time, dates, weather, attitudes, states of mind, physical descriptions, age, or locations. All circumstances described in the imperfect happened over an unspecified amount of time.

What happens if the narrator wants to tell about actions that occurred at a specific point in time? Let's pick up the story from the last sentence.

> Mis padres **dormían** y como yo no **quería** esperar más, **decidí** despertarlos. **Abrí** su puerta y **grité**: «¡Levántense! ¡Vamos a la playa!»

Which tense is used to describe the narrator's actions? _______________ Why?

ACTIVIDAD H

Write a short paragraph describing your early years. Complete each sentence with the imperfect of the verb in parentheses.

Cuando yo ______________ (ser) niño, mi familia ______________ (vivir) en Chicago, en un apartamento pequeño. Mi padre ______________ (trabajar) de mecánico en un garaje. Él siempre ______________ (llegar) temprano a casa y él y yo ______________ (salir) a jugar pelota al parque. En invierno mi madre ______________ (preparar) chocolate caliente y ______________ (sentarse) a contarme cuentos. Yo ______________ (ir) a una escuela cerca de casa.

ACTIVIDAD I

You are telling what you saw this morning on your way to school. Complete the paragraph with the correct form of the preterit or the imperfect of the verb in parentheses.

Esta mañana ______________ (llover) cuando yo ______________ (salir) de casa. Yo ______________ (caminar) rápidamente cuando yo ______________ (oír) a un señor que ______________ (gritar) en la calle. ______________ (ser) un hombre que ______________ (correr) detrás de un perro muy grande. Aparentemente el hombre ______________ (encontrar) a un amigo en la calle y el perro ______________ (escaparse) mientras los dos amigos ______________ (hablar).

ACTIVIDAD J

Imagine that you spent last summer in Mexico. Tell you friends in Spanish about a special excursion you took one day. Be careful! You have to decide when to use the imperfect and when to use the preterit.

1. It was August and I was in Mexico City.

____

2. I was living in a hotel.

____

3. One day I woke up early.

____

4. I was going to take a trip.

____

5. I opened the window and saw that the sun was shining.

____

6. We were going by bus.

____

7. I dressed quickly.

____

8. We were going to see the pyramids (*las pirámides*).

____

9. They were very beautiful.

____

10. I enjoyed myself.

____

5

Remember the verbs **saber** and **conocer**? They have special meanings in the preterit tense, different from their meanings in the imperfect. Let's first conjugate both in the preterit. **Conocer** is regular, but **saber** is irregular:

	conocer	saber
yo	**conoc*í***	**sup*e***
tú	**conoc*iste***	**sup*iste***
Ud., él, ella	**conoc*ió***	**sup*o***
nosotros, -as	**conoc*imos***	**sup*imos***
Uds., ellos, ellas	**conoc*ieron***	**sup*ieron***

Now look at these examples:

¿*Conocías* a Juan?	*Did you know Juan?*
Sí, lo *conocí* hace dos meses.	*Yes, I met him two months ago.*
¿*Sabías* que tenemos un examen hoy?	*Did you know that we have a test today?*
Sí, pero lo *supe* muy tarde ayer.	*Yes, but I found out late yesterday.*

RULE: In the imperfect tense, **conocer** means "knew (someone or something)"; in the preterit, it means "met."

In the imperfect tense, **saber** means "knew (something or how to do something)"; in the preterit, it means "found out."

ACTIVIDAD K

Work with a partner. Have the following conversation in Spanish.

1. Do you know María?

____

Yes, I met María at a party yesterday.

____

2. Do you know where she lives?

____

Yes, I found out that she lives near my house.

____

3. Did you also meet her sister, Rosa?

____

Yes, I met Rosa last week.

____

4. Did you know that they are Cuban?

____

No, I didn't know.

____

ACTIVIDAD L

Play the role of a telephone psychic. Tell the person on the line some things that he/she used to do in the past.

EXAMPLE: **De niño, *vivía* en una ciudad grande.**

Diálogo

You went to a fortune teller. To find out if she's any good, you asked her to tell you some things about your past. React to what she says.

Preguntas Personales

1. ¿Cuando eras niño(a), qué hacías para divertirte?

____

2. ¿Qué aprendías en la escuela elemental?

____

3. ¿Cómo era tu familia?

____

4. ¿Qué hacías durante las vacaciones?

____

5. ¿Te gustaba tu vida? ¿Por qué (no)?

____

Información Personal

You have been asked to "tell about yourself." Describe some interesting or important facts or events from your past. (You don't have to tell the truth. No one is going to check. So, go ahead, be outrageous!)

____

____

____

____

____

____

____

____

____

____

____

CÁPSULA CULTURAL

La Víspera de San Juan

En varios países de habla hispana existe una tradición muy interesante relacionada con el 23 de junio, el Día de San Juan. Este día anuncia la llegada del verano; y en la víspera, la gente se reúne para celebrar y practicar varios rituales, con la esperanza de recibir buena suerte.

En Puerto Rico, por ejemplo, la gente va a la playa y se tira tres veces. Según la tradición, eso les dará buena suerte. El ritual termina con una fiesta donde se sirven platos y bebidas tradicionales.

En las Islas Canarias de España también existe una tradición similar. En este caso las personas recogen ropa vieja, muebles rotos y otros artículos que no sirven. También hacen una lista de las cosas negativas que quieren cambiar en sus vidas. Entonces hacen una hoguera, casi siempre en la playa, y tiran al fuego las cosas que ya no quieren y la lista. Después de eso, las personas se tiran al mar inmediatamente. De esta manera dan la bienvenida al verano y esperan buena suerte y cosas positivas en el futuro.

víspera *eve*

se tiran *throw themselves*

hoguera *bonfire*

Para pensar

1. ¿Qué hace mucha gente para tener buena fortuna?
2. ¿Adónde va la gente de Puerto Rico y las Islas Canarias la Víspera de San Juan?
3. ¿Qué escriben en la lista?
4. ¿Por qué hacen las hogueras?
5. ¿Qué beneficios psicológicos tienen las tradiciones?

10

Los deportes

Demonstrative Adjectives and Pronouns

1 Vocabulario

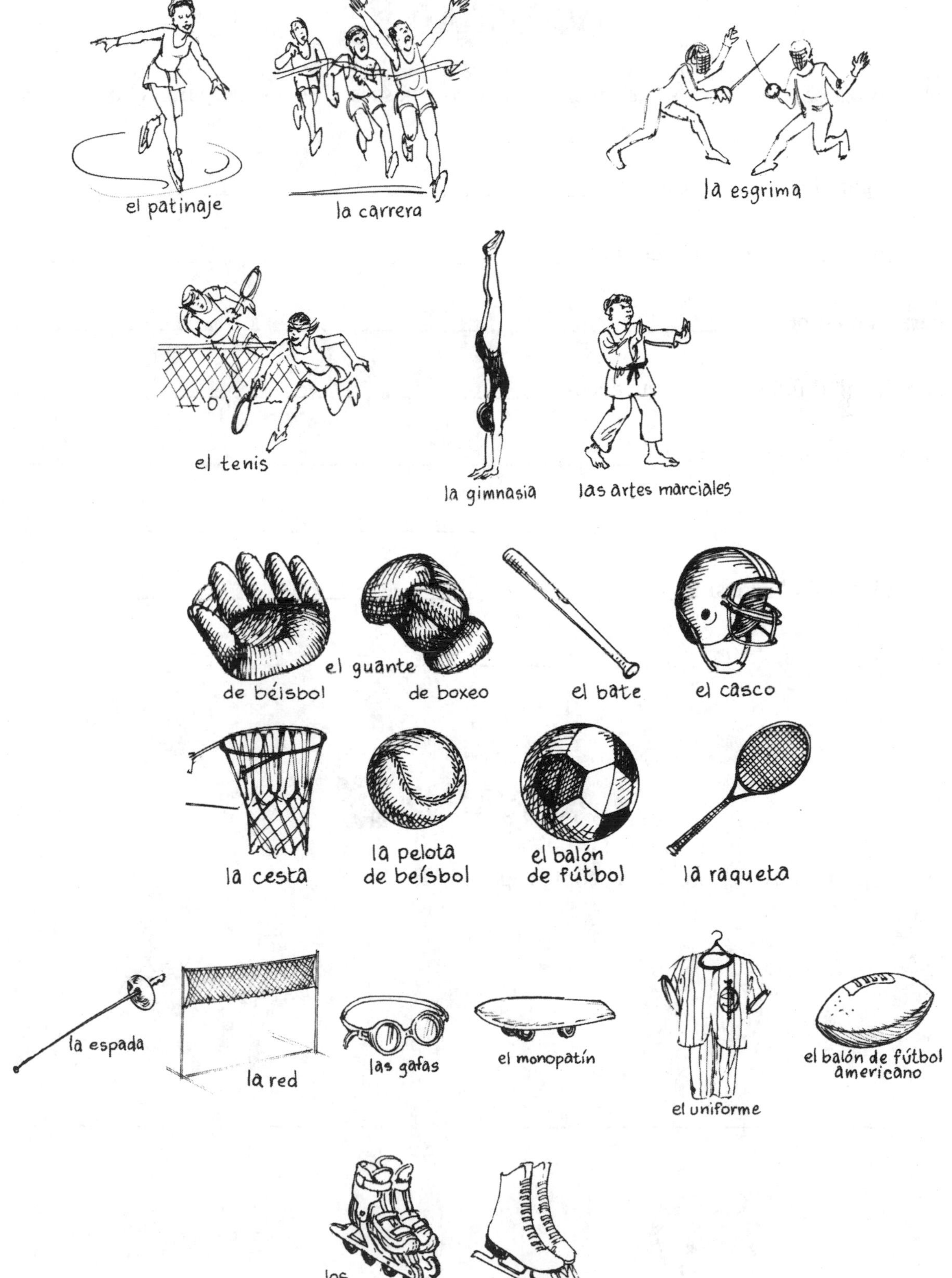
el patinaje
la carrera
la esgrima
el tenis
la gimnasia
las artes marciales
el guante
de béisbol
de boxeo
el bate
el casco
la cesta
la pelota
de béisbol
el balón
de fútbol
la raqueta
la espada
la red
las gafas
el monopatín
el uniforme
el balón de fútbol
americano
los
patines de rueda
los
patines de hielo

ACTIVIDAD A

Mr. Gonzalez needs sports equipment for his gym classes. Can you help him choose some items?

Para jugar al béisbol necesita ______________________________.

Para jugar al básquetbol necesita ______________________________.

Para esquiar necesita ______________________________.

Para jugar al fútbol americano necesita ______________________________.

Para la natación necesita ______________________________.

Para el tenis necesita ______________________________.

Para el voleibol necesita ______________________________.

Para el boxeo necesita ______________________________.

ACTIVIDAD B

What sports activities are these people engaged in?

1. ______________________________

2. ______________________________

3. ______________________________

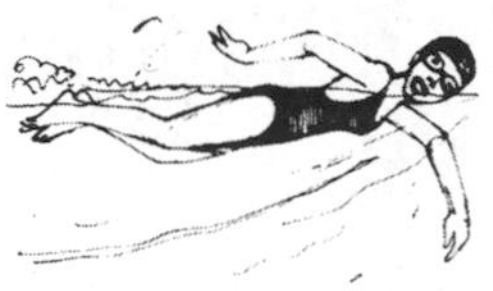

4. ______________________________

5. ______________________ 6. ______________________

El karate

Let's read about another popular sport, **el karate**:

Con un simple golpe de pie o de mano, una persona puede romper una tabla de madera o un ladrillo. ¿Imposible? No. Es muy posible si Ud. sabe ese antiguo arte japonés llamado karate. La palabra karate significa «mano vacía». Eso significa que no se usan armas. Para combatir se utilizan solamente ciertas partes del cuerpo como las manos, los pies, los codos y las rodillas.

el golpe *blow*
romper *to break*
la tabla *board*
el ladrillo *brick*
vacío *empty*

el codo *elbow*
la rodilla *knee*

El karate nació en la India hace más de dos mil años. Allí, unos budistas usaban una forma similar de combate para defenderse de los animales salvajes. Este sistema pasó a China, Japón y Corea, y se convirtió en un método de defensa personal. Hoy día, además, de ser un arte marcial, es un deporte de competición que se practica en todos los países del mundo.

Los estudiantes avanzan desde el grado de principiantes hasta el de expertos. Cada grado tiene un cinturón de un color diferente. Los principiantes, por ejemplo, llevan cinturón blanco y los expertos, negro. Muchas de las asociaciones de karate tienen reglas estrictas para evitar la violencia. Sus miembros aceptan

(1) dedicarse a la educación intelectual y física.

(2) ser corteses y modestos.

(3) respetar a todos, superiores e inferiores, amigos o enemigos.

(4) utilizar el karate sólo en emergencias.

(5) ser buenos.

El estudiante que quiere tener éxito tiene que pasar muchos años de práctica. Por ejemplo, tiene que demostrar su fuerza rompiendo dos o tres ladrillos con un solo golpe de pie. ¿Todavía está Ud. interesado en aprender? Buena suerte pero, ¡tenga cuidado con los dolores de pies!

tener éxito *to succeed*

Answer the following questions with complete sentences.

1. ¿Qué puede hacer con un golpe una persona que sabe karate?

____

2. ¿Qué quiere decir la palabra «karate» en japonés?

____

3. ¿Qué partes del cuerpo se usan en el karate?

____

4. ¿Quién usó originalmente el karate?

____

5. ¿Qué es el karate hoy día?

____

6. ¿Qué cinturón llevan los principiantes?

____

7. ¿Por qué muchas de las asociaciones de karate tienen reglas estrictas?

____

8. ¿Cómo debe demostrar su fuerza el estudiante?

____

2 The demonstratives *this, these, that,* and *those* are used in English to point out specific persons or things. In Spanish, there are many more demonstratives. Let's take a look.

How many possibilities are there in Spanish to point out things? ________

Este (this) refers to a person or thing that is *here* (**aquí**), next to you. **Ese** (that) refers to a person or thing that is *there* (**ahí**), away from you or close to the person you are talking to. **Aquel** *(that)* refers to a person or thing that is *over there* (**allí**), far from you and the person you are talking to. **Este, ese**, and **aquel** are demonstrative adjectives agreeing in number and gender with the noun they accompany.

Let's look at the forms of **este**:

est*e* hombre *this man* **est*os* hombres** *these men*

est*a* mujer *this woman* **est*as* mujeres** *these women*

Now write the appropriate form of **este** for the following words:

____________ traje ____________ guantes

____________ camisa ____________ medias

The forms of **ese** have the same endings:

es*e* árbol *that tree* **es*os* árboles** *those trees*

es*a* casa *that house* **es*as* casas** *those houses*

Write the appropriate form of **ese** for the following words:

____________ caballo ____________ gatos

____________ vaca ____________ gallinas

Finally, forms of **aquel** also have the same endings, but an extra **l** is placed before them.

aquel chico *that boy* **aquel*los* chicos** *those boys*

aquel*la* chica *that girl* **aquel*las* chicas** *those girls*

Now write the appropriate form of **aquel** for the following words:

________ disco ________ cuadros

________ ventana ________ puertas

Note that in Spanish demonstrative adjectives have to be repeated before each noun.

Quiero comprar *esos* periódicos y *esas* revistas. *I want to buy those newspapers and magazines.*

ACTIVIDAD D

You are in a sports store and want to find out how much various items cost. Ask questions using the appropriate form of **este**.

EXAMPLE: **esquíes** **¿Cuánto cuestan *estos* esquíes?**

1. guante ________________________________
2. bate ________________________________
3. balones ________________________________
4. raqueta ________________________________
5. cestas ________________________________
6. cascos ________________________________
7. pelota ________________________________
8. bicicletas ________________________________

ACTIVIDAD E

You're showing your friend what you would like for your birthday. Form sentences using the appropriate form of **ese**.

EXAMPLES: **camisa** **Me gusta *esa* camisa.**
suéteres **Me gustan *esos* suéteres.**

1. abrigo ______________________________
2. sortija ______________________________
3. gafas de sol ______________________________
4. zapatos ______________________________
5. reloj de pulsera ______________________________
6. perfume ______________________________
7. traje de baño ______________________________
8. cadena de oro ______________________________

ACTIVIDAD F

You are watching a parade with your friend and are calling each other's attention to things you see: Use a the appropriate form of **aquel.**

EXAMPLE: **caballo** **¡Mira *aquel* caballo!**

1. gigante ______________________________
2. músicos ______________________________
3. muchacha ______________________________
4. banderas ______________________________
5. banda ______________________________
6. soldados ______________________________
7. coche ______________________________
8. flores ______________________________

ACTIVIDAD G

You are going shopping at the supermarket. Say what you are going to buy.

EXAMPLES:	**pan (aquí)**	**Voy a comprar *este* pan.**
	torta (ahí)	**Voy a comprar *esa* torta.**
	frutas (allí)	**Voy a comprar aquellas frutas.**

1. helado (aquí) ____________________

2. sodas (allí) ____________________

3. pollo (ahí) ____________________

4. carne (aquí) ____________________

5. manzanas (ahí) ____________________

6. huevos (allí) ____________________

7. crema (ahí) ____________________

8. legumbres (aquí) ____________________

9. jugo (allí) ____________________

3 Now look at the following sentences:

Me gusta esta camisa pero no *aquélla.*	*I like this shirt but not that one.*
¿Qué película vas a ver, *ésta* o *ésa*?	*Which film are you going to see, this one or that one?*
Quiero comprar *ese* libro, no *éste.*	*I want to buy that book, not this one.*
¿Quieres escuchar *estos* discos o *ésos*?	*Do you want to listen to these records or those ones?*

When **aquel, este**, and **ese** are used by themselves (without nouns), they are called demonstrative pronouns. The form of the demonstrative pronoun depends on the gender and number of the noun it represents. Demonstrative pronouns have the same forms as demonstrative adjectives, except that the pronouns have an accent mark on the stressed syllable.

éste **ésta**	*this one*	**éstos** **éstas**	*these*
ése **ésa**	*that one*	**ésos** **ésas**	*those*
aquél **aquélla**	*that one*	**aquéllos** **aquéllas**	*those*

ACTIVIDAD H

Marcos went to summer camp and found signs telling him what to do everywhere. Select the demonstrative pronoun that completes the sentence correctly.

1. Ponga su ropa en esta silla, no en ________. (a) éste, (b) ésos, (c) aquélla

2. Entre por esa puerta, no por ________. (a) aquél, (b) ésta, (c) éste

3. Duerma en aquel cuarto, no en ________. (a) ése, (b) ésos, (c) aquélla

4. Abra estas ventanas, no ________. (a) aquéllos, (b) éstos, (c) ésas

5. Use esos zapatos, no ________. (a) éstas, (b) aquéllos, (c) ése

6. Báñese en este baño, no en ________. (a) ésa, (b) aquéllas, (c) ése

7. Siga esas reglas, no ________. (a) ésos, (b) éstas, (c) aquél

8. Corra por aquel patio, no por ________. (a) ésa, (b) éste, (c) éstas

ACTIVIDAD I

Complete the following sentences in Spanish.

1. Quiero ________________ (this) sombrero, no ________________ (that one).

2. Necesito ________________ libros, no ________________ .
(those) (those over there)

3. Prefiero ________________ flores rojas.
(these)

4. ________________ lección no es difícil, pero ________________ sí.
(that) (this one)

5. Abre ________________ ventana y cierra ________________ .
(this) (that one over there)

6. ________________ papeles son importantes.
(those over there)

7. ________________ soldados son españoles; ________________ son franceses.
(those) (these)

8. ________________ niño es mi hermano; ________________ es su amigo.
(that) (that one over there)

Preguntas Personales

1. ¿Practicas algún deporte? ¿Cuál(es)?

____

2. ¿Qué equipos de deporte hay en tu escuela?

____

3. ¿Sabes algún arte marcial? ¿Cuál(es)?

____

4. ¿Cuáles son algunos deportes populares hoy día?

____

5. ¿Deben participar las muchachas en todos los deportes? ¿Por qué (no)?

____

Diálogo

Rafael wants to join a team at school. He's talking with the head of the Physical Education Department.

Información Personal

You want to convince the coach of your favorite sport that you would be a good addition to the team. Complete the sentences that follow.

1. A mí me gusta mucho ______________________________.
2. Ese deporte es ______________________________.
3. Yo creo que soy ______________________________
4. El año pasado ______________________________
5. Quiero ______________________________

Composición

A group of visitors from different countries have come to your school. You are explaining to them the ways Americans spend their leisure time. Talk about some popular activities.

Los fines de semana, muchos norteamericanos ______________________________

____

____

____

____

____

____

____

____

____

CÁPSULA CULTURAL

El juego más rápido (y más peligroso) del mundo

Algunos lo llaman el juego más rápido; otros dicen que es el más peligroso, a causa de la velocidad en que la pelota va por el aire (150 millas por hora). El juego se llama *Jai Alai* o *Pelota Vasca*. Este juego antiguo se originó en el País Vasco, pero ahora se juega por toda España y el mundo entero.

Jai Alai es similar a la pelota de mano, pero hay mayores diferencias. Hay una competencia entre dos equipos, con dos jugadores en cada equipo. Se juega en una cancha larga y ancha de tres paredes, llamada el *frontón*. El objeto del juego es lanzar la pelota contra una de las paredes. Se gana un punto si el otro equipo no puede devolver la pelota.

La pelota es un poco más pequeña que una pelota de tenis y no parece peligrosa, pero está cubierta de cuero y es tan dura como una piedra. Las manos de los jugadores nunca tocan la pelota. Emplean un guante grande y curvo llamado *cesta* o *chistera*. Esta chistera es más de un pie de largo y tiene una ranura para atrapar y luego tirar la pelota; está atada a la muñeca del jugador con correas de cuero.

Una pared protectora de alambre separa a los jugadores de los espectadores. ¡Cuando ven la velocidad con que la pelota viaja, están muy contentos de estar detrás de esa protección!

la pelota de mano *handball*
el equipo *team*
la cancha *court*

devolver *to return*

peligroso *dangerous*
dura *hard*

la ranura *groove*
atrapar *to trap, catch*
la muñeca *the wrist*
la correa *strap*
el cuero *leather*
el alambre *wire*

Para pensar

1. ¿Qué es el Jai Alai? ¿Dónde se originó?
2. ¿Cómo se juega este deporte?
3. ¿Qué se necesita para jugar el juego?
4. ¿Qué juegos son similares? ¿Cómo son diferentes?
5. ¿Por qué participamos en actividades atléticas? ¿Qué beneficios derivamos de los deportes?

Repaso II

(Lecciones 6–10)

LECCIÓN 6

a. Reflexive verbs have a special pronoun, called a reflexive pronoun, to indicate that the subject and object of the verb refer to the same person or thing.

lavar*se*	**dormir*se***	**acostar*se***

b. Some Spanish reflexive verbs have nonreflexive English equivalents.

levantarse	*to get up*
divertirse	*to have fun*
acostarse	*to go to bed*

c. Different subjects require different reflexive pronouns.

yo	***me* visto**	**nosotros, -as**	***nos* vestimos**
tú	***te* vistes**		
Ud., él, ella	***me* visto**	**Uds., ellos, ellas**	***se* visten**

d. In Spanish reflexive constructions, the definite article is used instead of the possessive adjective with parts of the body or wearing apparel.

Tú te lavas *la* cara.	*You wash your face.*
Tú te pones *el* sombrero.	*You put your hat on.*

e. The reflexive pronoun normally stands directly before the verb.

Yo *me* acuesto temprano.
Tú no *te* vistes rápido.

The reflexive pronoun follows the verb and is attached to it in affirmative commands and when the reflexive verb is used as an infinitive.

AFFIRMATIVE COMMAND	INFINITIVE
Levánta*te*. **Levánte*se*.** **Levánten*se*.**	**No queremos levantar*nos*.** **¿Por qué quieres acostar*te* temprano?**

LECCIÓN 7

a. The preterit tense of regular verbs is formed by dropping the **-AR**, **-ER**, or **-IR** ending of the infinitive and adding preterit endings.

b. **Dar** takes **-ER** verb endings in the preterit tense: **di, diste, dio, dimos, dieron**.

c. **-AR** and **-ER** verbs with the stem changes in the present tense (**e** to **ie** and **o** to **ue**) have regular stems in the preterit:

	PRESENT TENSE		PRETERIT	
pensar (ie)	**p*ie*nso** **p*ie*nsas** **p*ie*nsa**	**pensamos** **p*ie*nsan** **p*ie*nsan**	**pensé** **pensaste** **pensó**	**pensamos** **pensaron** **pensaron**
volver (ue)	**v*ue*lvo** **v*ue*lves** **v*ue*lve**	**volvemos** **v*ue*lven** **v*ue*lven**	**volví** **volviste** **volvió**	**volvimos** **volvieron** **volvieron**

-IR verbs with stem changes in the present tense (**e** to **ie**, **o** to **ue**, and **e** to **i**) change **e** to **i** in the third-person singular and plural of the preterit.

	PRESENT TENSE		PRETERIT	
sentir (ie)	**s*ie*nto** **s*ie*ntes** **s*ie*nte**	**sentimos** **s*ie*nten** **s*ie*nten**	**sentí** **sentiste** **s*i*ntió**	**sentimos** **s*i*ntieron** **s*i*ntieron**
dormir (ue)	**d*ue*rmo** **d*ue*rmes** **d*ue*rme**	**dormimos** **d*ue*rmen** **d*ue*rmen**	**dormí** **dormiste** **d*u*rmió**	**dormimos** **d*u*rmieron** **d*u*rmieron**

d. Many Spanish verbs have irregular preterit forms. **Estar, hacer, poder, poner, querer, tener**, and **venir** have irregular stems and irregular endings common to all these verbs.

yo	**estuv**	***e***
tú	**hic**	***iste***
Ud.	**pud**	***o***
él, ella	**pus**	***o***
nosotros, -as	**quis**	***imos***
Uds.	**tuv**	***ieron***
ellos, ellas	**vin**	***ieron***

The preterit stem of **hacer** changes **c** to **z** in the third-person singular to keep the original sound: **hizo.**

e. **Ser** and **ir** share the same irregular forms in the preterit. Only the context makes the meaning clear.

ser	**fui, fuiste, fue, fuimos, fueron**

Yo *fui* al cine. *I went to the movies.*

Yo *fui* víctima de un robo. *I was the victim of a robbery.*

f. Verbs ending in a vowel + **-er** or **-ir** change **i** to **y** in the third-person singular and plural. In the other forms, the **i** has an accent:

leer	**le*í*, le*í*ste, le*yó*, le*í*mos, le*y*eron**

g. **Decir** and **traer** have irregular preterit tense forms.

	decir	**traer**
yo	***dije***	**tra*je***
tú	***dijiste***	**tra*jiste***
Ud., él, ella	***dijo***	**tra*jo***
nosotros, -as	***dijimos***	**tra*jimos***
Uds., ellos, ellas	***dijeron***	**tra*jeron***

LECCIÓN 8

a. The imperfect of regular verbs is formed by dropping the **-AR**, **-ER**, and **-IR** ending of the infinitive and adding imperfect endings.

b. There are only three verbs with irregular forms in the imperfect tense.

	ir	**ser**	**ver**
yo	***iba***	***era***	**veía**
tú	***ibas***	***eras***	**veías**
Ud., él, ella	***iba***	***era***	**veía**
nosotros, -as	***íbamos***	***éramos***	**veíamos**
Uds., ellos, ellas	***iban***	***eran***	**veían**

LECCIÓN 9

a. Uses of the preterit and the imperfect tenses.

IMPERFECT	PRETERIT
Describes repeated or habitual actions (equivalent to English *used* to):	Describes specific events that are not habitual:
Iba al cine todos los sábados.	***Fui* al cine el sábado pasado.**
Describes an ongoing or continuous action (equivalent to English *was (were) + . . . ing*):	Describes a particular action that happened while another action was in progress:

Miguel *dormía* profundamente cuando Jorge *llegó* a su casa.

LECCIÓN 10

a. Demonstrative adjectives.

este / esta *this* **ese / esa** *that* **aquel / aquella** *that*	**estos / estas** *these* **esos / esas** *those* **aquellos / aquellas** *those*

b. Demonstrative pronouns.

éste / ésta *this one* **ése / esa** *that one* **aquél / aquélla** *that one (over there)*	**éstos / éstas** *these* **ésos / ésas** *those* **aquéllos / aquéllas** *those*

ACTIVIDAD A

Here are nine pictures showing what Pepito did yesterday morning. Following the clues given, complete the sentence under each picture.

1. Ayer Pepito ________ a las seis.

2. ______________ de la cama inmediatamente.

3. Entró al baño a ______ ________________ .

4. ________________

5. Salió del baño y _____ ________________ .

6. ________________

7. Después de vestirse ____________ y fue a desayunar.

8. Después del desayuno ____________ .

9. ____________ «Adiós» a su mamá y ____________ de la casa.

ACTIVIDAD B

Buscapalabras Hidden in the puzzle are the names of 11 sports and 5 pieces of equipment needed for sports. Circle the words from left to right, right to left, up or down, or diagonally.

A	B	U	K	A	R	A	T	E	Í
L	E	T	A	B	U	E	N	U	L
O	Ñ	L	N	É	F	R	Q	O	U
B	A	O	A	I	V	S	L	O	C
T	T	B	T	S	E	L	O	M	H
E	E	T	A	B	S	B	B	S	A
U	U	Ú	C	O	A	P	I	I	L
Q	Q	F	I	L	S	N	L	L	I
S	A	L	Ó	B	E	B	O	C	B
Á	R	N	N	T	P	L	V	I	R
B	O	X	E	O	C	S	A	C	E

ACTIVIDAD C

These people used to do different things during the summer. Complete the sentence under each picture, using the imperfect of the appropriate verb.

1. Rosa ____ .

2. Juanita y Julia ____ .

3. El Sr. Gómez ____ .

4. Tú ____ .

5. Uds.  .

6. Jorge ____ .

7. Nosotros ____ .

8. Yo ____ .

ACTIVIDAD D

¿Es Ud. un buen testigo? You are walking down the street when a thief races out of a store and gets into a waiting car, which then speeds away. You have seen the whole incident and are asked to describe what you saw. Examine the following picture very carefully. Then cover the picture and try to answer the following questions.

1. ¿Qué hora era?

____

2. ¿Cómo era el carro?

____

3. ¿Cuál era el número de la placa?

____

4. ¿Tenía el ladrón la cara cubierta?

____

5. ¿Tenía barba o bigote?

____

6. ¿Llevaba sombrero?

____

7. ¿Cuántas personas había en el carro?

____

8. ¿Qué llevaba el ladrón en las manos?

____

9. ¿Qué vio el hombre con el periódico?

____

10. ¿Cuántas personas había en la calle? ¿Dónde estaban?

____

ACTIVIDAD E

Crucigrama

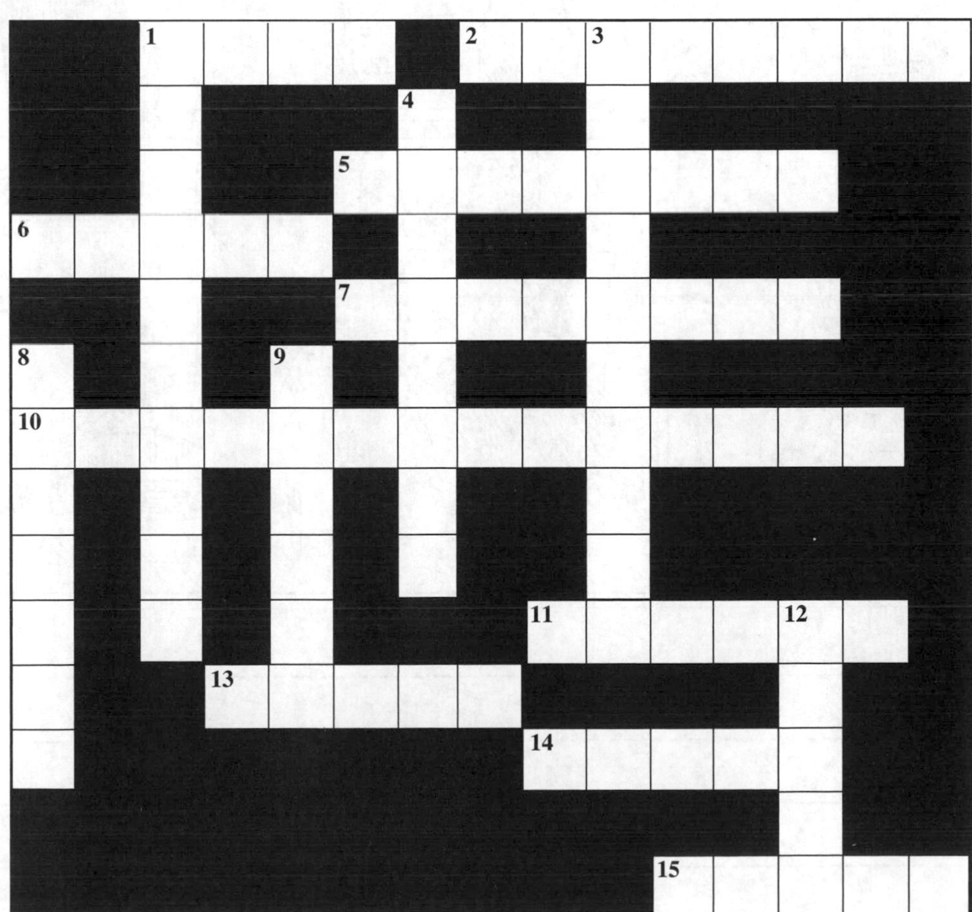

HORIZONTALES

1. baseball bat
2. volleyball (sport)
5. swimming
6. ski; skiing
7. gymnastics
10. martial arts
11. ball (baseball, tennis)
13. helmet
14. ball (basketball, football)
15. basket

VERTICALES

1. basketball (sport)
3. wrestling
4. skating
8. skates
9. sword
12. tennis

ACTIVIDAD F

Las seis diferencias

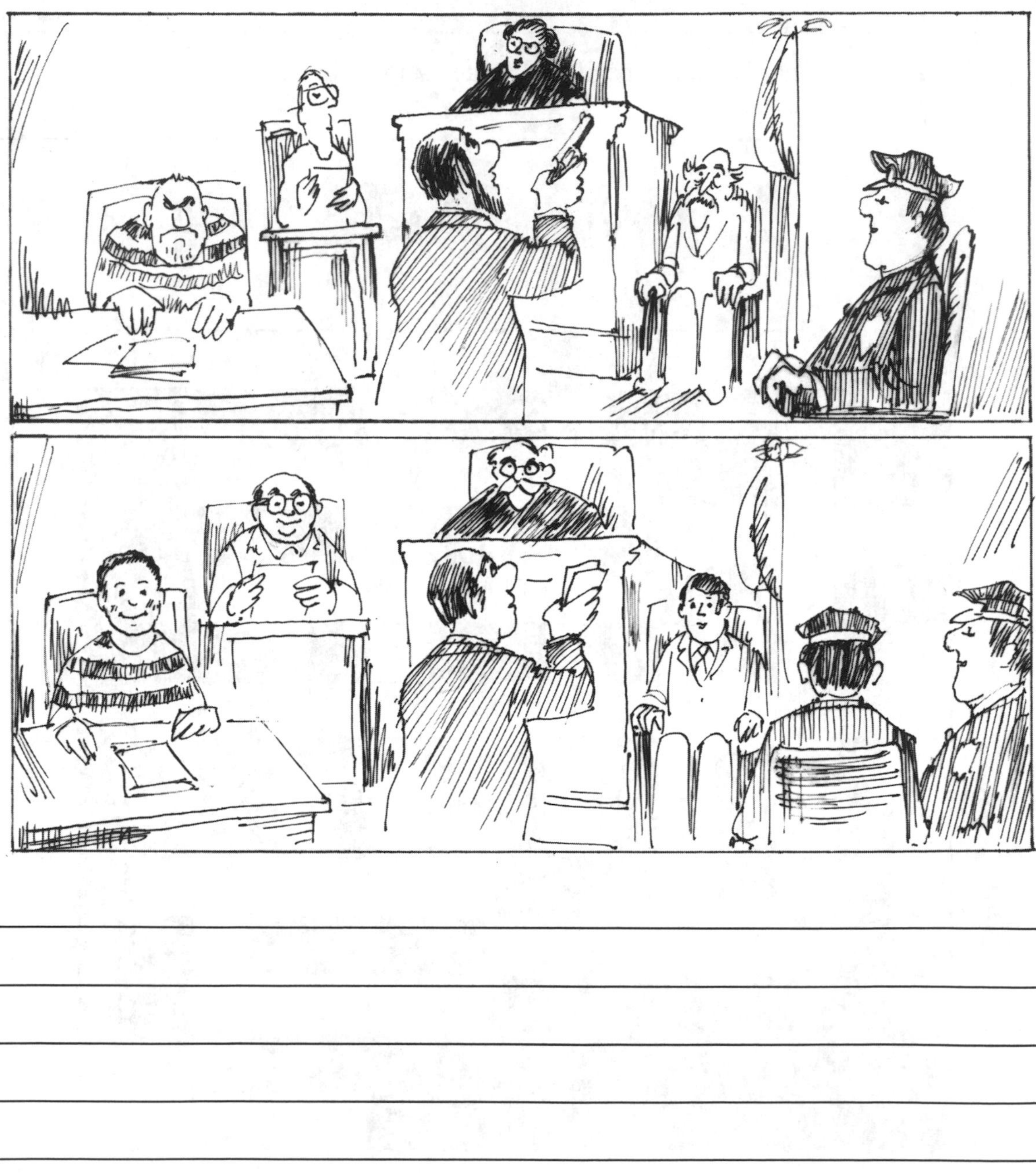

ACTIVIDAD G

Pablo arrived late to school today. Ms. Fernandez wants to know why. Write a short story in Spanish about the situation you see in the pictures.

Tercera Parte

11

En la tienda de ropa

Direct-Object Pronouns

1. Vocabulario

ACTIVIDAD A

You need to buy some clothes and you go shopping with a friend. What would you buy in this store? Work with a partner. One student says: **¿Te gusta esto? ¿Quieres ese saco? ¿Qué (más) necesitas?**

EXAMPLE: **¿Quieres *esta bufanda*?**
Sí, necesito *una bufanda* para el invierno.

1. ______________________ 5. ______________________

2. ______________________ 6. ______________________

3. ______________________ 7. ______________________

4. ______________________ 8. ______________________

ACTIVIDAD B

You are writing a story and have four characters in mind. Here are their descriptions. What clothes would you have them wear? Use the new words and those you already know. Here are some more helpful expressions.

de manga corta	*short-sleeved*	**el cuello**	*collar*
de manga larga	*long-sleeved*	**(ultra)moderno**	*(ultra)modern*
sin mangas	*sleeveless*	**estrecho**	*narrow*
el algodón	*cotton*	**el botón**	*button*
la lana	*wool*	**de tres botones**	*three-buttoned*
ancho	*wide*	**el raso**	*satin*

la tela *fabric, material*	**la seda** *silk*
a rayas *striped*	**de piel** *leather*
a cuadros *check, plaid*	**de goma** *rubber*

Some people are coming down from college. Read each of the descriptions that follow and select the correct person.

Tomás: Un joven de 20 años. Toma clases en la universidad. Tiene ideas muy modernas y originales. Quiere ser actor.

Mario: Un hombre de 30 años. Es un abogado serio, inteligente y práctico. Quiere ganar mucho dinero.

Dolores: Una chica de 21 años. Es refinada y elegante. Quiere ser modelo y le gusta la música moderna.

Sarita: Una chica de 19 años. De día, trabaja de secretaria y, de noche, toma cursos en la universidad. Quiere ser científica. Es alegre, simpática y estudiosa.

Tomás lleva ______________________________

____

____

Mario lleva ______________________________

____

____

Dolores lleva ______________________________

____

____

Sarita lleva ______________________________

____

____

Un vestido de fiesta

Liliana recibió el regalo de Navidad de sus padres— ¡doscientos dólares! ¿Qué va a hacer con tanto dinero? Pues hay una fiesta de año nuevo en casa de Blanquita. Sí, con el dinero que tiene puede comprar un vestido magnífico. Va a ser la chica más elegante de la fiesta. Necesita un vestido especial, y sabe exactamente en qué tienda **lo** puede comprar—la boutique francesa «Chez Fifí». Cuando entra en la tienda, una vendedora **la** saluda:

VENDEDORA: Buenas tardes, señorita. ¿En qué puedo servirle?

LILIANA: Necesito un vestido de fiesta de talla siete para un baile de año nuevo.

VENDEDORA: ¿Qué le parece este vestido de raso rojo?

LILIANA: No me gusta. Me parece muy ordinario.

VENDEDORA: Esta combinación de blusa blanca de encaje y minifalda negra es muy popular ahora. Sólo vale cien dólares.

LILIANA: No está mal. Pero yo prefiero algo más original, más sofisticado.

VENDEDORA: Ajá. Entiendo perfectamente. Aquí tiene un vestido de seda azul que es precisamente para Ud. Es único. No hay otro igual.

LILIANA: Oh, me encanta. ¿Puedo probar**lo**?

me encanta *I love it*
probar *to try on*

VENDEDORA: Sí, claro. Sígame, señorita.
(Liliana se **lo** prueba. Está encantada.)

VENDEDORA: El vestido le va muy bien. Es además muy «chic», muy de moda.

ir bien *to fit*
de moda *fashionable, in-style*

LILIANA: **Lo** compro. ¿Cuánto cuesta?

VENDEDORA: Para Ud., solamente 250 dólares.

LILIANA: Pero tengo sólo doscientos dólares. ¡Qué lástima! Entonces compro la blusa con minifalda.

La noche de la fiesta, Liliana entra en casa de Blanquita y ve a sus tres amigas, Conchita, Lolita y Panchita. Las tres tienen la cara triste y están vestidas exactamente igual— ¡con un vestido de seda azul!

LILIANA: ¿Qué pasó, chicas? ¿Por qué tan tristes? ¿Cómo es que llevan el mismo vestido?

CONCHITA: ¿No te gusta mi vestido muy «chic»?

LOLITA: Sí, es único. No hay otro igual en el mundo.

PANCHITA: Si veo a la vendedora de Chez Fifí **la** mato.

matar *to kill*

ACTIVIDAD C

Answer the following questions about the story.

1. ¿Cuánto dinero recibió Liliana?

____

2. ¿Qué tipo de fiesta hay en casa de Blanquita?

____

3. ¿Qué quiere comprar Liliana?

____

4. ¿En qué tienda piensa encontrar el vestido que busca?

____

5. ¿Por qué no le gusta a Liliana el vestido rojo?

____

6. Según la vendedora, ¿cómo es el vestido de seda azul?

____

7. ¿Por qué no compra Liliana el vestido azul?

____

8. ¿Qué ropa compra Liliana para la fiesta?

____

9. ¿Cómo se llaman las tres amigas de Liliana?

____

10. ¿Por qué están tristes?

____

2

Examine the following paragraph.

I have a Spanish book. I find my Spanish book very useful. I read my Spanish book, study my Spanish book, and refer to my Spanish book before taking a test.

Pretty repetitious! How about his version:

I have a Spanish book. I find it very useful. I read it, study it, and refer to it before taking a test.

Much better, isn't it? What have we done? We have substituted an object pronoun (*it*) instead of repeating the same noun (*Spanish book*). We can do the same thing in Spanish. Look at these sentences from the story.

Ella necesita un vestido especial y sabe dónde *lo* puede comprar.

She needs a special dress, and she knows where she can buy it.

Cuando la chica entra en la tienda, una vendedora *la* saluda.

When the girl enters the store, a saleswoman greets her.

Which noun in the first sentence is replaced by **lo**? ________________. What is the gender of **el vestido**? ________________. Which noun in the second sentence is replaced by **la**? ________________. What is the gender of **la chica**? ________________ .

Lo and **la** are direct-object pronouns; **lo** replaces a masculine singular noun, and **la** replaces a feminine singular noun. **Lo** and **la** have the plural forms **los** and **las**. **Lo, la, los**, and **las** may refer to people or things.

Look at these other examples.

¿Compras el impermeable? Sí, *lo* compro.

Are you buying the raincoat? Yes, I'm buying it.

¿Ves a la vendedora? No, no *la* veo.

Do you see the saleswoman? No, I don't see her.

¿Recibiste los regalos? Sí, *los* recibí.

Did you receive the books? Yes, I received them.

¿Venden batas aquí? No, no *las* venden.

Do they sell robes here? No, they don't sell them.

Where do **lo, la,** and **las** stand in relation to the verb? ________________. Contrary to English, the Spanish object pronoun comes directly before the verb.

ACTIVIDAD D

Substitute a direct-object pronoun for the word in italic type.

EXAMPLE: **Necesito *el libro*.** ***Lo* necesito.**

1. El doctor examina *los ojos*.

 ____

2. Ellos traen *un vaso*.

 ____

3. No veo *la pizarra*.

 ____

4. No escribimos *las cartas*.

 ____

5. El maestro explica *la lección*.

 ____

6. ¿Compras *los periódicos*?

 ____

7. La señora no vende *frutas*.

 ____

8. Tenemos *el abrigo* aquí.

 ____

ACTIVIDAD E

You are going on a trip and your mother wants to know what you are taking with you. Answer her questions.

EXAMPLE: **¿Llevas *la* camisa de seda?** **Sí, *la* llevo.**

1. ¿Llevas los pantalones negros?

 ____

2. ¿Llevas el impermeable?

____

3. ¿Llevas la bufanda azul?

____

4. ¿Llevas las botas de piel?

____

5. ¿Llevas ese sombrero viejo?

____

6. ¿Llevas la bata de casa?

____

7. ¿Llevas las pantuflas?

____

8. ¿Llevas los suéteres nuevos?

____

ACTIVIDAD F

You are giving a party and your best friend wants to know who is going and what foods you will serve. Answer his questions.

EXAMPLE: **¿Invitaste a Juan?** **Sí, *lo* invité.**

1. ¿Invitaste a Rosa?

____

2. ¿Invitaste a los hermanos Gómez?

____

3. ¿Invitaste a Julia y a María?

____

4. ¿Compraste los helados de chocolate?

____

5. ¿Preparaste sándwiches de queso?

____

6. ¿Hizo tu mamá la torta?

____

7. ¿Tienes bastantes sodas?

____

8. ¿Compraste el pastel?

____

ACTIVIDAD G

Carmen has just met Andrés at a party. They discover that they have a lot in common. Work with a partner.

EXAMPLE: CARMEN:—**Yo hago las tareas por la noche.**
ANDRÉS:—**Yo también *las* hago por la noche.**

CARMEN: Yo tomo el autobús para ir a la escuela.

ANDRÉS: _______________

CARMEN: Yo tengo amigos mexicanos.

ANDRÉS: _______________

CARMEN: Yo estudio matemáticas.

ANDRÉS: _______________

CARMEN: Yo toco el piano muy bien.

ANDRÉS: _______________

CARMEN: Yo escucho música clásica todos los días.

ANDRÉS: _______________

3 How can you tell your best friend in Spanish that you saw him? How do you ask him if he saw you? Look at this short dialog.

TÚ: **Ayer *te* vi por la calle con tus padres.**
TU AMIGO: **¿Sí? ¿*Nos* viste? ¿Por qué no *nos* saludaste?**
TÚ: **Uds. estaban muy lejos. ¿No *me* viste tú?**
TU AMIGO: **No, no *te* vi.**

Here's a complete table of the Spanish direct-object pronouns.

me	*me*
te	*you* (familiar)
lo	*you* (formal), *him, it* (masculine)
la	*you* (formal), *her, it* (feminine)
nos	*us*
los	*them, you* (masculine plural)
las	*them, you* (feminine plural)

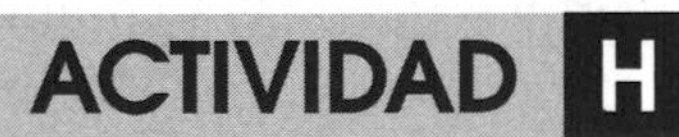

ACTIVIDAD H

Express the following in Spanish:

1. My mother called me an hour ago.

   ___

2. Our grandparents always take us to the movies.

   ___

3. Your friends visit you (*tú*) often.

   ___

4. You (*Ud.*) saw her this morning.

   ___

5. I invited them (*feminine*) to the party.

____

6. ¿Did you (*Uds.*) see us at the baseball game?

____

7. My parents don't understand me.

____

8. ¿Do your parents understand you (*tú*)?

____

We saw that the direct-object pronouns come before the verb. There are some situations, however, in which they take a different position. Look at these examples:

Compra el libro. Cómpra*lo*.	*Buy the book. Buy it.*
Abre la ventana. Ábre*la*.	*Open the window. Open it.*
Escriba Ud. las cartas. Escríba*las*.	*Write the letters. Write them.*
Visita a tus abuelos. Visíta*los*.	*Visit you grandparents. Visit them.*

Are these commands affirmative or negative? ______________ . Where is the direct-object pronoun in these commands? ______________ .

RULE: In affirmative (but NOT negative) commands, the direct-object pronoun follows the verb and is attached to it. In negative commands (informal and formal) the direct-object pronoun goes before the verb.

FORMAL: **No lo compre Ud.**
INFORMAL: **No lo compres.**

NOTE: When attaching a pronoun to an affirmative command, an accent mark is placed on the stressed vowel to keep the original stress. Why is this necessary?

First, let's review some rules of Spanish pronunciation:

- Words ending in a vowel, **n**, or **s** are stressed on the next-to-last syllable (the one just before the end):

casa	**Car**men	**te**nis
clase	**ha**blan	hambur**gue**sa
como		

- When a word ends in a consonant (except **n** or **s**), the stress is on the last syllable:

azul	hospi**tal**	profe**sor**
te**ner**	cami**nar**	liber**tad**

- Any word not following the above rules must have a written accent mark over the vowel of the syllable being stressed:

fútbol	te**lé**fono	cora**zón**	lec**ción**
lágrima	**mú**sica	**Bár**bara	Fran**cés**

Now let's look at some affirmative commands:

compra   **a**bre   es**cri**ba

The stress is on the next-to-the-last syllable. Now add a pronoun:

cómpralo   **á**brela   es**crí**balas

According to the rules of Spanish pronunciation, the stress should fall on the next-to-the last syllable of these words, but to keep the original stress, we must add an accent mark.

compralo: c**ó**mpralo   abrela: **á**brela   escribalas: escr**í**bales

Repeat the following commands, replacing the noun by a direct-object pronoun.

1. Aprende la lección.

   ____

2. Estudia los verbos.

   ____

3. No cierres la puerta.

   ____

4. Compra las revistas.

   ____

5. Llama a Juan.

____

6. No despiertes a tu hermana.

____

7. Escucha al profesor.

____

8. Lee esos capítulos.

____

9. Haz las tareas.

____

10. No prepares la comida.

____

5 Now look at these sentences:

I	II	MEANING
Quiero *verte* hoy.	**Te *quiero* ver hoy.**	*I want to see you today.*
Pedro va a *llamarme*.	**Pedro *me va* a llamar.**	*Peter is going to call me.*
Él viene a *visitarnos*.	**Él *nos viene* a visitar.**	*He is coming to visit us.*
Voy a *comprarlos*.	***Los voy* a comprar.**	*I'm going to buy them.*

How many verbs are in each Spanish sentence? ______________ . Which form does the second verb have? ______________ . Where is the direct-object pronoun in column I? ____________ . Is it attached to the infinitive? ____________ . Where is the direct-object pronoun in column II? ______________ .

RULE: When a direct-object pronoun is used with an infinitive, it may follow and is attached to the infinitive, or it may precede the conjugated form of the other verb.

ACTIVIDAD J

Work with a partner. You are told to do some things and you answer that you will do them:

EXAMPLE: lavar los platos
MADRE: **Lávalos.**
UD.: **Voy a lavarlos.**

1. hacer las tareas

MAESTRA: ______________________________

UD.: ______________________________

2. lavar el carro

PADRE: ______________________________

UD.: ______________________________

3. leer el artículo

PROFESOR: ______________________________

UD.: ______________________________

4. comer las legumbres

HERMANA: ______________________________

UD.: ______________________________

5. abrir la ventana

ESTUDIANTE: ______________________________

UD.: ______________________________

6. llamar al doctor

POLICÍA: ______________________________

UD.: ______________________________

7. comprar los zapatos

HERMANO: ______________________________

UD.: ______________________________

8. servir la comida

MAMÁ: ______________________________

UD.: ______________________________

9. escribir las cartas

PADRES: ______________________________

UDS.: ______________________________

10. traer el dinero

COMERCIANTE: ______________________________

UD.: ______________________________

ACTIVIDAD K

You are talking on the phone with a friend. Answer the questions, using a direct-object pronoun in each sentence: work with a partner who will ask the questions.

1. ¿Escuchaste las noticias hoy?

____

2. ¿Viste el vídeo nuevo que salió?

____

3. ¿Leíste el periódico esta mañana?

____

4. ¿Viste a Gloria y a Clara en el concierto?

____

5. ¿Quieres visitar a Raúl?

____

6. ¿Terminaste la tarea de biología?

____

7. ¿Miraste el partido de béisbol en la televisión?

____

8. ¿Vas a comprar las entradas para el cine?

____

9. ¿Conociste a la nueva profesora?

____

Preguntas Personales

1. ¿Cómo te vistes para ir a una fiesta elegante?

____

2. ¿Cómo te vistes para ir a la escuela?

____

3. ¿Qué ropa recibiste en tu último cumpleaños?

____

4. ¿Cuándo compras ropa nueva?

____

5. ¿Qué compraste la última vez que fuiste de compras?

____

Diálogo

You go into a department store to buy some presents.

Información personal

Your parents just gave you $300 to buy clothes. Make a list of some things you would buy, in what colors, material, and so on:

1. ____

____

2. ____

____

3. ____

____

4. ____

____

5. ____

____

6. ____

____

CÁPSULA CULTURAL

La ropa, los colores y la suerte

Es obvio que la ropa es esencial en nuestra sociedad de hoy. Una nota interesante son las prendas que se usan para ciertas fechas o festividades. Es importante la prenda y también el color de la prenda.

Por ejemplo, en la mayoría de los países hispanoamericanos existe una tradición curiosa para atraer la prosperidad y el amor en la Víspera de Año Nuevo. Hay que ponerse una prenda interior de cierto color. En Puerto Rico, las mujeres se ponen ropa interior amarilla para la buena suerte. Lo mismo pasa en Colombia, aunque en ese país hay que ponerse la prenda revés. En México los colores son el amarillo y el rojo: amarillo para la prosperidad y rojo para el amor. En España, la ropa interior es rosada. Además, estas prendas tienen que ser nuevas.

Otra costumbre que encontramos en algunas regiones de España es que las novias tienen que llevar algo viejo y algo prestado el día de su casamiento. Una costumbre bonita entre los mexicanos ocurre al principio de la primavera: la gente se viste de blanco, indicando así el fin de una temporada y el comienzo de otra, y van a las pirámides de Teotihuacán.

la prenda *article of clothing*

lo mismo *the same*
aunque *although*
al revés *inside out*

la novia *bride*
el casamiento *wedding, marriage*
vestirse *to get dressed*

Para pensar

1. ¿Cuáles son algunas costumbres curiosas de algunos países hispanoamericanos?
2. ¿Qué quiere la gente generalmente para Año Nuevo?
3. ¿Qué tradición de las novias hispanas es similar a la de las novias americanas?
4. ¿Qué hacen los mexicanos al principio de la primavera? ¿Por qué?
5. Describa algunas costumbres curiosas en los Estados Unidos.

12

Vivimos en la ciudad

Indirect-Object Pronouns

1 Vocabulary

ACTIVIDAD A

Your five-year-old nephew is visiting you from the country. You take a ride on the bus with him pointing out different things found in the city.

EXAMPLE: **Mira *el supermercado*.**

1. ______________________________

2. ______________________________

3. ______________________________

4. ______________________________

5. ______________________________

6. ______________________________

7. ______________________________

8. ______________________________

9. ______________________________

10. ______________________________

ACTIVIDAD B

Where are they going? Work with a partner. One student asks the questions; the other one answers, telling where each person is going.

EXAMPLE: **¿Adónde va el enfermo?** ***Va al doctor.***

1. ______________________________

2. ______________________________

3. ______________________________

4. ______________________________

5. ______________________________

6. ______________________________

7. ____

8. ____

9. ____

Pepita aprende a manejar

You have already learned the direct-object pronouns. Pay attention now to other pronouns you will find in this story.

Los padres de Pepita le van a dar un carro deportivo rojo para su cumpleaños. Antes de comprarlo, el papá decidió dar**le** unas clases de manejar a Pepita. Ella tiene hoy su primera clase y está muy nerviosa porque su padre le habla contínuamente.

manejar *to drive*

Primero, le muestra todas las diferentes partes del automóvil y **le** dice: —«Recuerda, hija, Maneja siempre muy despacio». Es importante. Pepita lo hace bastante bien. Sin embargo, su papá **le** grita: «Presta atención a las señales de tránsito. Maneja con cuidado. Tienes una parada en esa esquina. Mira los otros carros. Ten cuidado. Presta atención a los peatones, especialmente a los niños.» Y les grita a los otros choferes: «¡Cuidado! Mi hija está aprendiendo a manejar».

señales de tránsito *traffic signs*

Al final de la clase Pepita está completamente exhausta y más nerviosa que antes. Está muy contenta de ser pasajera otra vez. Su padre está contentísimo porque Pepita no tuvo un accidente. **Le** dice: «Gracias a Dios que no mataste a nadie, pero antes de comprar**te** el carro, tengo que dar**te** muchas clases más. Tienes mucho que aprender.»

De repente, oyen la sirena de un carro de policía que estaba en la esquina. Un policía sale del carro y **les** dice: «Señor, ¿no vio Ud. la luz roja? Lo siento, pero tengo que poner**le** una multa. Me parece que Ud. necesita algunas clases de manejar. ¿No es verdad, señorita?»

multa *fine, ticket*

Conteste con frases completas:

1. ¿Qué regalo va a recibir Pepita?

____

2. ¿Qué decidió su papá antes de comprarlo?

____

3. ¿Cómo está Pepita antes de la clase? ¿Por qué?

____

4. ¿Qué le muestra su padre?

____

5. ¿Cómo maneja Pepita?

____

6. ¿A quiénes debe prestar atención Pepita?

____

7. ¿Qué grita el padre a los otros choferes?

____

8. ¿Cómo está Pepita al final de la clase?

____

9. ¿Qué dice el policía al papá de Pepita?

____

10. ¿Qué hace el policía?

____

ACTIVIDAD C

There's been an accident at the corner of ______________ and ______________ . There were two witnesses. Unfortunately, they described the scene differently. Can you spot the six discrepancies?

Las seis diferencias

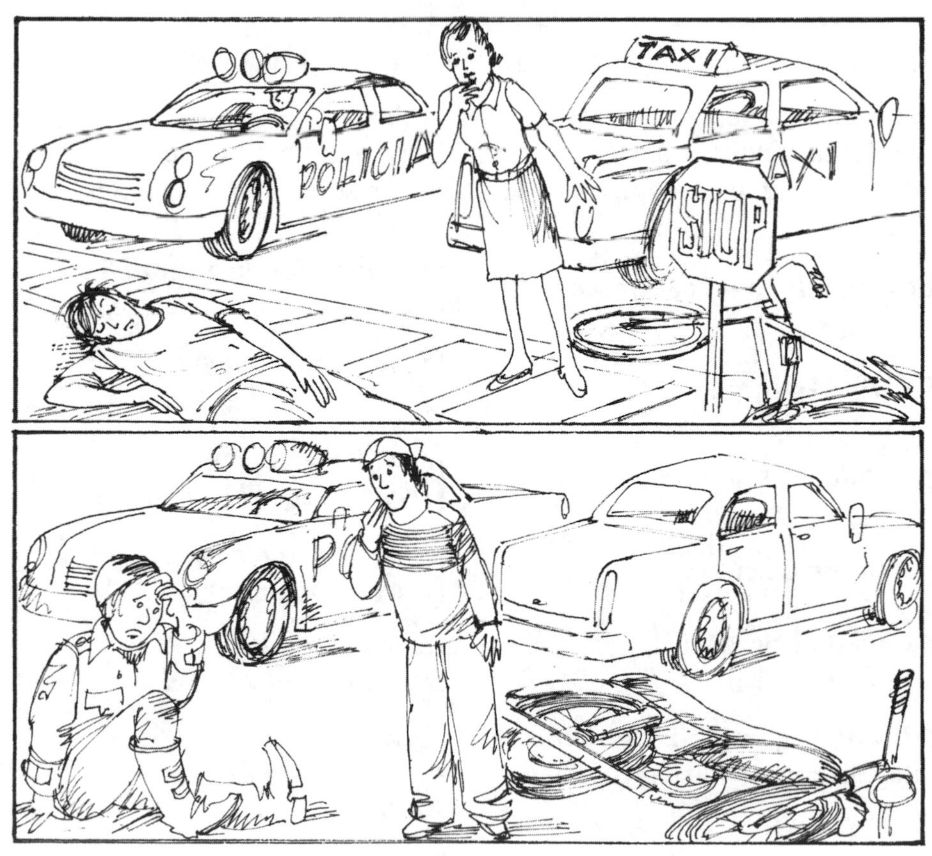

2 Look at the following sentences:

Él dio un regalo *a su mamá.* { *He gave her mother a present.* / *He gave a present to her mother.* }

Ella dio un regalo *a sus amigos*. — *She gave her friends a present.* / *She gave a present to her friends.*

What is the subject in both Spanish sentences? ________________ The verb? ________________ The direct object? ________________ . What are **a su madre** and **a sus amigos**? ________________ . They are indirect objects. An indirect object indicates *to whom* or *for whom* the action is done.

Now look at these sentences:

Ella *le dio* un regalo.	*She gave her a present.* *She gave a present to her.*
Ella *les dio* un regalo.	*She gave them a present.* *She gave a present to them.*

Which word has replaced **a su mamá** in the first sentence? ________________

Which word has replaced **a sus amigos** in the second sentence? ____________ .
Le and **les** are indirect-object pronouns. They stand before the verb and may refer to either masculine or feminine nouns. Here are some more examples:

***Le* doy un reloj a *mi hermano*.**	*I give my brother a watch.* *I give a watch to my brother.*
***Le* doy un reloj.**	*I give him a watch.* *I give a watch to him.*
***Le* presto un disco *a Ud*.**	*I lend you a record.* *I lend a record to you.*
***Le* presto un disco.**	*I lend you a record.* *I lend a record to you.*
Él *les* presta libros *a Uds*. **Él *les* presta libros.**	*He lends you books.* *He lends books to you.*
Les doy un regalo *a mis hermanas*. ***Les* doy un regalo.**	*I give a present to my sisters.* *I give them a present.*

NOTE: Indirect-object pronouns stand before the verb. In everyday Spanish indirect-object pronouns are normally used, even when the indirect-object noun is expressed.

***Les* digo la verdad *a mis padres*.**	*I tell the truth to my parents.*
***Le* sirvo el café *a Juan*.**	*I serve coffee to Juan.*

Here's a table of the indirect-object pronouns:

me	*(to, for) me*
te	*(to, for) you*
le	*(to, for) you* (formal), *him, her*
nos	*(to, for) us*
les	*(to, for) you* (plural), *them*

ACTIVIDAD D

Substitute an indirect-object pronoun for the expression in parentheses. Work with a partner.

EXAMPLE: Compañero: Presto dinero (*a mi hermano*)
Ud.: ***Le* presto dinero.**

1. La maestra enseña la lección (*a los alumnos*)

____

2. El Sr. Pérez da flores (*a su esposa*)

____

3. El policía pone una multa (*al chofer*)

____

4. José hace una pregunta (*a las muchachas*)

____

5. Muestro mi carro nuevo (*a mis amigos*)

____

6. Mi papá compró un regalo (*a mi mamá*)

____

7. El abuelo cuenta historias (*a los niños*)

____

8. Mi hermano presta su bicicleta (*a su amigo*)

____

9. La vendedora vendió un vestido (*a Mercedes*)

____

10. Ud. da trabajo (*a los jóvenes*)

____

3

Where do the direct-object pronouns stand in affirmative commands?

Cómpra*lo*. *Buy it.*

Escríba*los*. *Write them*

Where do they stand in sentences with an infinitive?

Voy a comprar*lo*.
***Lo* voy a comprar.** } *I'm going to buy it.*

The same rules apply to the indirect-object pronouns:

Escriba una carta a sus padres. *Write you parents a letter.*	***Escríbales* una carta.** *Write them a letter.*
Trae la comida a tu hermanito. *Bring the food to your brother.*	***Tráele* la comida.** *Bring him the food.*

Quiero *preguntarle* algo.
***Le quiero* preguntar algo.** } *I want to ask him (her, you) something.*

ACTIVIDAD E

You are on a trip with your parents and your mother is trying to decide what presents to buy and what postcards to send. You are helping her.

EXAMPLE: ¿Mando esta tarjeta a Pablo? **Sí, mánda*le* esta tarjeta.**

1. ¿Regalo esa bufanda? (*a mi hermana*)

____

2. ¿Mando esa tarjeta? (*a tus abuelos*)

____

3. ¿Compro esos discos? (*a mis amigos*)

____

4. ¿Escribo esas tarjetas? (*a los Gómez*)

____

5. ¿Mando aquella tarjeta? (*a José*)

____

6. ¿Compro este juguete? (*a tu hermanito*)

____

ACTIVIDAD F

Your brother always wants to do what you do:

EXAMPLE: Tú dices: Quiero dar flores a mamá.
Él dice: **Yo también quiero darle flores.**

1. Necesito hablar. (*a mis padres*)

____

2. Quiero escribir una carta. (*al editor*)

____

3. Debo servir refrescos. (*a mis amigos*)

____

4. Voy a prestar mi bicicleta. (*a Juan*)

____

5. Quiero dar unos discos. (*a Juan y a Tomás*)

____

6. Voy a hacer una pregunta. (*a la profesora*)

____

ACTIVIDAD G

Your mother is a wonderful cook and likes to prepare special dishes for each member of the family. Express in Spanish what she prepares for various family members.

EXAMPLE: arroz con pollo / mi papá
***Le prepara* arroz con pollo a mi papá.**

1. carne con papas / mis hermanos

   ____

2. flan / mi abuela

   ____

3. pollo / mis tías

   ____

4. pescado / mi hermana

   ____

5. legumbres / mi abuelo

   ____

4 Look at these sentences:

Mis padres *me* regalaron un carro deportivo.	*My parents gave me a sports car.*
¿Qué *te* dieron de regalo de cumpleaños?	*What did they give you as a birthday present?*
La profesora *nos* preparó una sorpresa.	*The teacher prepared a surprise for us.*

What object pronouns do you recognize in these sentences? ______________, ______________, and ______________. In Spanish, **me, te**, and **nos** are both direct and indirect-object pronouns.

ACTIVIDAD H

A friend asks you these questions. What are your answers? Work with a partner.

1. ¿Cuándo me darás el dinero?

____

2. ¿Qué tareas les dieron hoy?

____

3. ¿Me ayudas con el trabajo?

____

4. ¿Puedes explicarme la lección?

____

5. ¿Quién te compró esa bicicleta?

____

6. ¿Qué te dieron tus padres?

____

7. ¿Quién les dio la noticia?

____

8. ¿Qué te preguntó el policía?

____

ACTIVIDAD I

You are writing a letter to a friend. Complete it with the appropriate indirect-object pronouns:

Querida Rosario:

Hoy fui de compras. A mi mamá ____________ (*1.*) compré un suéter muy bonito y a mis hermanos ____________ (*2.*) compré juguetes. No ____________ (*3.*) escribí antes porque estuve muy ocupada. Ayer ____________ (*4.*) mandé tarjetas a todos los chicos de la clase. A

José, por supuesto, ____________ escribí una larga carta. El viaje ____________ gustó
5. *6.*
mucho; el guía ____________ prometió a nosotros una excursión para mañana. Bueno,
7.
ya ____________ conté muchas cosas. ¡Escribe ____________ pronto!
8. *9.*

ACTIVIDAD J

You are telling your friend Pablo what happened last night at a restaurant. Express the following in Spanish:

1. The waiter brought us the menu.

____

2. My mother told him: "Bring me a sandwich."

____

3. The waiter answered her: "I'm sorry, but at this hour I cannot serve you (plural) sandwiches."

____

4. "What can you serve us?" my mother asked him.

____

5. We didn't like anything.

____

6. We went out and my mother said to my father: "I told you (informal) that this restaurant is bad."

____

Preguntas Personales

1. ¿Qué instituciones te pueden ayudar en caso de emergencias?

____

2. ¿Adónde vas si tienes una enfermedad seria?

____

3. ¿Cómo viajas de una parte a otra en tu ciudad?

____

4. ¿Por qué es preferible ir de compras en un supermercado?

____

5. ¿Cuáles son las ventajas y desventajas de los rascacielos?

____

Información Personal

Tell how you get about town, how do you get to school, what means of transportation do you use when going out, etc.

____

____

____

____

____

____

____

____

____

____

Composición

Talk about the city you live in. What are some of the advantages and disadvantages of living there. Take a ride through you neighborhood and describe what you see in the streets.

Diálogo

Rosalinda is riding in a taxi.

CÁPSULA CULTURAL

La ciudad más grande del mundo

Cuando llegó a México, el conquistador Hernán Cortés descubrió la bella ciudad azteca de Tenochtitlán. La ciudad estaba construida sobre pequeñas islas en medio de un lago enorme—el Lago Texcoco. El lago, rodeado de montañas, estaba al lado de dos volcanes cubiertos perpetuamente de nieve—Ixtaccíhuatl y Popocatépetl. La ciudad con sus 300,000 (trescientos mil) habitantes tenía un sistema avanzado de puentes, grandes avenidas, templos, mercados y edificios públicos comparables a cualquier ciudad europea de ese tiempo.

rodeado *surrounded*

Había canales por toda la ciudad y los acueductos llevaban agua fresca a la ciudad desde manantiales de una colina cercana. Carreteras con puentes levadizos conectaban Tenochtitlán a la tierra que la rodeaba.

el manantial *(water) spring*
la colina *hill*
el puente levadizo *drawbridge*

Hoy día la ciudad de México D.F. (Distrito Federal), construida sobre las ruinas de la ciudad azteca de Tenochtitlán, es la capital más antigua del continente americano y la concentración urbana más grande del mundo. Esta ciudad enorme de edificios modernos y de rascacielos tiene una población de más de 20,000,000 (veinte millones) de habitantes y todavía está creciendo rápidamente mientras que miles de mexicanos llegan a la capital en busca de trabajo. En la Ciudad de México, hay más de 18,000 taxis y aproximadamente dos y medio millones más de vehículos de toda clase.

el rascacielos *skyscraper*

crecer *to grow*
en busca de *in search of*

Para pensar

1. Describa la ciudad azteca de Tenochtitlán en los tiempos de Cortés.
2. ¿Dónde estaba la ciudad? ¿Para qué servían las carreteras y puentes?
3. ¿Cuál es la capital de México hoy? ¿Qué significan las letras D.F.?
4. Describa la capital hoy. ¿Qué cree que son sus mayores problemas?
5. ¿Son demasiado grandes las ciudades de hoy? ¿Cuáles son algunas soluciones?

13
En la farmacia

Double-Object Pronouns; Pronouns After Prepositions

1 Vocabulario

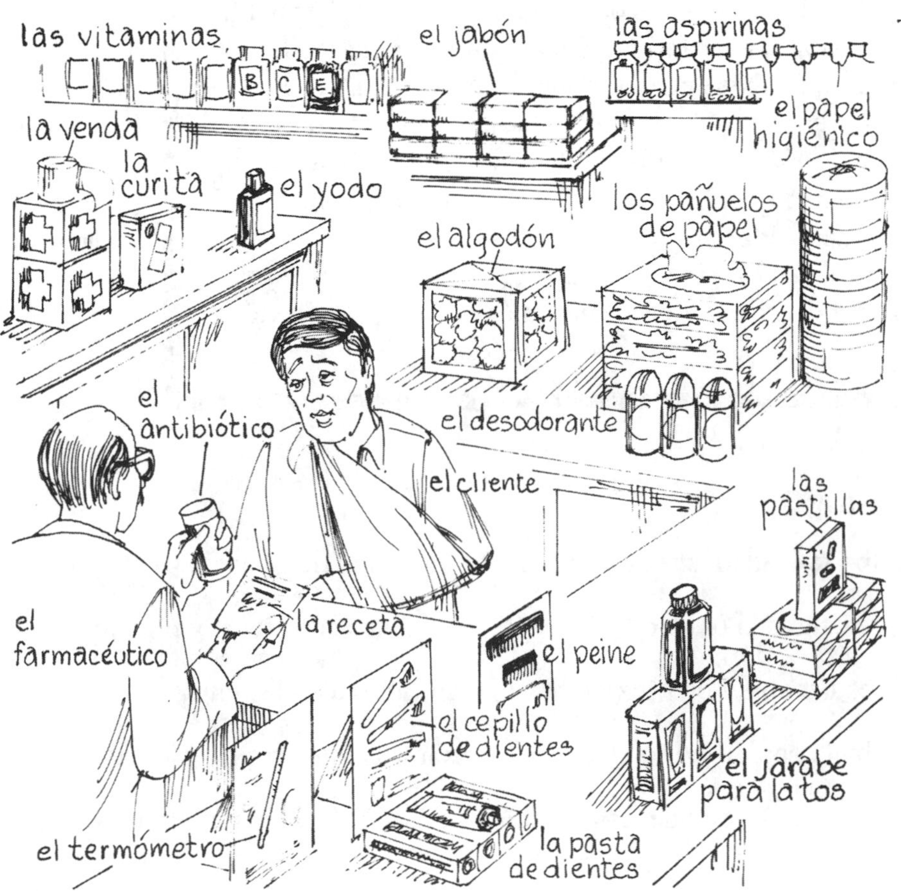

You have learned the names of certain things you can buy in a drugstore. Let's read a conversation between Isabel and a pharmacist. Isabel's little brother is sick and her mother has sent her to the drugstore to buy some things.

FARMACÉUTICO: ¿En qué puedo servirle?

ISABEL: Mi hermanito está enfermo y mi mamá dice que necesita varias medicinas y un termómetro.

FARMACÉUTICO: ¿Tiene fiebre su hermanito?

ISABEL: Creo que sí. Pero no tenemos termómetro para tomársela.

FARMACÉUTICO: ¿Qué más necesita?

ISABEL: Mi hermanito también tose y estornuda mucho. Le duelen la cabeza y la garganta.

toser *to cough*
estornudar *to sneeze*

FARMACÉUTICO: Seguramente tiene gripe o un catarro muy fuerte. Déle estas aspirinas cada cuatro horas. Aquí tiene también un jarabe para la tos y unas pastillas para la garganta.

la gripe *flu*
el catarro *cold*

ISABEL: Gracias. Como mi hermanito estornuda mucho, siempre tiene que sonarse las narices. Déme una caja de pañuelos de papel y un paquete de chicle, por favor.

sonarse las narices *to blow one's nose*
la caja *box*
chicle *chewing gum*

FARMACÉUTICO: Aquí está todo. Pero no comprendo por qué su mamá necesita chicle para su hermano.

ISABEL: El chicle no es para mi hermano. ¡Es para mí!

Your mother has sent you to the drugstore with a shopping list. Tell what you would like.
Necesito . . .

1.  ______________________ 2. ______________________

3.  ______________________ 4. ______________________

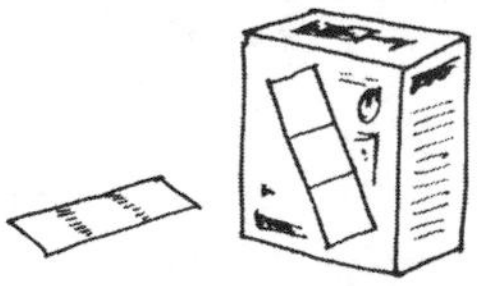

5.  ______________________ 6. ______________________

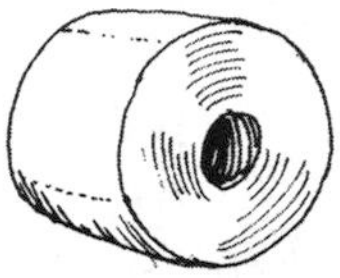

7.  ______________________ 8. ______________________

ACTIVIDAD B

Work with a partner. You are the pharmacist in the neighborhood drugstore. The people in the pictures below seem to be suffering from something. What do they need? (Some people may need more than one item!)

EXAMPLE: CLIENTE: No sé si tengo fiebre.
FARMACÉUTICO: **Ud. necesita *un termómetro.***

1. ______________________
____

2. ______________________
____

3. ______________________________

4. ______________________________

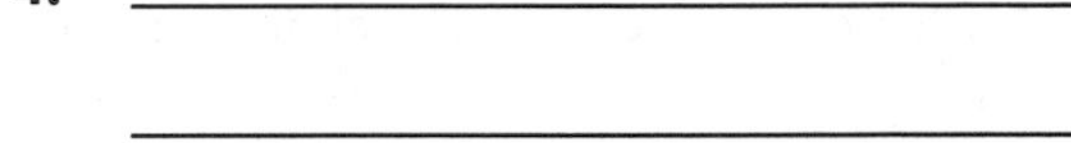

5. ______________________________

6. ______________________________

Do you think that advertisements influence your life? Let's read a story about them.

Los anuncios comerciales

La influencia de los anuncios comerciales está en todas partes—en los periódicos, en las revistas, en la televisión, en los autobuses y en carteleras por las carreteras. Para bien o para mal, son una parte importante de nuestra cultura y de nuestra vida diaria. Ellos nos dicen qué debemos comer, beber, llevar y comprar para vivir bien. ¿Tiene Ud. dolor de cabeza? Sólo cierta marca de aspirina puede ayudarle. ¿Va Ud. a una cita importante? Entonces necesita cierto desodorante o jabón para "estar seguro". Muchos niños aprenden las melodías y la letra de los anuncios comerciales antes de aprender a leer y a escribir. Aquí tiene varios anuncios comunes. ¿Reconoce algunos?

la cartelera *billboard*
la carretera *highway*

la cita *appointment*

la letra *lyrics*

Oportunidad única

¿Lo miran a Ud., tratando de no reírse, cuando Ud. pasa con su carro viejo y feo? Ud. puede ser la envidia de sus amigos y conocidos. Por solo unos pocos dólares, Ud. puede manejar el carro que siempre deseaba. ¿No tiene dinero? No hay problema. ¿Tiene crédito malo? No importa. Vaya hoy mismo a nuestro lote de carros usados de último modelo y siéntese dentro del volante del automóvil de sus sueños.

¡Yo tenía miedo de sonreír!

Iba por el mundo con la boca cerrada. No quería mostrar mis dientes amarillos y manchados. Me sentía tímido y extraño. Luego descubrí la pasta de dientes "*Dentiblanc*" y con ella el secreto de los dientes blancos y limpios. "*Dentiblanc*" está basada en una fórmula secreta europea de doble acción, que deja los dientes brillantes y el aliento agradable. Compre un tubo hoy, y si no está completamente satisfecho, puede devolvérnoslo para recibir todo el dinero que pagó. Le enviamos de vuelta el dinero que pagó por él. "*Dentiblanc*" le permite sonreír con confianza otra vez!

manchado *stained*

dejar *to leave*
el aliento *breath*
devolver *to return*

Conteste las preguntas en frases completas.

1. ¿Dónde hay anuncios comerciales?

____

2. ¿Qué nos dicen los anuncios?

____

3. ¿Qué aprenden muchos niños?

____

4. ¿Cómo son los automóviles que ofrece el anuncio?

____

5. ¿Adónde debe ir para verlos o comprarlos?

____

6. ¿Cuánto dinero necesita para vivir bien?

____

7. En el anuncio, ¿por qué iba el hombre por el mundo con la boca cerrada?

____

8. ¿Qué hace la fórmula secreta de la pasta de dientes?

____

9. Describe tu anuncio de televisión favorito.

____

2 You have already learned the direct- and indirect-object pronouns. Here they are again summarized.

DIRECT-OBJECT PRONOUNS		INDIRECT-OBJECT PRONOUNS	
me	*me*	**me**	(*to*) *me*
te	*you* (familiar)	**te**	(*to*) *you*
lo	*you* (formal), *him, it* (masculine)	**le**	(*to*) *you* (formal) *him, her*
la	*you* (formal), *her, it* (feminine)	**nos**	(*to*) *us*
nos	*us*	**les**	(*to*) *you* (plural), *them*
los	*them, you* (masculine plural)		
las	*them, you* (feminine plural)		

There are many times when you need to use the above pronouns together. Look at the following sentences:

Ella *me* da *la pasta de dientes.* — *She gives me the toothpaste.*
Ella *me la* da. — *She gives it to me.*

Tu mamá *te* compró *el peine.* — *Your mother bought you the comb.*
Tu mamá *te lo* compró. — *Your mother bought it for you.*

Juan *nos* prestó *los discos.* — *Juan lent us the records.*
Juan *nos los* prestó. — *Juan lent them to us.*

When you use two object pronouns together in Spanish, where do they stand in relation to the verb? ____________ . Which pronoun comes first? ____________ . Which pronoun comes directly before the verb?

RULE: In Spanish, contrary to English, the indirect-object pronoun comes before the direct-object pronoun and both stand before the verb.

Your little sister is always asking questions. Answer them in complete phrases.

EXAMPLE: ¿Me prestas tu raqueta de tenis? **Sí, *te la presto.***

1. ¿Me compras un helado? ____________________

2. ¿Me traes un vaso de agua? ____________________

3. ¿Te enseña ella el español? ____________________

4. ¿Te compró papá los zapatos? ______________________
5. ¿Te vendieron las pastillas para la tos? ______________________
6. ¿Me cuentas un cuento? ______________________
7. ¿Me prestas tu abrigo? ______________________
8. ¿Nos dijo mamá la verdad? ______________________
9. ¿Me muestras esos libros? ______________________
10. ¿Nos presta tu amigo la bicicleta? ______________________

Now study the following examples.

Pablo *le* dio *el peine* a María. **Pablo *se lo* dio.**	*Pablo gave the comb to Mary.* *Pablo gave it to her.*
Yo *le* compré *unos pañuelos* a papá. **Yo *se los* compré.**	*I bought some handkerchiefs for dad.* *I bought them for him.*
Mario *les* prestó *las vendas* a ellos. **Mario *se las* prestó.**	*Mario lent them the bandages.* *Mario lent them to them.*
Yo *les digo la verdad* a Uds. **Yo *se la* digo.**	*I am telling you the truth.* *I am telling it to you.*

Look at the first two sets of examples. What happened to the indirect-object pronoun (**le**) when it was used together with the direct-object pronoun **lo** or **los**? ______________

Now look at the last two sets of examples. What happened to the indirect-object pronoun les when it was used with the direct-object pronoun **la** or **las**? ______________

RULE: **Se** replaces **le** and **les** before direct-object pronouns **lo, la, los**, and **las**.

Yo le envié el dinero. **Yo *se lo* envié.**	*I sent him (her) the money.* *I sent it to him (her).*
Yo le envié la carta. **Yo *se la* envié.**	*I sent him (her) the letter.* *I sent it to him (her).*

As you can see, the pronoun **se** can have many meanings. Therefore, the indirect object is normally used together with **se**, either for clarification, emphasis, or reinforcement.

¿A quién le diste el periódico? ***Se* lo di a mi *papá*.**	*To whom did you give the newspaper?* *I gave it to my father.*
¿*Se* lo diste a *tu papá*? **Sí, *se* lo di *a él*.**	*Did you give it to your father?* *Yes, I gave it to him.*

Ella les mostró las fotos a sus amigos.	*She showed the pictures to her friends.*
Ella *se* las mostró *a ellos*.	*She showed them to them.*

ACTIVIDAD E

Work with a partner. You and your friend are playing a game in which you describe what different people do. Confirm you friend's statements.

EXAMPLE: Un médico da medicinas a los pacientes. **Sí, *se las* da.**

1. Un cartero lleva las cartas a la gente.

____

2. Un ladrón roba las joyas a las personas.

____

3. Un mesero sirve la comida a los clientes.

____

4. Una vendedora vende ropa a mi hermana.

____

5. Una profesora enseña el español a la clase.

____

6. Un banco presta dinero a mi papá.

____

7. Una abuela lee historias a los niños.

____

8. Un consejero da consejos al alumno.

____

9. Un policía pone multas a los choferes.

____

10. Un turista escribe tarjetas a los amigos.

____

ACTIVIDAD F

Work with a partner. You mother wants to know if you did certain things. Respond negatively:

EXAMPLE: ¿Escribiste la carta a tus abuelos? **No, no *se la* escribí.**

1. ¿Contaste el cuento a tus amigos?

   ____

2. ¿Explicaste tu problema al profesor?

   ____

3. ¿Diste el dinero a Manuel?

   ____

4. ¿Prestaste tus discos a tus amigos?

   ____

5. ¿Serviste el café a tu papá?

   ____

6. ¿Mandaste la tarjeta a tus tíos?

   ____

7. ¿Escribiste la nota al director?

   ____

8. ¿Diste las vitaminas a tu hermanita?

   ____

ACTIVIDAD G

Your teacher wants to know if you gave certain things to your classmates. Respond affirmatively:

EXAMPLE: el cuaderno / Rosa **Sí, *se lo* di a Rosa.**

1. el libro / Manuel ______________________________
2. los ejercicios / Ud. ______________________________

3. el examen / Juan y Javier ______________________

4. los lápices / los alumnos ______________________

5. la regla / Mercedes ______________________

6. las plumas / todos ______________________

Do you remember where the single-object pronoun stands in affirmative commands?

____

In sentences with an infinitive?

____

The same rules apply to double-object pronouns:

Dígame la verdad. **Díga*me*la.**	*Tell me the truth.* *Tell it to me.*
Cuéntele un cuento a Juan. **Cuénte*se*lo.**	*Tell a story to Juan.* *Tell it ot him.*
Quiero escribirle una tarjeta a Josefina.	*I want to write a postcard to Josefina.*
Quiero escribír*se*la. ***Se la* quiero escribir.**	*I want to write it to her.*

The double-object pronoun (first the indirect, then the direct) follows an affirmative command and may also follow an infinitive. When the double-object pronoun follows and is attached to a command or an infinitive, an accent mark is required on the stressed syllable.

ACTIVIDAD H

Work with a partner. Your friend tells you what she wants to do. Encourage her to do it:

EXAMPLE: Quiero mandarle un regalo a Mercedes. **Mánda*selo.***

1. Necesito comprarme un jarabe para la tos. ______________________

2. Voy a escribirle una carta al director. ______________________

3. Quiero mostrarles esas fotos a mis amigos. ______________________

4. Voy a leerte este artículo. ______________________

5. Necesito darle el dinero a la maestra. ______________________________

6. Quiero hacerte varias preguntas. ______________________________

7. Voy a contarte mi problema. ______________________________

8. Quiero comprarme unos pañuelos de papel. ______________________________

ACTIVIDAD I

Work with a partner. You are going shopping for holiday presents with a friend. Respond to your friend.

EXAMPLE: Voy a comprarle ese disco a José. { **Sí, debes comprár*selo*.** / **Sí, *se lo* debes comprar.** }

1. Voy a comprarle esa bufanda a mi mamá.

____

2. Voy a comprarme ese radio.

____

3. Voy a comprarles esos juguetes a mis hermanos.

____

4. Voy a comprarte ese casete.

____

5. Voy a comprarle aquel reloj a mi papá.

____

6. Voy a comprarles esos dulces a mis amigos.

____

7. Voy a comprarle esas pantuflas a mi abuela.

____

8. Voy a comprar helado.

____

ACTIVIDAD J

Express in Spanish the following conversation between two friends.

1. I need a new bicycle.

___

2. Why don't you buy it?

___

3. I don't have enough money to buy it.

___

4. Your parents can buy it for you.

___

5. They say that I don't need it.

___

6. They don't want to give me the money.

___

7. My grandparents can buy it for me.

___

8. If they buy it for you, can you lend it to me?

___

Preguntas Personales

1. ¿Por qué algunos anuncios son más efectivos que otros?

___

2. ¿Qué valor tienen los anuncios?

___

3. ¿Por qué no compras todos los productos que ves en los anuncios de la televisión?

___

4. ¿Qué importancia tienen los antibióticos?

____

5. ¿Qué compras en una farmacia cuando tienes gripe?

____

Información Personal

Write five sentences in Spanish about things you do for other people. Then rewrite the sentences using object pronouns:

EXAMPLE: Le sirvo el café a mi mamá. ***Se lo* sirvo.**

1. (a) ____
   (b) ____
2. (a) ____
   (b) ____
3. (a) ____
   (b) ____
4. (a) ____
   (b) ____
5. (a) ____
   (b) ____

Composición

You are being interviewed for a job in an advertising agency. You are asked to compose a sample advertisement for any product you want (soda, toothpaste, deodorant, and the like) to see how imaginative you are:

____

____

____

____

____

____

____

____

____

____

3 You have been learning about personal pronouns that are direct or indirect objects of the verb. Other personal pronouns are used after prepositions. You already know most of them. First, let's recall the most common prepositions in Spanish:

a *to*	**en** *in, on, at*
cerca de *near*	**hacia** *toward*
con *with*	**hasta** *as far as; up to; until*
contra *against*	**lejos do** *far from*
de *of, from*	**para** *for*
debajo de *under, beneath*	**por** *for*
delate de *in front of*	**sin** *without*
detrás de *behind*	**sobre** *on, over*

Now look at these sentences:

Juan vive *cerca de nosotros*.	*John lives near us.*
Voy a salir *sin ellos* (*ellas*).	*I am going to go out without them.*
La casa está *lejos de Ud.* (*Uds.*).	*The house is far from you.*
Tú vas de compras *con él* (*ella*).	*You go shopping with him (her).*

What do you notice about the pronouns that follow the prepositions? ______________

____

They are the same as the subject pronouns.

ACTIVIDAD K

Replace the expression in bold type by an appropriate pronoun:

EXAMPLE: Les llevo la comida **a Jorge y a Juan**.
Les llevo la comida *a ellos*.

1. Yo estudio con María.

____

2. ¿Quieres trabajar para mi padre?

____

3. Siempre hablan de Elisa y de Juana.

____

4. No salgas sin tu hermana.

____

5. Enrique se sienta detrás de Josefina.

____

6. El gato está debajo de la cama.

____

7. El avión vuela sobre los edificios.

____

8. Mi hermana quiere vivir lejos de mis padres y yo.

____

Did you notice that we did not use the pronouns **yo** and **tú**? That's because they are the only ones that change after a preposition:

Este vestido es para *ti*.	*This dress is for you.*
No puedes salir sin *mí*.	*You can't go out without me.*

Furthermore, when used with the preposition con, **mi** and **ti** form a new word:

Venga Ud. *conmigo*.	*Come with me.*
El director quiere hablar *contigo*.	*The principal wants to speak with you.*

ACTIVIDAD L

You went shopping and your friend is trying to guess for whom you bought presents.

EXAMPLE: El suéter es para Luis, ¿verdad? **Sí, es para *él*.**

1. La blusa es para Ana, ¿verdad?

____

2. Los dulces son para tu hermano y para ti, ¿verdad?

____

3. Esa camisa es para ti, ¿verdad?

____

4. Los pantalones son para tu papá, ¿verdad?

____

5. Los chocolates son para papá y para mí, ¿verdad?

____

6. Este regalo es para tus padres, ¿verdad?

____

ACTIVIDAD M

You are in a contrary mood today. Your father is trying to convince you to go out and do something.

EXAMPLE: Los muchachos van a jugar al fútbol. **No quiero jugar *con ellos*.**

1. Elena va a ir al parque. ______________________________
2. Tu hermano va a jugar al tenis. ______________________________
3. Tu papá y yo vamos a ir al cine. ______________________________
4. Yo voy a ir al supermercado. ______________________________
5. Gloria y María van a nadar. ______________________________
6. Tus amigos van a jugar al béisbol. ______________________________

ACTIVIDAD N

Answer your little sister's questions, using prepositional pronouns:

1. ¿Vas a salir con Mónica el sábado por la noche?

____

____

2. ¿Puedo salir con Uds.?

____

____

3. ¿Quién se sienta delante de ti en la clase?

____

____

4. ¿Puedo ir contigo a la escuela?

____

____

5. ¿Quieres ir conmigo al cine?

____

____

6. ¿Puedes devolver este libro a la biblioteca por mí?

____

____

7. ¿Compraste esa camiseta para ti?

____

____

8. ¿Vas a salir sin mí?

____

____

Diálogo

An announcer is interviewing you about a particular product:

CÁPSULA CULTURAL

El curandero

El curandero es una figura común en los países de Hispanoamérica. Es una persona que se dedica a curar a los enfermos con remedios caseros, especialmente en los pueblos pequeños o en áreas remotas donde no hay hospitales o doctores. Básicamente hay tres tipos de curandero: el yerbero, que trata las enfermedades con plantas y productos naturales; la partera (casi siempre una mujer), que ayuda a las mujeres durante el parto; y el sobador, que se especializa en masajes.

Alguna gente cree que los curanderos tienen poderes sobrenaturales y por eso los consultan cuando creen ser víctimas de algún mal. El tratamiento prescrito por los curanderos consiste generalmente en rituales religiosos, remedios herbales y oraciones; pero quizás lo más importante es la fe del paciente.

curandero *healer*
casero *home (made)*
el yerbero *herbalist*
la partera *midwife*
el parto *birth*
el sobador *masseur*
prescrito *prescribed*
la fe *faith*

Para pensar

1. ¿Qué es un curandero?
2. ¿Por qué hay generalmente curanderos en áreas remotas?
3. ¿Cuántos tipos de curandero hay? ¿En qué se especializan?
4. ¿Tienen valor los remedios naturales? ¿Por qué?
5. Menciona algunos remedios caseros que utiliza la gente.

14
En la mueblería

Cardinal and Ordinal Numbers

1 Vocabulario

ACTIVIDAD A

Does this kitchen look all right to you? There are seven items you don't normally find in a kitchen and seven that do.

En la cocina hay	En la cocina no hay
______________________	______________________
______________________	______________________
______________________	______________________
______________________	______________________
______________________	______________________
______________________	______________________
______________________	______________________

¡Qué precios!

Let's read a story about a couple who goes shopping for furniture. See if you can figure out how much money they spend.

ANITA: Ricardo, nunca podemos invitar a nadie al apartamento. Todos nuestros muebles son tan viejos . . . ¡Vamos a comprar muebles nuevos!

RICARDO: Está bien. Pero hoy día todo es muy caro. No quiero gastar una fortuna en cosas innecesarias.

ANITA: Para mí una casa bonita es una necesidad. Además, hay una venta especial de verano en

«La Casa Elegante,» la mueblería más grande de la ciudad.

RICARDO: Bueno, vamos a ver qué tienen.

Un poco más tarde, llegan a la mueblería. En el primer piso están los muebles de dormitorio.

ANITA: Me encanta ese juego de dormitorio. Es muy moderno.

juego *set*

RICARDO: Pero mira el precio, quinientos cincuenta dólares.

ANITA: ¿Qué importa? Es un sueño.

En el segundo piso hay muebles de sala.

ANITA: Vamos a comprar ese sofá blanco, las dos butacas y la mesita.

RICARDO: Ay, no, mujer. Cuestan un ojo de la cara—casi seiscientos dólares.

costar un ojo de la cara *to cost a fortune*

ANITA: Para eso tenemos dinero, mi amor, para gastarlo.

En el tercer piso están los muebles de comedor.

ANITA: ¡Qué bonito ese juego con las seis sillas!

RICARDO: Pero, el precio, el precio . . . No estás considerando el precio. Cuestan casi setecientos dólares.

ANITA: Amorcito, no seas tacaño.

tacaño *stingy*

Al final, Anita hace una lista de todos los muebles que quiere y se la muestra a un vendedor.

VENDEDOR: Bueno, señora. El precio de todo, con el impuesto del ocho por ciento y menos el descuento del veinticinco por ciento, es mil trescientos ochenta y nueve dólares.

el impuesto *tax*

RICARDO: ¡Casi mil cuatrocientos dólares! ¡No puedo gastar tanto dinero, no soy millonario! Con esos precios, prefiero vivir con mis muebles viejos.

VENDEDOR: Señor, es evidente que Ud. es inteligente y muy prudente. Espere, tengo la solución. Les propongo un trato especial a Uds., mis queridos amigos. Sólo tiene que pagarme quinientos dólares por ahora. El resto lo puede pagar a plazos, en pequeños pagos cada mes.

el trato *deal*

a plazos *in installments*

RICARDO: Eso parece mejor. Déme el contrato. Tú ves, Anita, es importante pensar antes de hacer una compra. Así se ahorra dinero.

ahorrar *to save*

Al salir de la tienda, Anita lee el contrato: quinientos dólares ahora, y después, setenta dólares al mes durante dieciocho meses.

ANITA: (sarcásticamente) Oh, sí, Ricardo. ¡Ahorraste mucho dinero!

ACTIVIDAD B

Conteste en frases completas.

1. ¿Por qué quiere Anita comprar muebles nuevos?

____

2. ¿Dónde hay una venta especial?

____

3. ¿En qué piso están los muebles de dormitorio?

____

4. ¿Cuánto cuesta el juego de muebles que le gustó a Anita?

____

5. ¿Qué hay en el segundo piso?

____

6. ¿Qué quiere comprar Anita allá?

____

7. ¿Qué quiere Anita para el comedor?

____

8. ¿Cuál es el precio de todo lo que compran?

____

9. ¿Cuánto tiene que pagar Ricardo inmediatamente?

____

10. ¿Cuánto paga Ricardo por los muebles con el trato especial del vendedor?

____

2

You have already learned the cardinal numbers from 0 to 100. Let's review them.

0	**cero**	**13**	**trece**	**50**	**cincuenta**
1	**uno**	**14**	**catorce**	**54**	**cincuenta y cuatro**
2	**dos**	**15**	**quince**	**60**	**sesenta**
3	**tres**	**16**	**dieciséis**	**65**	**sesenta y cinco**
4	**cuatro**	**17**	**diecisiete**	**70**	**setenta**
5	**cinco**	**18**	**dieciocho**	**76**	**setenta y seis**
6	**seis**	**19**	**diecinueve**	**80**	**ochenta**
7	**siete**	**20**	**veinte**	**87**	**ochenta y siete**
8	**ocho**	**21**	**veintiuno**	**90**	**noventa**
9	**nueve**	**30**	**treinta**	**98**	**noventa y ocho**
10	**diez**	**32**	**treinta y dos**	**100**	**cien**
11	**once**	**40**	**cuarenta**		
12	**doce**	**43**	**cuarenta y tres**		

Numbers over 100.

200	**doscientos**	**600**	**seiscientos**	**1.000**	**mil**
300	**trescientos**	**700**	**setecientos**	**100.000**	**cien mil**
400	**cuatrocientos**	**800**	**ochocientos**	**200.000**	**doscientos mil**
500	**quinientos**	**900**	**novecientos**	**1.000.000**	**un millón (de)**

NOTE: Periods are used instead of commas to separate numbers. Commas are used instead of periods to mark decimals.

ACTIVIDAD C

You are a clerk in a large hotel. Several people come to check in. Tell them their room number and then write it in Spanish.

EXAMPLE: Sra. Ramírez / 118 **Sra. Ramírez, su cuarto es el *ciento dieciocho.***

1. Doctor López / 213

____

2. Srta. Gómez / 304

____

3. Sr. y Sra. Pérez / 521

____

4. Doctora Peláez / 417

____

5. Srta. Casas / 745

____

6. Sres. Ramos / 132

____

7. Sra. Montes / 866

____

8. Srta. Gallo / 901

____

9. Sr. Torres / 658

____

ACTIVIDAD D

Match the numbers on the left with the numerals on the right.

1.	ciento ochenta y cuatro	_______________	523
			120.000
2.	doscientos cincuenta y seis	_______________	10.730
			256
3.	cuatrocientos ochenta y nueve	_______________	100.340
			489
4.	ochocientos quince	_______________	1.550
			815
5.	quinientos veinte y tres	_______________	184
			3.910
6.	mil quinientos cincuenta	_______________	
7.	tres mil novecientos diez	_______________	
8.	diez mil setecientos treinta	_______________	
9.	ciento veinte mil	_______________	
10.	cien mil trescientos cuarenta	_______________	

ACTIVIDAD E

Write in Spanish the year in which the following things happened:

EXAMPLE: Cristóbal Colón llegó a América en 1492.
mil cuatrocientos noventa y dos

1. La independencia de los Estados Unidos se declaró en 1776.

___

2. Juan Ponce de León llegó a la Florida en 1512.

___

3. Jorge Washington nació en 1732.

___

4. La Guerra de Independencia Mexicana comenzó en 1810.

___

5. La Organización de las Naciones Unidas se estableció en 1945.

___

6. El nuevo milenio comenzó en el año 2001.

___

3 The numbers 200 to 900 agree in gender with the nouns they accompany.

trescient*as* mesitas **ochocient*as* cincuenta alfombras**

trescient*os* escritorios **ochocient*os* cincuenta floreros**

What happens to the number 100? Look at these examples:

cien **lámparas**
ciento veinte lámparas

cien espejos
ciento veinte espejos

cien **mil habitantes**
cien **millones de habitantes**

Ciento becomes **cien** before any noun, masculine or feminine, and before the numbers **mil** and **millones**.

ACTIVIDAD F

Write in Spanish the numerals in parentheses.

1. (500) ______________________________ casas.
2. (1,400) ______________________________ alumnos.
3. (750) ______________________________ personas.
4. (100,000) ______________________________ soldados.
5. (365) ______________________________ días.
6. (872) ______________________________ páginas.
7. (680) ______________________________ camas.
8. (250,000,000) ______________________________ de norteamericanos.

Let's look again at the number **uno**.

Quiero comprar *un* horno y *una* butaca. — *I want to buy one oven and one easy chair.*

Uno becomes **un** before a masculine singular noun. It changes to **una** before a feminine singular noun. This also applies to compound numbers (**31**, **41**, **51**, etc.).

Veintiún has an accent mark.

Anoche leí *veintiún* capítulos y escribí cuarenta y *una* páginas.
Last night I read thirty-one chapters and wrote forty-one pages.

ACTIVIDAD G

The teacher is making a list of materials needed for the class. Write the numbers in Spanish.

1. (21) ______________________________ libros.
2. (51) ______________________________ lápices.
3. (31) ______________________________ reglas.

4. (61) ______________________________ cuadernos.

5. (41) ______________________________ plumas.

6. (71) ______________________________ mesas.

ACTIVIDAD H

You are the teller in the foreign-exchange division of a bank. Several people need different types of currency. Can you help them?

EXAMPLE: Sr. López / 1.120 dólares
El Sr. López necesita mil ciento veinte dólares.

1. Sra. Martínez / 350.100 pesos mexicanos ______________________
2. Srta. Gómez / 8.671 pesetas ______________________
3. Sr. Pérez / 989 dólares ______________________
4. Sr. Ramos / 25.500 pesos colombianos ______________________
5. Sra. Vélez / 10.431 colones ______________________
6. Doctor Villa / 5.500 quetzales ______________________

5

Do you remember the adjectives **primero** and **tercero**? They are ordinal numbers. Ordinal numbers are used to rank people or things and put them in a certain order. Ordinal numbers are adjectives and agree in number and gender with the noun they describe. **Primero** and **tercero** drop the **o** before a singular masculine noun.

1º	**primer(o)**	*first*
2º	**segundo**	*second*
3º	**tercer(o)**	*third*
4º	**cuarto**	*fourth*
5º	**quinto**	*fifth*
6º	**sexto**	*sixth*
7º	**séptimo**	*seventh*
8º	**octavo**	*eighth*
9º	**noveno**	*ninth*
10º	**décimo**	*tenth*

Enero es el *primer* mes del año. — *January is the first month of the year.*

Carlos *V (Quinto)* fue un rey muy importante.* — *Charles the Fifth was a very important king.*

Vivo en la Cuarta (4º) Avenida. — *I live on 4th Avenue.*

Alfonso XIII (*Trece)* fue un rey español. — *Alphonso the Thirteenth was a Spanish king.*

NOTE: In Spanish, a numbered street is expressed with a cardinal number.

Vamos al festival de la Calle *Ocho*. — *Let's go to the Eight Street Festival.*

Ordinal numbers used with royalty names are usually expressed with Roman numerals.

Felipe II (Segundo) fue muy famoso. — *Philip II was very famous.*

ACTIVIDAD I

You are going shopping in a large department store. On which floor do you find the following things?

EXAMPLE: muebles / 4º **Los muebles están en el *cuarto piso*.**

1. ropa de hombre / 8º ______________________________
2. ropa de mujer / 5º ______________________________
3. televisores / 9º ______________________________
4. cafetería / 2º ______________________________
5. zapatos / 3º ______________________________
6. toallas / 6º ______________________________
7. sombreros / 1º ______________________________

There were tryouts for the track team in your school. You are telling the order of arrival in the first race.

EXAMPLE: Rosa / 1º **Rosa fue *la primera*.**

1. Jorge / 3º ____________________
2. María / 5º ____________________
3. Raúl / 2º ____________________
4. Mercedes / 4º ____________________
5. Josefina / 8º ____________________
6. Mario / 9º ____________________
7. Elisa / 7º ____________________
8. Miguel / 6º ____________________

Diálogo

You are in a furniture store. Tell the salesman what you want.

Preguntas Personales

1. ¿Qué muebles hay en la sala de tu casa?

___

2. Es mejor comprar cosas a crédito o al contado. ¿Cuáles son las ventajas y desventajas de comprar a crédito?

___

3. ¿Qué es un tacaño? ¿En qué situaciones eres tacaño?

___

4. ¿Qué porciento de impuesto pagas cuando compras algo?

___

5. ¿Qué puedes comprar con mil dólares?

___

Información Personal

1. Voy a terminar la escuela superior en al año ___ .
2. Tengo un televisor que costó ___ .
3. El carro que más me gusta cuesta ___ .
4. Estoy en el ___ año de español.
5. Yo nací en el año ___ .

Composición

Describe your room. (Tell what kind of furniture you have, when it was bought, how much you think it cost, whether you like it or not, what color the curtains, the rug, etc.)

CAPSÚLA CULTURAL

Casas sin muebles

Muchas veces cuando una familia va a mudarse a una casa o apartamento, la primera necesidad es ir a comprar muebles nuevos para poder amueblar el lugar.

Pero en la provincia de Esmeralda, al norte del Ecuador, vive una comunidad distinguida por su autosuficiencia. Es principalmente una comunidad de campesinos que han podido mantener sus costumbres sencillas, poco influenciadas por la modernidad. Lo que llama la atención de esta comunidad es que viven en casas construidas con una especie de bambú. Son construidas sobre unos palos y así tienen bastante altura para protegerlas de posibles inundaciones.

En el interior de estas casas, casi no hay muebles. Viven estrictamente con lo necesario. Por ejemplo, a la hora de la comida, la familia se sienta en círculo en el suelo y ponen la comida en el centro del círculo, en el piso.

Para dormir en vez de camas, duermen sobre petates de paja, que ellos fabrican. También, hacen sus propias sábanas y almohadas, bordadas con colores.

Sin duda, esta comunidad representa un ejemplo de sencillez y vivienda ecológica para el resto del mundo.

la autosuficiencia *self-sufficiency*

el palo stilt

la inundación *flood*

el petate *sleeping mat*

paja *straw*

la sábana *bedsheet*

la almohada *pillow*

bordado *embroidered*

Para pensar

1. ¿Dónde está situada la provincia de Esmeralda?
2. ¿Por qué se distingue la comunidad mencionada en la lectura?
3. Da algunos ejemplos de la autosuficiencia de los campesinos de Esmeralda.
4. ¿Son necesarios los muebles? ¿Por qué (no)?
5. Algunos científicos dicen que nuestras sociedades modernas consumen demasiado y destruyen el ambiente. ¿Qué debemos hacer?

Repaso III

(Lecciones 11–14)

LECCIÓN 11

a. Direct-object pronouns

me	*me*	**nos**	*us*
te	*you* (informal)	**los**	*them, you* (masculine plural)
lo	*you* (formal), *him, it* (masculine)	**las**	*them, you* (feminine plural)
la	*you* (formal), *her, it* (feminine)		

b. Direct-object pronouns normally come directly before the verb.

Yo *te* vi ayer.	*I saw you yesterday.*
Él no *la* llamó.	*He didn't call her.*

There are two situations, however, in which direct-object pronouns take a different position:

1. In affirmative commands, direct-object pronouns follow the verb and are attached to it. An accent mark is required on the stressed syllable.

Llláma*me*.	*Call me.*
Acompáña*los*.	*Accompany them.*

2. When the direct-object pronoun is used with an infinitive, it may follow and is then attached to the infinitive, or it may precede the conjugated form of the other verb.

Quiero comprar*la*.	*I want to buy it.*
***La* quiero comprar.**	*I want to buy it.*

LECCIÓN 12

a. Indirect-object pronouns

me	(to, for) *me*	**nos**	(to, for) *us*
te	(to, for) *you*	**les**	(to, for) *you* (plural), *them*
le	(to, for) *you* (formal), *him, her*		

b. Indirect-object pronouns normally come before the verb.

***Te* escribo una carta.** *I write a letter to you.*

Like direct-object pronouns, indirect-object pronouns follow the verb and are attached to it in affirmative commands.

Cómpra*le* el regalo. *Buy him the present.*

When used with an infinitive, indirect-object pronouns may follow the infinitive and are then attached to it, or they may precede the conjugated form of the other verb.

Quicro comprar*le* un regalo. *I want to buy him a present.*

***Le* quiero comprar un regalo.** *I want to buy him a present.*

c. In Spanish, the indirect-object pronoun is normally used even when the indirect-object noun is expressed:

Le escribí una carta a mi amigo. *I wrote a letter to my friend.*

LECCIÓN 13

Double-object pronouns

a. When using two-object pronouns in Spanish, the indirect-object pronoun comes before the direct-object pronoun and both stand before the verb.

La profesora *nos lo* dio. *The teacher gave it to us.*

b. **Se** replaces **le** and **les** before the direct-object pronouns **lo, la, los**, and **las**.

Yo *se* lo di *a ella*. *I gave it to her.*

c. Double-object pronouns (first the indirect, then the direct) follow an affirmative command and may also follow an infinitive. When the double-object pronoun follows and is attached to a command or an infinitive, an accent mark is required on the stressed syllable:

Tráe*melo*. *Bring it to me.*

Tengo que comprár*tela*.
***Te la* tengo que comprar.** } *I have to buy it for you.*

d. Common prepositions

a	*to*	**en**	*in, on, at*
cerca de	*near*	**hacia**	*toward*
con	*for*	**hasta**	*as far as, until, up to*
contra	*with*	**lejos de**	*far from*
de	*of, from*	**para**	*for*
***debajo* de**	*under*	**por**	*for*
delante de	*in front of*	**sin**	*without*
detrás de	*behind*	**sobre**	*on, over*

e. Personal pronouns used after prepositions

mí	**nosotros**
ti	**Uds.**
Ud.	**Uds.**
él	**ellos**
ella	**ellos**

f. **Mí** and **ti** form a new word with the preposition **con**: **conmigo** and **contigo.**

Ella fue al cine *conmigo*. *She went to the movies with me.*

LECCIÓN 14

a.

200	**doscientos**	**600**	**seiscientos**	**1.000**	**mil**
300	**trescientos**	**700**	**setecientos**	**100.000**	**cien mil**
400	**cuatrocientos**	**800**	**ochocientos**	**200.000**	**doscientos mil**
500	**quinientos**	**900**	**novecientos**	**1.000.000**	**un millón (de)**

The numbers 200 to 900 agree in gender with the nouns they accompany.

El libro tiene *trescientas* páginas.

b. **Ciento** becomes **cien** before any noun, masculine or feminine, and before the numbers **mil** and **millones**.

Anoche leí *cien* páginas del libro.

La biblioteca tiene *cien* mil libros.

c. **Uno** becomes **un** before a masculine singular noun. It changes to **una** before a feminine singular noun.

Enero tiene treinta y *un* días.

En la clase hay cuarenta y *una* sillas.

d. Ordinal numbers

1º primer(o)

2º segund(o)

3º tercer(o)

4º cuart(o)

5º quint(o)

6º sext(o)

7º séptim(o)

8º octav(o)

9º noven(o)

10º décim(o)

After ten, cardinal numbers are normally used.

Ordinal numbers are adjectives and agree in gender and number with the noun they describe.

Vivo en el *segundo* edificio de la avenida *quinta.*

e. **Primero** and **tercero** drop the final **o** before a singular masculine noun.

Terminé el *primer* capítulo.

Subí al *tercer* piso.

ACTIVIDAD A

Los siete errores

ACTIVIDAD B

En la tienda de ropa.

Unscramble the words. Then unscramble the letters to find out what Carmen bought in the clothing store.

ASTIECAM ☐☐☐◯☐◯☐◯

TARCEAR ☐☐◯☐◯☐☐

APZALLITAS ☐☐◯☐☐☐◯☐☐☐

SOBAT ED AGOM ◯☐☐☐☐ ☐◯ ☐☐◯☐

IMAPAJ ☐☐☐☐◯☐

Carmen compró un ☐☐☐☐☐☐☐☐☐☐☐

ACTIVIDAD C

Your mother asks you to bring in one of the clothing articles hanging on the line. Pick it out from her description. Place an X in the correct circle.

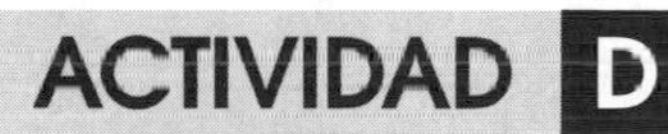

1. Tiene mangas.
2. Tiene un bolsillo pequeño.
3. Tiene botones.
4. Tiene cuello.
5. La tela es a rayas.

ACTIVIDAD D

Crucigrama

HORIZONTALES

4. syrup
5. comb
7. vitamin
9. toothpaste
11. prescription
12. antibiotic

VERTICALES

1. pharmacist
2. deodorant
3. bandage
6. tablet
8. aspirin
10. cotton

ACTIVIDAD E

Picture Story Can you read this story? Whenever you come to a picture, read it as if it were a Spanish word.

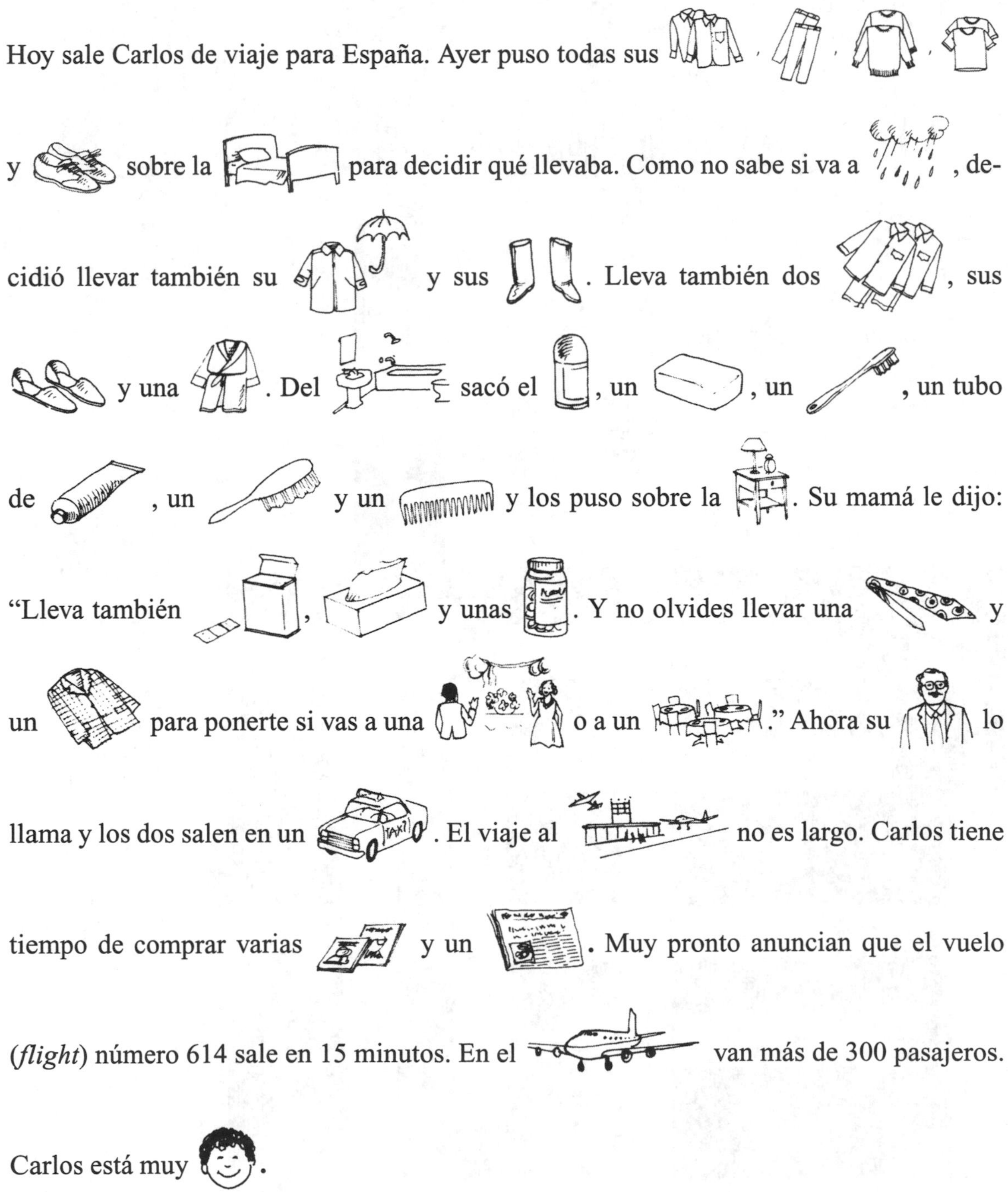

Hoy sale Carlos de viaje para España. Ayer puso todas sus , , , y sobre la para decidir qué llevaba. Como no sabe si va a , decidió llevar también su y sus . Lleva también dos , sus y una . Del sacó el , un , un , un tubo de , un y un y los puso sobre la . Su mamá le dijo: "Lleva también , y unas . Y no olvides llevar una y un para ponerte si vas a una o a un ." Ahora su lo llama y los dos salen en un . El viaje al no es largo. Carlos tiene tiempo de comprar varias y un . Muy pronto anuncian que el vuelo (*flight*) número 614 sale en 15 minutos. En el van más de 300 pasajeros.

Carlos está muy .

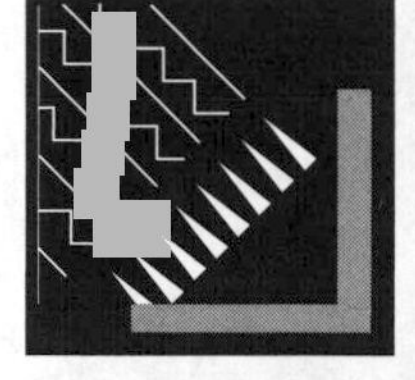

Cuarta Parte

15
La superstición

Verbs With Spelling Changes

1 Vocabulario

ACTIVIDAD A

Work with a partner. One person reads the statement in Column A and asks the question **¿Qué es?** The other person answers, using the phrases in Column B.

A

1. Estudio de la influencia de las estrellas. ______
2. Según la superstición, el día que trae mala suerte. ______
3. La consecuencia de romper un espejo. ______
4. Persona que crea ilusiones. ______
5. Vuela en una escoba. ______
6. Un mal sueño. ______
7. Una creación de la imaginación. ______
8. Animal que vuela por la noche. ______

B

a. el cementerio
b. la bruja
c. la pesadilla
d. la fantasía
e. la mala suerte
f. el viernes trece
g. el mago
h. la astrología
i. el murciélago

ACTIVIDAD B

Describe what's happening in the following pictures.

1. ______________________________

2. ______________________________

3. ______________________________

4. ______________________________

5. ______________________________

6. ______________________________

7. ______________________________

8. ______________________________

Las supersticiones

Are you superstitious? Read this story about superstitions and see if you recognize any of them. Pay attention to the spelling of the verbs in boldface.

Acérquese, por favor. Quiero preguntarle algo. ¿Es Ud. una persona supersticiosa? ¡Claro que no! La idea es ridícula. Ud. es inteligente, moderno, lógico y no cree en cosas como la mala suerte. La superstición es para los viejos y los ignorantes.

acercarse *to come near*
¡Claro que no! *of course not*

Y sin embargo . . . dígame, ¿qué hacen algunas personas cuando un gato negro pasa por delante de ellas, cuando tienen que pasar por debajo de una escalera, cuando rompen un espejo o cuando alguien abre un paraguas dentro de su casa? ¿Tocan madera? ¿Cruzan los dedos?

el paraguas *umbrella*

¿Qué piensa Ud. cuando ve que es viernes trece? (¿Sabe Ud. que en los aviones no hay asientos con el número trece y que en muchos edificios no hay pisos con ese número?)

Como ve, el mundo está lleno de supersticiones. Muchos científicos afirman que la superstición se basa en la ignorancia y en el miedo. No obstante, muchas veces la superstición tiene influencia en nuestra vida diaria. Muchas de estas supersticiones son universales. Otras se ven en ciertas culturas solamente. Entre los hispanos supersti-

no obstante *nevertheless*

ciosos, por ejemplo, es mala suerte casarse o viajar los martes, especialmente si es el día 13.

Al contrario, si tienen un sueño con toros es porque van a ganar la lotería. Y si ven a tres curas juntos, van a recibir un regalo. Además, algunos creen que hay objetos que traen buena suerte: una pata de conejo, un trébol de cuatro hojas o una estatua de un elefante blanco. Y si no quiere visitas aburridas en la casa, **coloque** una escoba detrás de la puerta: la visita se irá pronto.

el cura *priest*

la pata de conejo *rabbit foot*
trébol *clover*

colocar *to place*

¿Está confundido ahora? Entonces, **siga** todas las supersticiones y **aprenda** así a evitar la mala suerte. **Toque** madera, **cruce** los dedos, no **llegue** de viaje el día trece. El problema es que muchas veces las supersticiones tienen significados **contrarios** en diferentes lugares del mundo. La vida es complicada, ¿verdad?

ACTIVIDAD C

Conteste con frases completas.

1. ¿Qué tipo de persona no cree en la mala suerte?

___

2. ¿Quiénes creen en las supersticiones?

___

3. ¿Por qué los supersticiosos no pasan por debajo de una escalera?

___

4. ¿Qué no abre en su casa una persona supersticiosa?

___

5. ¿Qué hacen con los dedos muchos supersticiosos para tener buena suerte?

___

6. ¿Según algunos, qué número trae mala suerte?

___

7. ¿En qué está basada la superstición, según muchos científicos?

___

8. ¿En qué día no debe uno viajar o casarse, según algunos supersticiosos?

____

9. ¿Cuáles son algunos objetos que traen buena suerte?

____

10. ¿Es posible creer en todas las supersticiones? ¿Por qué no?

____

2

Note the following sentences.

***Toque* madera.**	*Knock on wood.*
No *llegue* de un viaje el trece.	*Don't arrive from a trip on the thirteenth.*
***Cruce* los dedos.**	*Cross your fingers.*

What are the infinitives of these verbs?

toque ______________

llegue ______________

cruce ______________

What happened to the **c** in **tocar**? ______________________

What happened to the **g** in **llegar**? ______________________

What happened to the **z** in **cruzar**? ______________________

The **c** changed to **qu**, and **g** changed to **gu**, and the **z** changed to **c**.

RULE: Verbs ending in –**car**, -**gar**, and –**zar** change their spelling in the first person (**yo**) of the preterite and in the formal commands in order to maintain the original sound of the infinitive.

c to **qu**
g to **gu** } before **e**
z to **c**

Here are more examples:

expli*car*: **Yo *expliqué* la lección.** *I explained the lesson.*
***Explíquela* Ud. ahora.** *Explain it now.*

jug*ar*:	**Yo ya *jugué* con ese juego. *Jueguen* Uds. con él.**	*I already played with that game. Play with it.*
almor*zar*:	**Ya *almorcé*. Almuerce (Ud.) sin mí.**	*Thanks, I had lunch. Have lunch without me.*

Note that some verbs with spelling changes also have stem changes: **jugar (ue), almorzar (ue), comenzar (ie), empezar (ie)**, and others.

ACTIVIDAD D

What did you do yesterday?

EXAMPLE: pescar en el lago **_Pesqué_ en el lago.**

1. buscar un libro en la biblioteca ______________________
2. sacar una buena nota en el examen ______________________
3. tocar la guitarra ______________________
4. explicar las tareas a mi hermanito ______________________
5. acercarse a la escuela por la tarde ______________________

ACTIVIDAD E

Give the following commands.

EXAMPLE: empezar a trabajar ya (Uds.) **_Empiecen_ a trabajar ya.**

1. almorzar en la cafetería (Uds.) ______________________
2. cruzar la calle con cuidado (Uds.) ______________________
3. comenzar a hacer las tareas (Ud.) ______________________
4. pagar la cuenta del gas (Ud.) ______________________
5. no jugar en la sala (Uds.) ______________________
6. llegar temprano a la casa (Uds.) ______________________

ACTIVIDAD F

Answer the following questions.

1. ¿A qué hora almorzaste ayer?

____

2. ¿Con quién jugaste el sábado pasado?

____

3. ¿Qué nota sacaste en el último examen de español?

____

4. ¿A qué hora comenzaste a ver televisión anoche?

____

5. ¿Cruzaste muchas calles para llegar a la escuela?

____

6. ¿A qué hora llegaste a casa ayer por la tarde?

____

7. ¿Tocaste a la puerta?

____

8. ¿Buscaste palabras en el diccionario para la tarea de español?

____

3

Other verbs undergo different spelling changes to maintain the original sound of the infinitive. Look at these examples.

recog*er*:	**Yo *recojo* los juguetes.**	*I pick up the toys.*
	***Recoja* Ud. su ropa.**	*Pick up your clothes.*
dirig*ir*:	**Yo *dirijo* la obra de teatro.**	*I direct the play.*
	***Dirija* Ud. el coro.**	*Direct the choir.*

What happened to the **g** in **recoger** an **dirigir**? ______________

The **g** changed to **j** in the first person (**yo**) singular of the present tense and in the formal commands.

RULE: Verbs ending in **-ger** or **-gir** change the **g** to **j** before the vowels **a** and **o** to keep the original sound of the infinitive. Some **-ger** and **-gir** verbs also have stem changes: **corregir (i)** *to correct* (**yo corr*ij*o**) and **elegir (i)** *to elect* (**yo el*ij*o**).

ACTIVIDAD G

Give the following commands.

EXAMPLE: recoger los platos sucios (Ud.)
Recoja los platos sucios.

1. corregir los errores en la composición (Uds.) ______________________
2. proteger a los animales (Uds.) ______________________
3. escoger una película cómica (Ud.) ______________________
4. coger la pelota (Ud.) ______________________
5. elegir al presidente de la clase (Uds.) ______________________
6. dirigir el coro en la clase de música (Ud.) ______________________

Finally, verbs ending in **-guir** undergo a spelling change in the first person (**yo**) singular of the present tense and in the formal commands.

extin*guir*:	**Yo siempre *extingo* el fuego.**	*I always put out the fire.*
	***Extinga* el fuego.**	*Put out the fire.*

In these sentences, **gu** changes to **g** before **o** and **a** to maintain the original sound of the infinitive. Note that some verbs with spelling changes also have stem changes: **seguir (i)** *to follow*, **perseguir (i)** *to pursue*, and **conseguir (i)** *to obtain, get*.

***Sigan* a ese señor.** *Follow that man.*

Answer the following questions.

1. ¿Escoges a tus maestros en la escuela?

____

2. ¿Sigues algún curso de arte?

____

3. ¿Recoges los platos sucios después de la comida?

____

4. ¿Consigues siempre entradas para los conciertos que quieres ver?

____

5. ¿Proteges a los animales?

____

6. ¿Diriges algún proyecto en la escuela?

____

ACTIVIDAD I

Here are some statements you heard from some political candidates. Express them in Spanish.

1. I follow the advice of the people.

____

2. I knocked on every door.

____

3. I embraced (**abrazar**) a hundred babies.

____

4. I do not protect criminals.

____

5. I arrived in this city twenty years ago.

____

6. I always choose the correct solutions.

____

7. I correct my mistakes.

____

Preguntas Personales

1. ¿En cuáles supersticiones cree mucha gente?

____

2. En tu opinión, ¿cuál es la superstición más ridícula?

____

3. ¿Tuviste mala suerte el año pasado? ¿Qué pasó?

____

4. ¿Tienes algún objeto de buena suerte?

____

5. ¿Cuál es tu cuento de hadas favorito?

____

Información Personal

You are a successful person. Using the following expressions, show the steps to your success.

escoger una carrera	**elegir una compañía**
seguir mis estudios	**conseguir un empleo**
comenzar a trabajar	**jugar en un equipo**
sacar buenas notas	

EXAMPLE: ***Saqué*** **buenas notas en la escuela.**

____

____

____

____

____

____

Diálogo

Your friend Francisco (a very superstitious person) is always a nervous wreck when he walks down the street. Anita is trying to calm him down.

CÁPSULA CULTURAL

El dios malo: Juracán

Cada año, tormentas violentas con vientos de más de 100 millas por hora se forman en los océanos de las regiones tropicales.

Estos vientos destructivos pueden cubrir un área de miles de millas cuadradas, trayendo nubes que producen lluvias torrenciales y olas tremendas. Estas olas pueden inundar la tierra, ahogar a miles de personas y causar billones de dólares en daños.

Los vientos son tan fuertes que derrumban árboles y edificios y aún levantan automóviles. Estas tormentas, llamadas huracanes, son las más fuertes que existen en la tierra.

¿Pero, de dónde viene su nombre? Antes de la llegada de los españoles al Nuevo Mundo, una tribu de indios, los taínos, vivían en muchas de las islas del Mar Caribe. Fue esta gente quien dio a Puerto Rico su nombre original: Borinquen. Los taínos eran una gente apacible y trabajadora. Nos dieron muchas palabras indias que forman parte de la lengua española y de ahí pasaron al inglés, por ejemplo: la hamaca, el tabaco, la canoa y el maíz.

Como todos los pueblos antiguos y modernos, los taínos tenían sus supersticiones y creencias. Crearon una mitología para explicar la naturaleza y su mundo. Inventaron cuentos de sus dioses y sus poderes. Había muchos cuentos del dios malo, Juracán, que causaba tormentas terribles cuando estaba enojado. No es difícil ver por qué los taínos llamaron "huracán" a esas tormentas terribles que destruían su tierra.

la tormenta *storm*
cuadrado *square*
la ola *wave*
inundar *to flood*
ahogar *to drown*
el daño *damage*
derrumbar *to knock down*
fue *it was*
apacible *peaceful*
la creencia *belief*
el poder *power*

Para pensar

1. Describa lo que pasa durante un huracán.
2. ¿Quiénes eran los taínos? ¿Cómo eran?
3. Mencione algunas palabras taínas que son ahora parte de nuestra lengua.
4. ¿Quién era Juracán y que hacía?
5. ¿Cómo explicaban los eventos naturales los pueblos antiguos, como los romanos y los griegos?

16

Las maravillas del reino animal

Comparing People and Things

1 Vocabulario

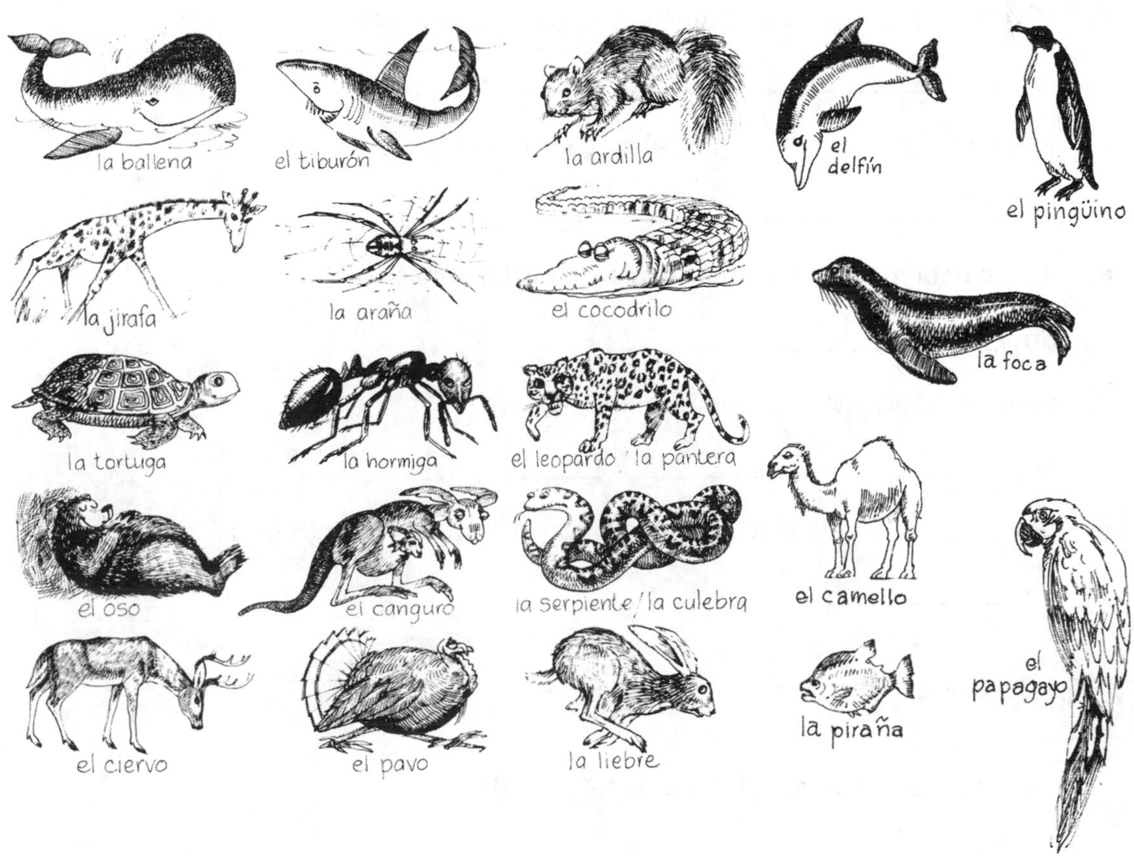

ACTIVIDAD A

Did you ever play **"¿Quién soy?"**? This time we are going to play it with animals. See if you can guess the animal by what it says.

1. Soy un reptil, camino despacio y vivo por mucho tiempo.

   Soy ______________________________ .

2. Soy un pájaro que no puede volar. Vivo en las tierras frías del Antártico.

   Soy ______________________________ .

3. No tengo patas. Me muevo silenciosamente.

   Soy ______________________________ .

4. Vivo en el río. Soy feroz y la gente me tiene mucho miedo.

   Soy ______________________________ .

5. Salto en vez de correr y vengo de Australia.

   Soy ______________________________ .

6. Vivo en los árboles. Soy pequeña y tengo una cola larga y bonita.

   Soy ______________________________ .

7. Soy muy inteligente y vivo en el mar, pero no soy un pez.

   Soy ______________________________ .

8. Tengo ocho patas y atrapo insectos en mis telarañas.

   Soy ______________________________ .

9. Salto rápidamente y tengo orejas muy largas.

   Soy ______________________________ .

10. Soy muy grande y peludo. Duermo todo el invierno en una cueva.

    Soy ______________________________ .

¡Es increíble!

Let's read a story about some world records.

En todo el mundo a la gente le gusta discutir sobre cuál es la cosa más grande, la más pequeña, la más fría, la más caliente, la más alta, la más vieja, etc. Hacen preguntas como: ¿quién es el hombre más pesado del mundo?, ¿quién es el más rápido?, ¿quién bateó el «jonrón» más largo?, ¿cuál es el animal más grande?

Puede encontrar las respuestas a todas estas preguntas, y a miles más, en un solo libro, «El libro Guinness de récords». La compañía Guinness produce cerveza y es la compañía más grande de Irlanda. Cuando publicó su libro por primera vez, no tenía la menor idea del éxito que iba a tener. El libro está publicado hoy día en 23 idiomas y hasta ahora ha vendido más de 30 millones de copias.

la cerveza *beer*

Aquí tenemos algunos récordes mundiales interesantes: la persona más alta del mundo, un hombre que medía 8 pies, 11 pulgadas; la persona más pequeña; una mujer que medía 23 pulgadas; la persona más pesada; un hombre que pesaba 1,069 libras; la persona más vieja; un japonés que murió a la edad de 120 años; el animal más grande y más pesado; una ballena azul que medía 110 pies y pesaba 195 toneladas; el animal más alto; una jirafa que medía 20 pies; el animal más veloz, el leopardo cazador; que puede correr de 96 a 101 kilómetros por hora (60–63 millas por hora); el animal terrestre más grande; un elefante africano que medía 13 pies de alto y pesaba 26,328 libras; el perro más pequeño, un chihuahua que pesaba 10 onzas; la serpiente más larga y más pesada, una anaconda que medía 27 pies, 9 pulgadas; el reptil más grande y más pesado, un cocodrilo que medía 27 pies y pesaba 1,100 libras; el pez marino más grande, un tiburón que medía 60 pies, 9 pulgadas y pesaba 90,000 libras; el árbol más alto, una secoya gigante de California que medía 366 pies; el árbol más viejo, un pino de los Estados Unidos que tenía 4,900 años.

la pulgada *inch*

la libra *pound*

pesado *heavy*

la tonelada *ton*

el leopardo cazador *cheetah*

la secoya *sequoia*

¿Le pareció interesante la información? ¿Sabe la respuesta a las siguientes preguntas? Algunas parecen ridículas, pero sin embargo están en el libro oficial de records mundiales. ¿Sabe Ud. cuál es . . .

(a) la pizza más grande del mundo?

(b) el mayor peso levantado por un ser humano?

(c) el perfume más caro?

(d) la perla más grande?

(e) la iglesia más grande?

(f) el «jonrón» más largo?

Las respuestas

(a) una que medía 80 pies y pesaba 18,664 libras

(b) 6,270 libras

(c) una esencia de jazmín que costaba más de $200 por onza

(d) una que pesó 14 libras, una onza

(e) San Pedro en Roma, con un área de 18,110 yardas cuadradas

(f) 618 pies de distancia

ACTIVIDAD B

Conteste con frases completas.

1. ¿Qué le gusta discutir a la gente?

____

2. ¿Cuáles son algunas preguntas que hace la gente?

____

3. ¿Dónde se encuentran las respuestas a esas preguntas?

____

4. ¿En qué país está la compañía?

____

5. ¿En cuántas lenguas está publicado el libro?

____

6. ¿Cuánto medía el hombre más alto del mundo, según el libro?

____

7. ¿De qué nacionalidad era el hombre más viejo?

____

8. ¿De qué país viene el perro más pequeño?

____

9. ¿Cuál es el animal más grande y más pesado del mundo?

____

10. ¿Dónde está el árbol más alto del mundo?

____

2

In order to arrive at the facts you read in the story, people had to make comparisons. Let's look at some examples:

El elefante medía trece pies de alto.	*The elephant was 13 feet tall.*
La jirafa medía veintitrés pies de alto.	*The giraffe was 23 feet tall.*
La jirafa era *más alta que* el elefante.	*The giraffe was taller than the elephant.*
El elefante era *menos alto que* la jirafa.	*The elephant was less tall than the giraffe.*

In Spanish, to form a comparison stating that one thing (or person) is MORE than another, use **más** + adjective + **que**. To form a comparison stating that one thing (or person) is LESS than another, use **menos** + adjective + **que**. Remember that the adjective has to agree in gender and number with the noun it refers to:

***María* es más estudios*a* que Juan.**	*María is more studious than Juan.*
***Juan* es menos estudios*o* que María.**	*Juan is less studious than María.*

ACTIVIDAD C

Compare the animals illustrated using **más** and the clues given.

EXAMPLE: pequeño **El gato es *más pequeño que* el cochino.**

1. alto

____

2. grande

____

3. rápidos

____

4. inteligente

____

5. feroces

6. bonito

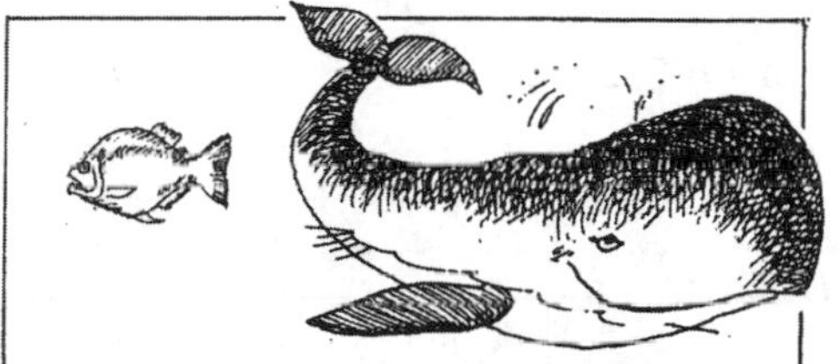

7. pequeño

Give your opinion of the following things.

EXAMPLE: las películas románticas / las películas de horror (*emocionante*)
Las películas románticas son *más emocionantes que* las películas de horror.

1. el tenis / el béisbol (*popular*)

2. el fútbol / el fútbol americano (*violento*)

3. la comida en un picnic / la comida en un restaurante (*sabroso*)

4. la playa / la piscina (*divertido*)

____

5. la clase de español / la clase de matemáticas (*difícil*)

____

ACTIVIDAD E

Using **más** or **menos**, compare the following things.

EXAMPLE: **novela policíaca / novela histórica** (*interesante*)
La novela policíaca *es menos interesante que* la novela histórica.
La novela policíaca *es más interesante que* la novela histórica.

1. Cristóbal Colón / Francisco Núñez de Coronado (*famoso*)

____

2. el dinero / la salud (*importante*)

____

3. los trenes / los aviones (*rápidos*)

____

4. el periódico / la radio (*necesario*)

____

5. los automóviles / las bicicletas (*útiles*)

____

3 Now look at the following type of comparison.

Las serpientes son *tan largas* como los cocodrilos.	*Snakes are as long as crocodiles.*
Yo soy *tan alto(a)* como tú.	*I am as tall as you.*

To form a *comparison of equality* in Spanish, use **tan** + adjective + **como**.

ACTIVIDAD F

Using **tan . . . como**, compare the following people.

EXAMPLE: Juan / Elisa (*amable*) **Juan *es tan amable como* Elisa.**

1. el profesor / el director (*serio*) ____________________
2. las frutas / las legumbres (*bueno*) ____________________
3. el policía / el bombero (*valiente*) ____________________
4. el perro / el gato (*inteligente*) ____________________
5. yo / tú (*sincero*) ____________________

What happens if you want to express a superlative — that is, say that something or somebody is the greatest or the most intelligent? Look at the following examples.

Pablo es *el más alto de la clase.*	*Pablo is the tallest in the class.*
Rosa *es la menos tímida de la clase.*	*Rosa is the least timid in the class.*
Andrés y Mario son *los más pequeños del grupo.*	*Andrés and Mario are the smallest in the group.*
Elisa y Luisa son *las menos serias del grupo.*	*Elisa and Luisa are the least serious in the group.*

RULE: In Spanish, the superlative is expressed as follows:

definite article **(el, la, los, las)** + **más / menos** + adjective + **de**
(*the* + *most / least* + *adjective* + *in*)

ACTIVIDAD G

Using the following adjectives, state who in your family is the most or the least:

EXAMPLE: estricto
Mi papá es *el más estricto de* la familia.
Mi mamá es *la menos estricta de* la familia.

1. alegre ______________________________

____

2. serio ______________________________

____

3. ambicioso ______________________________

____

4. amable ______________________________

____

5. divertido ______________________________

____

6. generoso ______________________________

____

ACTIVIDAD H

In your opinion, which are *the most* and *the least* in each category?

EXAMPLE: animal rápido
El leopardo es *el más rápido*.
La tortuga es *la menos rápida*.

1. deporte interesante

____

____

2. animal inteligente

____

____

3. programa de televisión aburrido

____

____

4. película divertida

____

____

5. actor guapo

____

____

6. automóvil elegante

____

____

5

There are four adjectives with irregular comparative forms.

bueno *good*	**mejor** *better, best*	**Pablo es *mejor que* Jorge. Él es *el mejor alumno de la* clase.**
malo *bad*	**peor** *worse, worst*	**Ellos son *peores que* sus amigos. Ellos son *los peores de la* escuela.**
grande *big*	**mayor** *older, oldest* **más grande** *bigger, biggest*	**Francisco es *mayor que* yo, pero yo soy *más grande que* él. Él es *el mayor* y yo soy el *más grande de los* hermanos.**
pequeño *small*	**menor** *younger, youngest* **más pequeño** *smaller, smallest*	**María es mi hermana *menor* y es *la más pequeña de la* familia.**

Mayor and **menor** refer to age, **más grande** and **más pequeño** refer to physical size.

ACTIVIDAD I

In your opinion, which was or is the best and the worst of these things?

EXAMPLE: novela de ciencia ficción
***La mejor novela de ciencia ficción* es «El planeta desconocido».**
***La peor novela de ciencia ficción* es «Noche de horror».**

1. película del año

____

____

2. actor de televisión

____

____

3. equipo de fútbol profesional

____

____

4. automóvil deportivo

____

____

5. grupo de rock

____

____

ACTIVIDAD J

Write a description of your family (real or imaginary). Mention who is smaller, bigger, older, taller, smarter, etc.

EXAMPLE: **Tengo un hermano. Se llama Raúl. Raúl *es más estudioso* que yo, pero yo soy *más inteligente*.**

Información Personal

1. La mejor película qué vi el año pasado fue ______________________ .
2. El programa de televisión que más me gustó es ______________________ .
3. La experiencia más interesante que tuve fue ______________________ .
4. La clase que más me gustó fue ______________ porque ______________ .
5. Yo soy el / la mejor ______________ de mi familia (de mi clase, de mi escuela).

Diálogo

Your sister Carmencita is a very curious child. She's forever asking you difficult questions. Give your answers:

Composición

You are a camp counselor and have gone to the zoo with a group of small children. Write some of the questions the children ask you about the animals. For example, they want to know whether the leopard is as strong as the tiger; whether the crocodile is as dangerous as the shark; which is the longest snake in the zoo; which is the smallest animal in the zoo, and so on:

____

____

____

____

____

CÁPSULA CULTURAL

Los animales de la selva

El Amazonas es la selva más grande de nuestro planeta y ocupa un área de más de 2,5 millones de millas cuadradas e incluye grandes partes de nueve países sudamericanos. El Río Amazonas, el más grande de la tierra, tiene su origen en un pequeño arroyo en las alturas de los Andes. Este «río mar» corre 4.000 (cuatro mil) millas por Perú y Brasil hasta

e *and*

el arroyo *brook*
el río mar *river sea*
correr *flow*

el Océano Atlántico. Más que un río, el Amazonas es una red de ríos, arroyos, lagos, islas y pantanos que se unen con la selva tropical para crear el ecosistema más grande que ha producido la naturaleza. La diversidad y abundancia de plantas y animales no tienen igual en ninguna otra parte de la tierra. Hay más especies de peces en el Río Amazonas que en el océano. En este ecosistema hay más pájaros (8.600 especies), más plantas (25.000 especies identificadas), más árboles, más mariposas — en efecto, más de casi todos los organismos.

Vamos a mencionar algunos de los animales hallados en esta selva:

el caimán: un reptil relacionado al cocodrilo y que crece hasta 15 pies de largo.

la piraña: un pez conocido por su ferocidad. Un grupo de pirañas puede comerse un animal grande en pocos minutos.

el jaguar: el gato salvaje más grande del hemisferio occidental.

la capibara: el roedor más grande del mundo. Mide 4 pies y pesa más de 100 libras.

la anaconda: una culebra gigante que puede crecer hasta 32 pies de largo.

Desafortunadamente, mucho de este mundo está desapareciendo como resultado de la deforestación causada por operaciones de minería, explotación forestal y el desmonte de la tierra para hacer sitio para la gente que huye de las áreas sobrepobladas. Si no se para esta destrucción, la tierra se hará un desierto y la vida que depende de ella se extinguirá.

la red *web*
el pantano *marsh*
en efecto *in fact*
el roedor *rodent*
el desmonte *clearing*
hacer sitio *to make room*
pararse *to stop*

Para pensar

1. ¿Por qué se llama al Río Amazonas el «río mar»? Descríbalo.
2. ¿Por qué es única la selva del Amazonas?
3. Nombra y describe algunos de los animales de la selva.
4. Menciona algunas causas de la destrucción de la selva. ¿Cuáles son las consecuencias de esta destrucción?
5. ¿Cómo te afecta personalmente esta destrucción? ¿Qué podemos hacer para pararla?

17

¿Cuál será tu profesión?

Future Tense of Regular Verbs

1 Vocabulario*

*In this **Vocabulario**, we illustrate sometimes male, sometimes female professionals. Most of the professions, however, have both male and female practitioners.

ACTIVIDAD A

Who does the following? Complete the sentences with the appropriate noun.

1. ____________________ corta el pelo a la gente.
2. ____________________ vende carne.
3. ____________________ prepara y vende el pan.
4. ____________________ trata a los animales cuando están enfermos.
5. ____________________ hace o arregla zapatos.
6. ____________________ vende estampillas en el correo.
7. ____________________ saca fotos artísticas.
8. ____________________ escribe programas para las computadoras.
9. ____________________ entrena a la gente.
10. ____________________ maneja el avión.
11. ____________________ escribe en los periódicos.
12. ____________________ trabaja en el banco.
13. ____________________ combate los fuegos.
14. ____________________ ayuda a los pasajeros en el avión.
15. ____________________ supervisa un grupo de personas en una compañía.
16. ____________________ conecta los cables para la electricidad.

El horóscopo

Todo el mundo quiere saber qué **pasará** en el futuro? Los astrólogos dicen que nuestra personalidad y nuestro futuro están influenciados por las estrellas. Todos nacimos bajo uno de los doce signos del zodíaco, y hay personas que no toman ninguna decisión importante sin consultar su horóscopo. ¿Qué **traerá** el día de mañana? ¿Qué sorpresas **revelarán** las estrellas? Diviértase leyendo el siguiente horóscopo.

Acuario 21 de enero al 18 de febrero

Ud. es una persona generosa, romántica y poética. Muy pronto **recibirá** una noticia de gran importancia para su felicidad. **Realizará** su sueño de hacer un viaje largo.

Piscis 19 de febrero al 20 de marzo

Ud. es una persona sensitiva, idealista y sentimental. En los próximos meses **conocerá** a alguien que **será** muy importante en su vida.

Aries 21 de marzo al 20 de abril

Ud. es una persona valiente y decidida. Siempre **conseguirá** las cosas que quiere. Le **llegarán** noticias de un amigo querido.

Tauro 21 de abril al 21 de mayo

Ud. tiene mucho sentido común. Es una persona práctica y realista. Este año le **sonreirá** la fortuna. **Recibirá** un dinero que no esperaba.

Géminis 22 de mayo al 21 de junio

Ud. es impaciente e impulsivo(a). Los próximos meses **estará** muy ocupado(a) con actividades sociales. **Ganará** la admiración de una persona importante para Ud.

Cáncer 22 de junio al 22 de julio

Ud. tiene un gran sentido común, es simpática y le gusta ayudar a los demás. Pronto **resolverá** muchos de sus problemas. El próximo año **será** muy interesante.

Leo 23 de julio al 23 de agosto

Ud. es una persona segura de sí misma, con cualidades de líder. En las próximas semanas **establecerá** contactos importantes con personas que le **ayudarán** en el futuro.

Virgo 24 de agosto al 23 de septiembre

Ud. es perfeccionista. Antes de hacer algo, estudia todos los detalles y lo piensa bien. Los resultados de un examen que Ud. **tomará serán** brillantes.

Libra 24 de septiembre al 23 de octubre

Ud. es una persona tranquila, que busca la armonía en las cosas. **Ganará** mucho dinero este año, pero tenga cuidado porque, si no, lo **gastará** pronto.

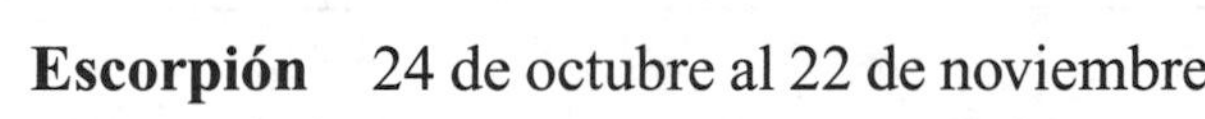

Escorpión 24 de octubre al 22 de noviembre

A Ud. le gusta trabajar y es una persona determinada que no acepta el fracaso. Ud. **tratará** de cambiar su vida este año, pero los cambios no le **traerán** satisfacción.

Sagitario 23 de noviembre al 20 de diciembre

Ud. es una persona alegre, sincera y honesta, pero necesita tener más confianza misma. Los nuevos proyectos que **comenzará** pronto le **darán** prestigio.

Capricornio 21 de diciembre al 20 de enero

Ud. es independiente y ambicioso(a), pero también melancólico(a) y pesimista. Sus problemas de dinero no **durarán** mucho. Este año Ud. **empezará** un proyecto ambicioso.

durar *to last*

ACTIVIDAD B

Answer the following questions with complete sentences.

1. ¿Qué dicen los astrólogos?

   ____

2. ¿Qué hacen muchas personas antes de tomar una decisión importante?

   ____

3. ¿Qué tipo de persona es un Leo?

   ____

4. ¿Qué problema tiene un Sagitario?

   ____

5. Según el horóscopo, ¿qué recibirá pronto un Acuario?

   ____

6. ¿Qué tipo de persona es un Cáncer?

   ____

7. ¿Bajo qué signo nacieron las personas sensitivas, idealistas y sentimentales?

   ____

8. ¿Bajo qué signo naciste?

   ____

2

Up to now, we have been talking in the present and the past tenses. How do we describe actions and events that will happen in the future? The horoscope in the story told you some things that will happen in the future. Let's look at some examples:

Ud. *realizará* su sueño.	*You will fulfill your dream.*
¿Qué *traerá* el día de mañana?	*What will tomorrow bring?*
Ud. *recibirá* una noticia importante.	*You will receive important news.*

Which are the infinitives of the three verbs used in these sentences?

_______________ , _______________ , and _______________ . What ending was added to all three infinitives? _______________ . It's easy to form the future tense in Spanish. There is only one set of endings for all verbs**: -ar, -er, ir**. You simply add the following endings to the infinitive: **-é, -ás, -á, -emos, -án.**

	INFINITIVE		
SUBJECT	**habl*ar***	**com*er***	**viv*ir***
yo	**hablar*é***	**comer*é***	**vivir*é***
tú	**hablar*ás***	**comer*ás***	**vivir*ás***
Ud., él, ella	**hablar*á***	**comer*á***	**vivir*á***
nosotros, -as	**hablar*emos***	**comer*emos***	**vivir*emos***
Uds., ellos, ellas	**hablar*án***	**comer*án***	**vivir*án***

Now try to supply the forms of the future tense for these verbs:

	estar	**ser**	**abrir**
yo	__________	__________	__________
tú	__________	__________	__________
Ud., él, ella	__________	__________	__________
nosotros, -as	__________	__________	__________
Uds., ellos, ellas	__________	__________	__________

Note that all endings, except for nosotros, have an accent.

You are going to spend your vacation at the beach. What will you do there?

EXAMPLE: tomar el sol **Yo tomaré el sol.**

1. nadar en el mar ______________________________
2. correr por la playa ______________________________
3. construir castillos de arena ______________________________
4. comer en restaurantes ______________________________
5. recoger conchas ______________________________

ACTIVIDAD D

Here's a list of things your mother will do tomorrow.

EXAMPLE: comprar carne en la carnicería **Ella *comprará* carne en la carnicería.**

1. ir con el gato al veterinario

____

2. hablar con el fotógrafo

____

3. leer el artículo de la periodista española

____

4. dar instrucciones al electricista

____

ACTIVIDAD E

You are going to spend tomorrow afternoon at a friend's house. What will the two of you do there?

EXAMPLE: mirar la televisión ***Miraremos* la televisión**

1. estudiar para el examen ______________________________

2. terminar las tareas ______________________________

3. escribir la composición ______________________________

4. leer el periódico ______________________________

5. escuchar unos discos ______________________________

ACTIVIDAD F

Your school is going to have a party. How will everyone help?

EXAMPLE: la profesora / mandar las invitaciones
La profesora *mandará* las invitaciones.

1. los muchachos / traer los discos

____

2. las muchachas / escoger la música

____

3. tú / servir el ponche

____

4. Uds. / ayudar a decorar

____

5. el director / tocar la guitarra

____

6. las madres / preparar los sándwiches

____

7. tú / comprar los platos de papel

____

8. yo / abrir la puerta

____

9. Ud. / recoger la basura (*garbage*)

____

10. todos nosotros / cantar y bailar

____

ACTIVIDAD G

Next week you are going to the flea market with some friends. Write what each of you will be doing, using the suggestions:

yo	estar allí temprano
Uds.	pasar el día allí
tú y yo	comprar muchas cosas

Carlos y Ana	vender los juguetes viejos
tú	comer hamburguesas
Roberto	gastar mucho dinero
todos nosotros	escoger libros de uso

EXAMPLE: **Tú y yo *pasaremos* el día allí.**

1. ______________________________
2. ______________________________
3. ______________________________
4. ______________________________
5. ______________________________
6. ______________________________

3

You know that the future tense is used in Spanish to describe future actions or events. But look at these sentences.

¿Qué hora *será*?	*I wonder what time it is. (What time can it be?)*
No sé. *Serán* las seis.	*I don't know. It's probably six o'clock.*
¿Dónde estará tu mamá?	*I wonder where your mother is. (Where can your mother be?)*
No sé. *Estará* en la cocina.	*I don't know. I guess she's in the kitchen.*

In Spanish, the future tense is sometimes used to express wonder or probability in the present. It is then equivalent to English *I wonder, I guess, probably.*

ACTIVIDAD H

You have been told that a new Spanish teacher will join the school and you are wondering about him.

EXAMPLE: ser simpático **¿Será simpático?**

1. ser estricto ______________________________
2. dar muchos exámenes ______________________________

3. hablar sólo en español ____________________
4. escribir mucho en la pizarra ____________________
5. llegar puntualmente ____________________

Preguntas Personales

1. ¿Qué tipo de persona eres?

____

2. ¿En qué profesión piensas trabajar en el futuro? ¿Por qué?

____

3. ¿Bajo que signo del zodíaco naciste? ¿Tiene alguna relación con tu personalidad?

____

4. ¿Conoces a otras personas con tu personalidad? ¿Nacieron bajo el mismo signo?

____

5. ¿Qué tipo de persona consulta su horóscopo antes de tomar una decisión importante?

____

Diálogo

You are talking with your brother, wondering about the future.

Composición

Mis planes para el fin de semana. Tell what you will do this weekend. Here are some suggested verbs.

comenzar	**comer**	**ir**	**ver**
comprar	**hablar**	**jugar**	**visitar**

1. ______________________________

2. ______________________________

3. ______________________________

4. ______________________________

5. ______________________________

CÁPSULA CULTURAL

Ocupación: Vaquero

A la pregunta: «¿cuál es una ocupación típica y exclusiva de los Estados Unidos?» muchos contestan: «vaquero, por supuesto».

Muchas de las personas que crecieron leyendo novelas y mirando películas y programas de televisión del oeste, consideran a los vaqueros un símbolo típicamente norteamericano; pero en realidad el vaquero nació en México.

El primer vaquero fue el indio de la misión. Las misiones fueron las primeras instituciones que se ocuparon de ganado, y usaban estos vaqueros nativos para rodear los caballos salvajes, descendientes de los que trajeron los españoles al Nuevo Mundo.

Estos vaqueros (de donde viene la palabra *buckaroo* en inglés) tenían nombres diferentes: por ejemplo, en Chile se les llama *huasos*, y en Argentina y Uruguay se les llama *gauchos*. Hoy, hay alrededor de medio millón de gauchos trabajando en las pampas, los inmensos prados que contienen más de ochenta millones de cabezas de ganado.

El gaucho, quien era originalmente una mezcla de indio y español, es quizás el más pintoresco de todos los vaqueros suramericanos. Vestido con un poncho y bombachas, el gaucho es un vaquero auténtico que trabaja duro en las estancias de Suramérica.

el vaquero *cowboy*

el ganado *cattle*
rodear *to round up*
salvaje *wild*

el prado *meadow, grassland*

bombachas *loose baggy riding pants*

Para pensar

1. ¿De dónde reciben su información muchos norteamericanos sobre los vaqueros?
2. ¿Quiénes fueron los primeros vaqueros y cómo se originaron?
3. ¿Cómo se llaman los diferentes tipos de vaqueros hispanoamericanos y de dónde vienen?
4. Describa dos prendas de vestir de los gauchos.
5. ¿Por qué es importante el trabajo del vaquero en la economía de un país como el nuestro? ¿Cuáles son algunas características de un vaquero? ¿Por qué son tan romantizados en nuestra historia?

18

La exploración del espacio

Future Tense of Irregular Verbs

1 Vocabulario

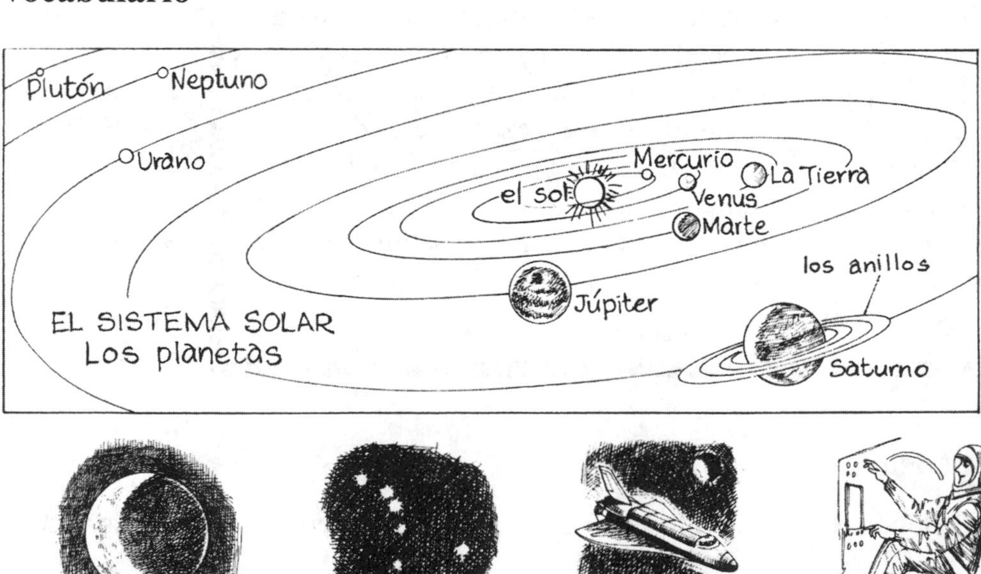

la luna

las estrellas

la nave espacial/ la astronave

el astronauta/ el cosmonauta

el traje espacial

el cohete

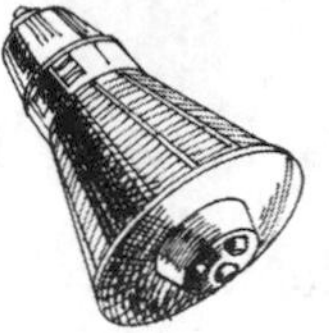
la cápsula espacial

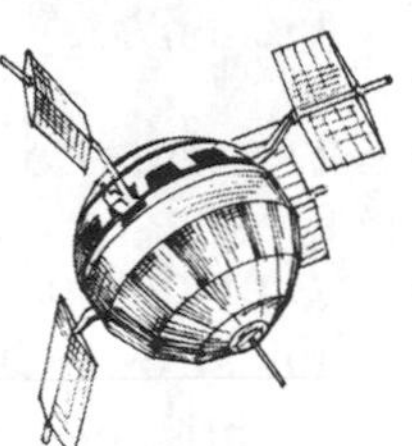
el satélite

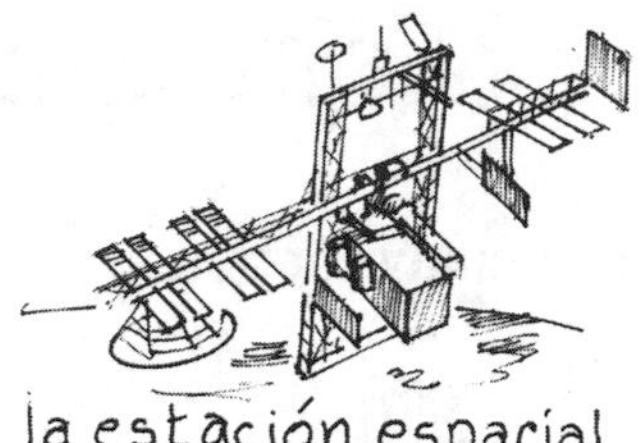

ACTIVIDAD A

Picture story Can you read this story? Whenever you come to a picture, read it as if it were a Spanish word.

La  es un  en el 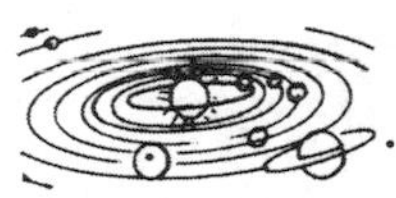. Este sistema es parte de la Vía Láctea, una de las galaxias del Universo. La  viaja alrededor del , y la 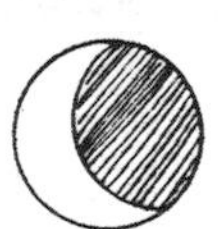 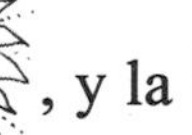 alrededor de la Tierra.

La  que vemos durante el 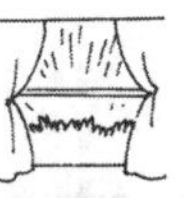 es la  del . Por la  podemos ver la , las  y otros cuerpos celestes. Uno de los  que podemos reconocer fácilmente es  porque tiene .

ACTIVIDAD B

Humor espacial Make up a funny caption for each situation.

______________________ ______________________

ACTIVIDAD C

Identify the five pictures and write the names in the spaces below. Each name has a different number of letters.

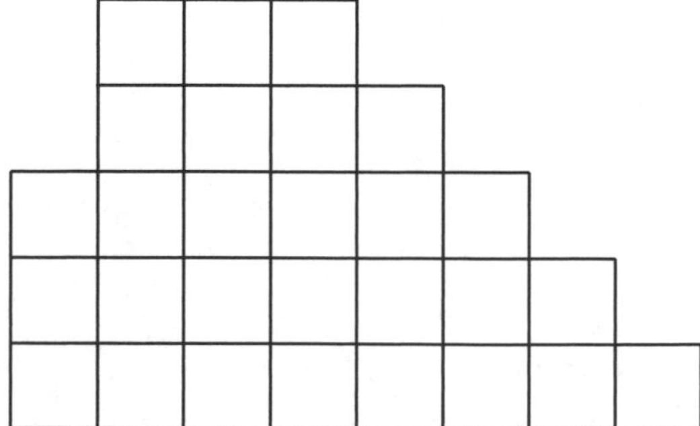

Una aventura en el espacio

Let's read a story about an adventure in space. Pay attention to the verbs in boldface.

CONTROL: ¿Listos para aterrizar en el planeta XGB-37 (equis, ge, b, treinta y siete)?
PILOTO: Estaremos listos en algunos minutos.
CONTROL: ¿Necesitarán nuestra ayuda?
PILOTO: No, no **tendremos** ningún problema. El conteo regresivo comenzará inmediatamente. 10, 9, 8, 7, 6, 5, 4, 3, 2, 1 . . . ¡Contacto!

el conteo regresivo *countdown*

CONTROL: ¿Quiénes **pondrán** pie en el planeta?
PILOTO: Paco y Flaco, nuestros dos astronautas hispanos, serán los primeros. Ellos **saldrán** de la cápsula, **observarán** todo y nos **dirán** qué vieron. Por fin **sabremos** si hay vida en ese planeta o no.
CONTROL: Bueno, en un minuto Uds. estarán al otro lado del planeta y no **podremos** comunicarnos más.

Paco y Flaco aterrizan; salen de la cápsula y sólo ven unas plantas enormes por todas partes. De repente las plantas comienzan a moverse y rodean a los dos astronautas.

rodear *to surround*

PACO: ¡Ay, Flaco, esto no me gusta nada! ¿Qué crees que **harán** estas plantas?

Una de las plantas empieza a hablar.

PLANTA: ¿Por qué interrumpen la paz y la tranquilidad de nuestro mundo? ¿Uds. son seres terrestres, verdad? ¿**Vendrán** otros detrás de Uds.?
FLACO: Sí, pero . . .
PLANTA: ¡Silencio! Conocemos muy bien las crueldades de su planeta. En la Tierra hacen ensaladas mixtas de nuestros hermanos. Preparan guacamole de nuestros primos, los aguacates. ¡Uds. son todos unos asesinos!

el aguacate *avocado*

PACO: Claro que hacemos eso. Pero no somos asesinos. Los aguacates son solamente vegetales.
VEGETAL: ¡Solamente vegetales! Uds. **pagarán** ese insulto con la vida. ¡**Morirán** ahora mismo! Pronto, tráiganme la sal.

FLACO:	Oh, no. Los vegetales nos van a comer. ¡Qué manera tan horrible de morir!		
VEGETAL:	Les **pondremos** también un poco de salsa.		
PACO:	No, no quiero morir así. ¡Auxilio! ¡Socorro! (Miguelito oye la voz de la mamá.)	**¡Auxilio! ¡Socorro!**	*Help!*
MAMÁ:	Miguelito, son las once. Apaga ya el televisor. Seguro que **tendrás** pesadillas a causa de esa basura de ciencia ficción.	**apagar**	*to turn off*

ACTIVIDAD D

Answer the following questions with complete sentences.

1. ¿Dónde están los astronautas?

____

2. ¿Cuándo comenzará el conteo regresivo?

____

3. ¿Quiénes pondrán pie en el planeta?

____

4. ¿Qué ven Paco y Flaco cuando aterrizan en el planeta desconocido?

____

5. ¿Cómo reciben las plantas a los astronautas? ¿Están contentas de verlos?

____

6. ¿Qué opinión tienen las plantas de los seres terrestres?

____

7. ¿Qué quieren hacer las plantas con Paco y Flaco?

____

8. ¿Qué les pondrán a los astronautas las plantas?

____

9. ¿Qué hacía Miguel cuando le habló su mamá?

____

10. ¿Qué piensa la mamá de Miguel sobre la ciencia ficción?

____

ACTIVIDAD E

Look at the pictures to solve the following puzzle. The boxed letters will answer the question:

¿Cómo se llama la galaxia donde está nuestro planeta?

__ uz

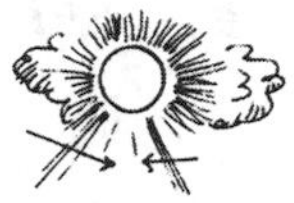

__ steroide

na __ e

T __ erra

s __ télite

So __

Lun __

__ onteo **10-9-8-7-6-5-4-3-2-1-0**

es __ rella

coh __ te

astron __ uta

Solución:

2

Did you pay attention to the verbs in bold type in the story? They are all in the future tense. They have regular endings, but their stem is not the infinitive.

No podremos comunicarnos.	*We won't be able to communicate.*
Por fin *sabremos* si hay vida en ese planeta o no.	*Finally we will know if there is life on that planet or not.*

What are the stems of **podrá** and **sabremos**? ___________ and ___________ .

What are the infinitives of these verbs? ___________ and ___________ . Can you figure out what happened to the infinitive to become **podr-** and **sabr-.**

Poder and **saber** drop the **e** of the infinitive and then add the endings of the future tense. **Querer** also belongs in this category.

Complete the verb tables below.

	poder	**querer**	**saber**
yo	**podré**	**querré**	**sabré**
tú	___________	___________	___________
Ud., él, ella	___________	___________	___________
nosotros, -as	___________	___________	___________
Uds., ellos, ellas	___________	___________	___________

ACTIVIDAD F

You have invited a friend from another city to visit you and she has called to ask you some questions. Work with a partner and answer them.

1. ¿Podrás ir al aeropuerto a recibirme?

____

2. ¿Querrán tus padres ir contigo?

____

3. ¿Sabrás cómo llegar al aeropuerto?

____

4. ¿Sabrán Uds. en qué puerta esperarme?

____

5. ¿Podré llamar por teléfono a mis padres desde tu casa?

____

6. ¿Podremos salir el sábado por la noche?

____

7. ¿Querrá tu hermano salir con nosotros?

____

8. ¿Podrán tus padres prestarte el carro?

____

3

Look now at these sentences from the story:

Les *pondremos* también salsa.	*We will also put salsa on them.*
No *tendremos* ningún problema.	*We won't have any problem.*
Ellos *saldrán* de la cápsula.	*They will leave the capsule.*
¿*Vendrán* otros detrás de Uds.?	*Will others come behind you?*

Can you figure out how the stems of these verbs were formed?

INFINITIVE	STEM OF FUTURE TENSE
Poner	**pondr-**
Tener	**tendr-**
Salir	**saldr-**
Venir	**vendr-**

The **e** of **poner** and **tener** and the **i** of **salir** and **venir** change to **d**. Complete the following tables:

	poner	**tener**	**salir**	**venir**
yo	**pondré**	**tendré**	**saldré**	**vendré**
tú	________	________	________	________
Ud., él, ella	________	________	________	________
nosotros, -as	________	________	________	________
Uds., ellos, ellas	________	________	________	________

ACTIVIDAD G

You are writing a letter to some friends who will come to visit you. Complete the letter with the appropriate form of the future tense:

Queridos amigos:

Yo ____________ (salir) de la escuela temprano y ____________ (poder) ir a la estación a recibirlos. Sé que Paula y Mario ____________ (querer) ir conmigo. Como Uds. son cuatro, yo ____________ (tener) que hacer dos viajes a la estación. Mientras yo hago un viaje, los demás ____________ (poder) esperarme en un café. Según me dicen, Uds. ____________ (venir) en el tren de las cuatro.

ACTIVIDAD H

You are going camping with some friends. Write what the subjects will do, using the following suggestions.

yo	salir a las seis
mis amigos y yo	ponerse ropa cómoda
Ud.	querer ser el (la) guía
Roberto y Rosa	poder nadar en el lago
tú	tener que levantarse temprano

Mario	venir a visitarnos
Uds.	saber cómo llegar al campamento

EXAMPLE: **Usted *vendrá* a visitarnos.**

1. ______________________________
2. ______________________________
3. ______________________________
4. ______________________________
5. ______________________________
6. ______________________________

4

There are two more verbs with irregular future tense forms, **decir** and **hacer**:

Ellos nos *dirán* qué vieron.	*They will tell us what they saw.*
¿Qué *harán* estas plantas?	*What will these plants do?*

The stem of the future tense of **decir** is __________ . The stem of the future tense of **hacer** is __________ . Complete the following tables.

yo	**dir** __________	**har** __________
tú	__________	__________
Ud., él, ella	__________	__________
nosotros, -as	__________	__________
Uds., ellos, ellas	__________	__________

ACTIVIDAD I

Using the suggested expressions, write when the following people will do certain things.

más tarde	el año que viene	el próximo verano
los fines de semana	pasado mañana	mañana
de hoy en quince	de hoy en ocho	el mes que viene

EXAMPLE: mis padres / ir a Europa
Mis padres *irán* a Europa *el próximo verano.*

1. Enrique / tener que trabajar

____

2. nosotros / venir a comer

____

3. tú / hacer las tareas

____

4. Uds. / querer salir

____

5. Marta y Rosa / hacer una torta

____

6. yo / salir de vacaciones

____

7. Ud. / poder viajar

____

8. tú y yo / saber hablar español

____

ACTIVIDAD J

Your father wants to know your plans for next weekend. Answer his questions. Work with a partner.

1. ¿Saldrás con tus amigos el sábado?

____

2. ¿A qué hora te encontrarás con ellos?

____

3. ¿Te dirán ellos adónde quieren ir?

____

4. ¿Sabrás qué autobús coger?

____

5. ¿Querrá tu hermano ir contigo?

____

6. ¿Tendrás suficiente dinero?

____

7. ¿Qué ropa te pondrás?

____

8. ¿Qué harán Uds. el domingo?

____

9. ¿Podrás lavar el carro?

____

10. ¿Me dirás si piensas regresar muy tarde a casa?

____

Preguntas Personales

1. ¿Cuántos años tendrás en el año 2025?

____

2. ¿Por qué es importante explorar el espacio?

____

3. ¿Qué crees que podrás hacer en el futuro?

____

4. ¿Qué cualidades debe tener un astronauta? ¿Las tiene Ud.?

____

5. ¿En qué nuevas formas nos comunicaremos en el futuro?

____

Diálogo

You are looking at a TV science-fiction movie with a friend. Complete the dialog.

Información Personal

What will you do when you graduate from high school?

Después de graduarme, yo ______________________________

____

____

____

____

Composición

What will your life be like when you are 25 years old? Write about where you think you will live, what type of job you will have, how much money you will earn, whether you will be married or not, what kinds of clothes you will be wearing, and what kind of music will be in style, etc.

____

____

____

____

____

CÁPSULA CULTURAL

La gente en el espacio

Uno de los sueños más grandes de la humanidad ha sido el de viajar y explorar el espacio. Nuestra tierra es solo un planeta que gira en órbita alrededor de una estrella — el sol. El sol es sólo una de más de 100 billones de estrellas en nuestra galaxia, o grupo de estrellas – la Vía Láctea. La Vía Láctea es sólo una de más de 100 billones de galaxias en el universo conocido. Así, se puede ver que no somos muy grande y que aún con nuestros telescopios más potentes nuestra habilidad de ver muy lejos es limitada.

girar *to revolve*

En 1961, un cosmonauta ruso llegó a ser el primer hombre en el espacio; un año después, un astronauta norteamericano hizo órbita alrededor de la tierra. En 1969, Neil Amstrong fue el primer hombre que pisó la superficie de la luna.

El sueño de explorar el espacio ha sido compartido por todos, incluyendo a los hispanohablantes. El primer astronauta de habla española en ir al espacio fue el costarricense Franklin Chang Díaz, el segundo fue el español Miguel López Alegría y el español Pedro Duque fue el tercero.

Es interesante que la Universidad de Puerto Rico tiene el porcentaje más alto de ingenieros contratados por la Administración de Aeronáutica del Espacio del Espacio (NASA). El programa de estudio que ofrece la Universidad de Puerto Rico en materia de ingeniería es conocido y reconocido a nivel mundial, de manera que mucha gente fuera de Puerto Rico va a estudiar allí. La universidad está a la vanguardia en el campo de la ingeniería y su aplicación en la exploración del espacio.

llegar a ser *to become*

pisar *to step on*
la superficie *surface*

compartido *shared*

el nivel *level*

Para pensar

1. ¿Cómo es nuestro planeta en relación al universo total?
2. ¿Qué es la Vía Láctea?
3. ¿De qué nacionalidad fue el primer hombre en el espacio? ¿Y el primer hombre que puso pie en la luna?
4. ¿Cómo figura la Universidad de Puerto Rico en el campo de la exploración del espacio?
5. ¿Tiene sentido gastar nuestros recursos en la exploración del espacio en vez de usarlos aquí en la tierra? ¿Cuál es su opinión?

Repaso IV

(Lecciones 15–18)

LECCIÓN 15

Some Spanish verbs change their spelling in certain forms to maintain the original sound of the infinitive.

a. Verbs ending in **–car, -gar,** and **–zar** change the **c** to **qu**, the **g** to **gu**, and the **z** to **c** before **e**:

tocar:	**Yo to*qué* a la puerta.**	**Toque Ud. ahora.**
pagar:	**Yo no pag*ué* la cuenta.**	**Páguela Ud.**
comenzar:	**Yo ya comen*cé* a hacer las tareas.**	**Comience Ud. también.**

b. Verbs ending in **–ger** or **–gir** change the **g** to **j** before **a** and **o**:

coger:	**Yo co*jo* esta pelota.**	**Co*ja* Ud. la otra.**
corregir:	**Yo corri*jo* los ejercicios.**	**Corrí*j*anlos Uds. también.**

c. Verbs ending in **–guir** change the **gu** to **g** before **a** and **o**:

seguir:	**Yo si*g*o su ejemplo.**	**Sí*g*anlo Uds. también.**

LECCIÓN 16

a. **más** + adjective + **que** are used to form a comparison stating that one thing or person is more than another:

Ese edificio es *más alto que* éste.

menos + adjective + **que** are used to form a comparison stating that one thing or person is less than another:

Esta tarea es *menos difícil que* la otra.

b. **tan** + adjective + **como** are used to form a comparison of equality:

Este diccionario es *tan bueno como* ése.

c. In Spanish, the superlative is expressed as follows:

definite article (**el, la, los, las**) + **más / menos** + adjective + **de**

María es *la alumna más seria de la* clase.

d. Four adjectives have irregular comparative forms:

bueno	*good*	**mejor**	*better, best*
malo	*bad*	**peor**	*worse, worst*
grande	*big*	**mayor**	*older, oldest*
pequeño	*small*	**menor**	*younger, youngest*

Más grande and **más pequeño** refer to size, **mayor** and **menor** refer to age.

LECCIÓN 17

a. The future of regular verbs is formed by adding the fututre endings to the infinitive:

yo		**-é**
tú	**estudiar**	**-ás**
Ud., él, ella	**aprender**	**-á**
nosotros, -as	**escribir**	**-emos**
Uds., ellos, ellas		**-án**

b. In Spanish, the future tense is sometimes used to express wonder, or probability in the present:

¿Quién *llamará* a esta hora? *I wonder who's calling at this hour.*

***Será* Carlos.** *It's probably Carlos.*

LECCIÓN 18

a. **Poder, querer, and saber** drop the **e** of the infinitive before adding the regular endings of the future tense.

Yo *podré* visitarte mañana. *I'll be able to visit you tomorrow.*

Ella *querrá* ir conmigo. *She will want to go with me.*

Mañana *sabremos* los resultados del examen. *Tomorrow we'll learn the test results.*

b. **Poner, tener, salir**, and **venir** change the **e** and the **i** of the infinitive to **d** before adding the regular endings of the future tense.

Tú *pondrás* los libros en la mesa.	*You'll put the books on the table.*
Él *tendrá* que estudiar hoy.	*He'll have to study today.*
Uds. *saldrán* mañana para Europa.	*You will leave for Europe tomorrow.*
Ellas *vendrán* temprano.	*They will come early.*

c. **Decir** and **hacer** have irregular stems in the future tense forms:

Ud. me *dirá* la verdad.	*You will tell me the truth.*
Ellos *harán* las tareas esta noche.	*They will do their homework tonight.*

ACTIVIDAD A

Put yourself in Lupe's place. Say that you've done all the activities pictured. Use the suggested verbs that follow.

almorzar	**llegar**	**cruzar**
pagar	**perseguir**	**recoger**
explicar	**jugar**	**sacar**

1. Ayer ____________ con Juan.

2. ____________ muy buenas notas.

3. Fui a la pizarra y ____________ .

4. ____________ $30 por una falda.

5. Cuando ________________ la calle, ayudé a un señor.

6. Anoche ____________ .

7. ______________________________ .

8. Ayer ____________ a casa a las tres y media.

9. Y ____________ a la una.

ACTIVIDAD B

Look at the pictures and compare the objects in them with the clues given. The answer depends sometimes on your point of view.

1. rápido: ____ .

2. importante: ____ .

3. pequeño: ____ .

4. interesante: ____ .

5. alto: ____ .

6. nuevo: ____ .

7. grande: ____ .

8. divertido: ____.

ACTIVIDAD C

¿Qué será? Everyone has plans for the future. Tell what these people will do.

1. (salir) Yo ____.

2. (venir) Ellos ____.

3. (decir) Usted ____.

4. (hacer) Nosotros ____.

5. (tener) María ____.

6. (querer ir) el niño ____.

7. (saber) Él no ____.

8. (poner) Pepito ____ .

8. (poder) Tú no ____ .

ACTIVIDAD D

Word search There are 16 words hidden in the puzzle. They are all related to travel, on earth and in space. Can you find them? The words may be read from left to right, right to left, up or down, or diagonally.

A	N	A	U	D	A	M	N	D	I	E
A	S	T	R	O	N	A	V	E	A	J
T	Q	C	R	U	S	T	T	S	E	A
U	N	Á	E	A	A	E	I	P	T	P
A	Ó	P	N	T	T	V	E	E	R	I
N	I	S	Í	A	É	L	R	G	O	U
O	V	U	T	F	L	R	R	A	P	Q
R	A	L	E	A	I	S	A	R	A	E
T	N	A	L	Z	T	Z	U	U	S	B
S	M	C	A	A	E	L	U	N	A	L
A	Q	R	M	O	T	O	L	I	P	P

ACTIVIDAD E

Jumble Unscramble the words. Then unscramble the letters above the numbers to find out what Juanita dreamed (or had a nightmare) about.

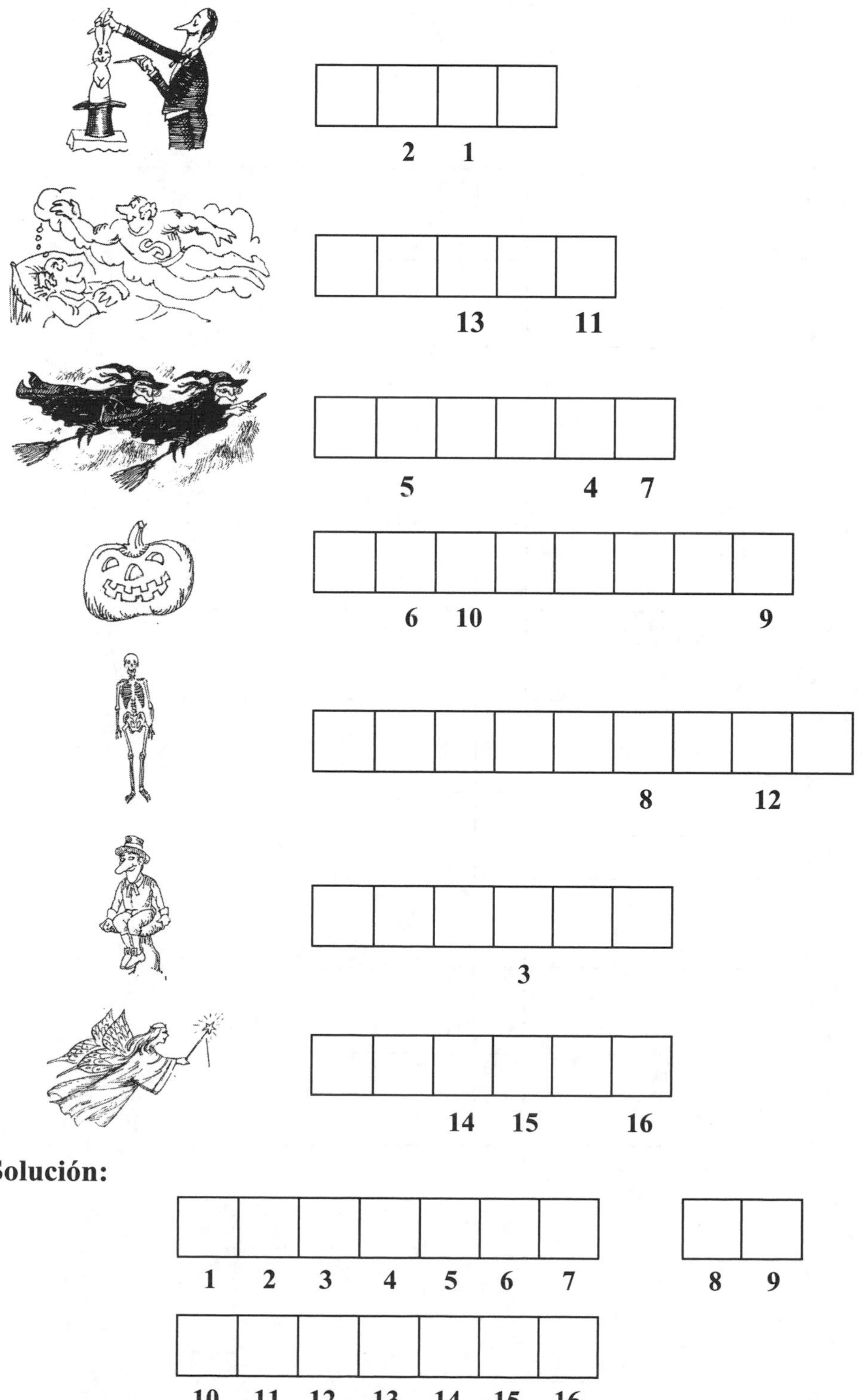

Solución:

1	2	3	4	5	6	7		8	9

10	11	12	13	14	15	16

ACTIVIDAD F

How many of these jobs do you remember? Fill in the Spanish words, then read down the boxed column to find the answer to this question: **¿Cuál es el trabajo de la señorita Gómez?**

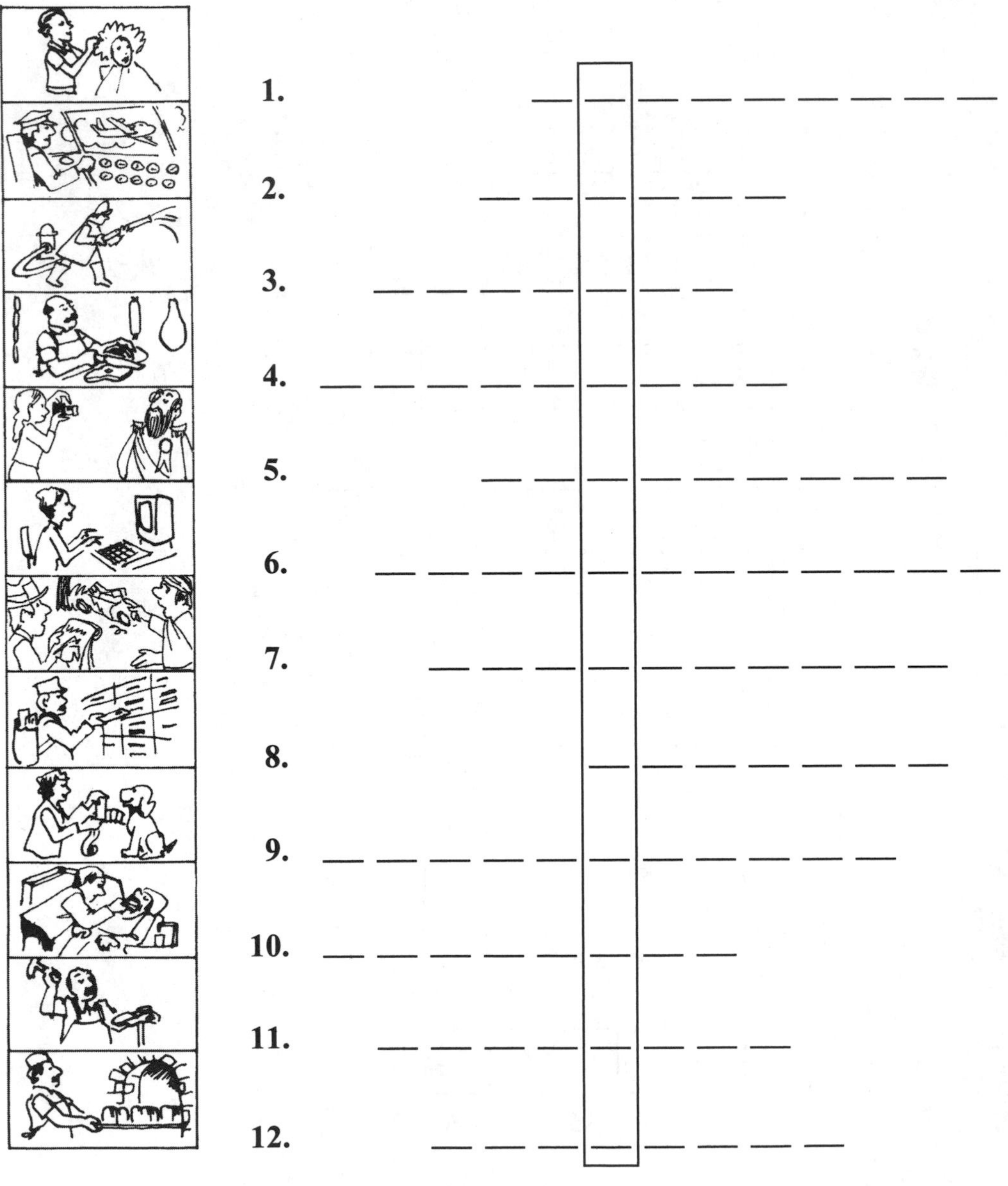

ACTIVIDAD G

You are one of a group of astronauts exploring a new planet. Describe your trip:

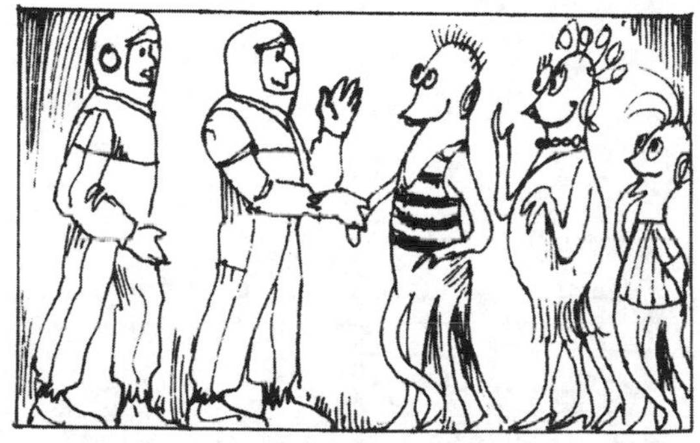

ACTIVIDAD H

It's the year 3000 and you, an inspector in the Earth's Department of Immigration, are interviewing newcomers from outer space. You have just received word to keep on the lookout for a particular creature that reproduces itself every 24 hours. You can see what a problem that would create. Spot this creature from the information given.

Le gustan los deportes.

No tiene aretes, pero sí una cadena larga.

Tiene antenas en vez de orejas.

Parece estar siempre contento.

Tiene tres ojos y lleva gafas.

Lleva botas.

Quinta Parte

19
La personalidad

The Conditional Tense

1 Vocabulario

Personality Character Traits

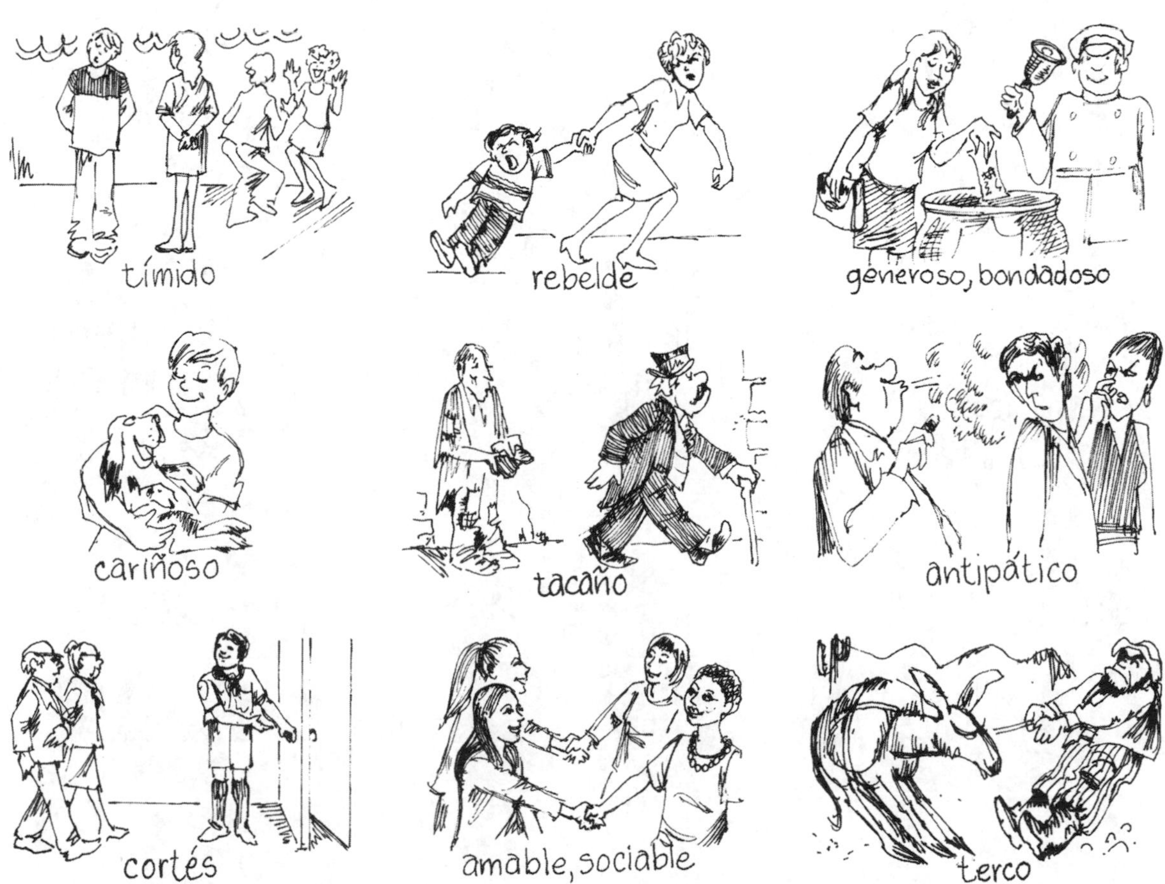

egoísta
optimista
LOTERÍA
travieso
pesimista
Lotería
paciente
envidiosa
gracioso
celoso
considerado
mentiroso
trabajador
sincero
perezoso
curioso
aburrido

ACTIVIDAD A

Here are some people you might know. Say something about their personality.

1. ____________________ 2. ____________________

3. ____________________ 4. ____________________

5. ____________________ 6. ____________________

7. ____________________ 8. ____________________

9. ____________________ 10. ____________________

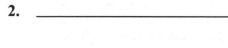

ACTIVIDAD B

Do you recognize some of these personality types? Match the characteristics on the right with the descriptions on the left. Work with a partner.

EXAMPLE: Student 1: **Nunca dice la verdad.**
Student 2: **Es un *mentiroso*.**

1. No quiere gastar dinero.

 ____

2. Tiene miedo. Casi no habla.

 ____

3. Siempre espera las cosas malas.

 ____

4. No está satisfecho. Quiere las cosas del otro.

 ____

5. Es muy bueno con todo el mundo.

 ____

6. Siempre dice lo que piensa.

 ____

7. No le gusta trabajar. Prefiere dormir.

 ____

8. Siempre hace cosas cómicas.

 ____

9. Ayuda a sus amigos. Les presta dinero.

 ____

10. Nunca cambia sus opiniones.

 ____

a. envidioso
b. simpático
c. perezoso
d. gracioso
e. generoso
f. terco
g. tímido, callado
h. pesimista
i. tacaño
j. honesto, sincero

2 Un examen psicológico

¿Qué tipo de persona es Ud.? ¿Es simpático o antipático? ¿Tímido o agresivo? ¿Hace sus decisiones con confianza? Lea las siguientes situaciones e indique sus reacciones. Calcule los puntos que están al lado de sus respuestas. El total revelará su carácter.

1. Es sábado por la noche. Ud. quiere ir al cine. Sus amigos quieren ir a otro lugar que a Ud. no le interesa. ¿Qué haría?
   a. Iría al cine sin ellos. ❏ 5
   b. Seguiría a mis amigos. ❏ 1
   c. Propondría otra alternativa. ❏ 3

2. Está en un restaurante. El mesero le da la cuenta y Ud. encuentra un error. ¿Qué haría?
   a. Le diría cortésmente al mesero que hay un error en la cuenta. ❏ 4
   b. Pagaría la cuenta sin decir nada. ❏ 1
   c. Le diría al mesero: «Ud. no sabe calcular». ❏ 5

3. Una persona de importancia le cuenta una historia cómica que Ud. ya conoce. ¿Qué haría?
   a. Lo interrumpiría y le diría que Ud. ya conoce la historia. ❏ 5
   b. No diría nada. Escucharía toda la historia y reiría cortésmente. ❏ 2
   c. Reiría histéricamente al final de la historia. ❏ 1

4. Una amiga compra un vestido nuevo. A Ud. no le gusta. Su amiga le pide su opinión. Ud. le diría:
   a. Yo no saldría contigo con ese vestido horrible. ❏ 5
   b. No sé. No soy experto(a) en esas cosas. ❏ 3
   c. Me gusta mucho. Te va muy bien. ❏ 1

5. Ud. tiene una cita con alguien a las dos. Él llega a las dos y media y no ofrece ninguna excusa. ¿Qué haría?
   a. Miraría su reloj y preguntaría: «¿Qué pasó?». ❏ 4
   b. Saludaría sin mencionar que llegó tarde. ❏ 1
   c. Se pondría furioso(a) por su actitud egoísta. ❏ 5

6. Ud. está en una fiesta. Una persona muy aburrida lo atrapa en la cocina y no cesa de hablar. ¿Qué haría?
   a. Le diría: «Perdón, pero tengo que ir al baño». ❏ 4
   b. Escucharía todo, pero pensaría en otra cosa. ❏ 3
   c. Mostraría mucho interés en la conversación. ❏ 2

7. Alguien le ofrece una posición en una oficina con buen sueldo y muchas oportunidades. Pero Ud. no tiene ninguna experiencia. ¿Qué haría?
   a. Aceptaría el trabajo sin decir nada. ❏ 5
   b. Explicaría que no tiene la preparación necesaria. ❏ 3
   c. No aceptaría la posición. ❏ 1

8. Sus padres le dicen que no puede salir el fin de semana con sus amigos. ¿Qué haría?
a. Saldría con ellos sin permiso. ❑ 5
b. Trataría de resolver el asunto con sus padres. ❑ 4
c. Aceptaría la decisión de sus padres. ❑ 2

9. Un compañero de clase le pide prestados cinco dólares, que le pagaría mañana. Ud. sabe que él es un mentiroso. ¿Qué haría Ud.?
a. Le prestaría un dólar y le diría: «No tengo más dinero conmigo». ❑ 2
b. Le prestaría los cinco dólares. ❑ 1
c. No le prestaría nada. ❑ 5

10. Ud. hace una cita para ir a un juego de pelota por la noche. Pero al volver a casa se acuerda de que tiene un examen importante al día siguiente y tiene que estudiar. ¿Qué haría Ud.?
a. Trataría de estudiar antes del juego. ❑ 1
b. Llamaría al amigo y le diría que no puede salir porque está enfermo. ❑ 2
c. Llamaría al amigo y le explicaría que no puede salir porque tiene que estudiar. ❑ 4

Interpretación de los resultados

39–48 puntos: Tiene un carácter fuerte e independiente. Toma sus decisiones con confianza. Es una persona muy determinada, directa e impulsiva. Muchas veces no es diplomático y puede ofender a la gente. Ud. se considera honesto, pero la gente puede creer que es arrogante o antipático.

27–38 puntos: Ud. es amable y simpático y generalmente tiene buenas relaciones con todo el mundo. Es paciente y sabe tratar a la gente. Tiene un carácter bastante fuerte pero es diplomático cuando es necesario.

amable *kind, nice*

12–26 puntos: Ud. es reservado y un poco tímido. Muchas veces tiene miedo de decir la verdad. Nunca ofende a nadie. Necesita ser más dinámico y tener más confianza.

Conteste con frases completas.

1. ¿Qué tipo de examen es éste?

____

2. ¿Qué revela el examen?

___

3. ¿Qué hay al lado de cada respuesta?

___

4. ¿Qué es necesario hacer con los puntos al final?

___

5. ¿Qué carácter tiene una persona que recibe más de 39 puntos?

___

6. ¿Qué problemas puede tener esa persona?

___

7. ¿Cómo es una persona que recibe 30 puntos en el examen?

___

8. ¿Qué problemas puede tener una persona tímida?

___

9. ¿Qué necesita una persona tímida?

___

10. ¿Cuántos puntos recibió Ud.? ¿Refleja realmente su personalidad el examen?

___

ACTIVIDAD D

Using an adjective of personality, describe the following people.

EXAMPLE: su cartero **Mi cartero *es muy trabajador*.**

1. su profesor(a) de español ___
2. su mamá ___
3. su papá ___
4. su hermano(a) ___
5. el director de la escuela ___
6. el Presidente de los Estados Unidos ___

7. un americano típico ______________________

8. un alumno típico de su escuela ______________________

9. su mejor amigo(a) ______________________

10. Ud. ______________________

ACTIVIDAD E

One can often tell peoples' personality by their actions. Different people like to do different things. Here is a list of activities. Work with a partner and tell him (her) what you do or don't do. He (she) will then use an adjective to describe you.

EXAMPLE: **seguir las instrucciones**
***No sigo* las instrucciones de mis padres.**
Ud. es *rebelde*.

1. dormir hasta mediodía

____

2. dar dinero a los pobres

____

3. considerarse la persona más importante

____

4. no decir nunca la verdad

____

5. no querer gastar dinero

____

6. investigar siempre las cosas

____

7. no querer cambiar sus ideas y sus opiniones

____

8. decir siempre «por favor»

____

9. demostrar mucho amor

____

10. querer las cosas de otras personas

____

3

When you took the personality test, do you remember seeing the following sentences?

¿Qué *haría* Ud.?	*What would you do?*
***Iría* al cine.**	*I would to to the movies.*
No *diría* nada.	*I would not say anything.*
Yo no *saldría* contigo.	*I would not go out with you.*

All of the verbs were in the *conditional tense*. The conditional tense expresses the idea of *would* in English.

Me *gustaría* ir.	*I would like to go.*
***Sería* muy triste.**	*It would be very sad.*
Me dijo que *escribiría*.	*He told me he would write.*

The conditional tense, like the future tense, has only one set of endings for all three conjugations: **-AR, -ER,** and **-IR** verbs. These endings **-ía, -ías, -ía, -íamos**, and **-ían** are attached to the whole infinitive of the verb.

	habl*ar* *to speak*	**respond*er*** *to answer*	**recib*ir*** *to receive*
yo	**hablar*ía***	**responder*ía***	**recibir*ía***
tú	**hablar*ías***	**responder*ías***	**recibir*ías***
Ud., él, ella	**hablar*ía***	**responder*ía***	**recibir*ía***
nosotros, -as	**hablar*íamos***	**responder*íamos***	**recibir*íamos***
Uds., ellos, ellas	**hablar*ían***	**responder*ían***	**recibir*ían***

NOTE: The endings **ía, ías, ía,** etc. are the same as the imperfect endings of **-ER** and **-IR** verbs.

ACTIVIDAD F

Express what the following people would do.

EXAMPLE: (comprar) **Lupe *compraría* un regalo para sus padres.**

1. (hablar) Los estudiantes ______________ español con un cubano.
2. (vender) Mi padre no ______________ nuestra casa.
3. (vivir) Yo ______________ en México.
4. (llamar) Nosotros ______________ a la policía en una emergencia.
5. (comer) Tú ______________ bien en ese restaurante.

There is a group of verbs that are irregular in the conditional. Just as in the future tense, they have regular endings, but their stem is not the infinitive. All irregular future verbs undergo the same changes they did in the future.

Irregular Verbs in the Future and Conditional Tenses

VERB	FUTURE TENSE (WILL)	CONDITIONAL TENSE (WOULD)
poder	**podr*é, -as, -á, -emos, -án***	**podr*ía, -ías, -ía, íamos, ían***
querer	**querr*é, -ás, -á, -emos, -án***	**querr*ía, -ías, -ía, -íamos, -ían***
saber	**sabr*é, -ás, -á, -emos, -án***	**sabr*ía, -ías, -ía, -íamos, -ían***
poner	**pondr*é, -ás, -á, -emos, -án***	**pondr*ía, -ías, -ía, -íamos, -ían***
salir	**saldr*é, -ás, -á, -emos, -án***	**saldr*ía, -ías, -ía, -íamos, -ían***
tener	**tendr*é, -ás, -á, -emos, -án***	**tendr*ía, -ías, -ía, -íamos, -ían***
venir	**vendr*é, -ás, -á, -emos, -án***	**vendr*ía, -ías, -ía, -íamos, -ían***
decir	**dir*é, -ás, -á, -emos, -án***	**dir*ía, -ías, -ía, -íamos, -ían***
hacer	**har*é, -ás, -á, -emos, -án***	**har*ía, -ías, -ía, -íamos, -ían***

ACTIVIDAD G

Express the following in the conditional tense.

1. (ir) Paco dijo que ______________ a la fiesta.
2. (querer) ¿Qué ______________ para tu cumpleaños?
3. (saber) Ellos no ______________ la diferencia.

4. (poner) ¿Dónde ________________ Ud. la lámpara?

5. (salir) Yo ________________ hoy.

6. (tener) No sé cuando nosotros ________________ el dinero.

7. (venir) Ellos me dijeron que ________________ mañana.

8. (poder) Ella no ________________ vivir sin su perro.

9. (decir) ¿Te ________________ tu amigo la verdad?

10. (hacer) ¿Qué ________________ Ud. en esa casa grande?

5

To express the idea of *probably* or *I wonder if*. . . , Spanish uses the future and conditional tenses. The future is used to express probability in the present; the conditional to express probability in the past.

Mi mamá *estará* en casa.	*My mother is probably at home.*
Mi mamá *estaría* en casa.	*My mother was probably at home.*
¿Qué hora *será*?	*I wonder what time it is.*
¿Qué hora *sería*?	*I wonder what time it was.*
¿Adónde *irán*?	*I wonder where they're going.*
¿Adónde *irían*?	*I wonder where they went.*

ACTIVIDAD H

Express the following using the future or conditional tenses.

1. I wonder if she's sick. ______________________________
(estar enferma)

2. He probably did the work. ______________________________
(hacer el trabajo)

3. They're probably coming tomorrow. ______________________________
(venir mañana)

4. She probably took the train. ______________________________
(tomar el tren)

5. I wonder if we'll go to the beach. ______________________________
(ir a la playa)

6. You (*tú*) will probably have the money. ______________________
(tener dinero)

7. They probably left for Spain. ______________________
(salir para España)

8. I wonder if she's telling the truth. ______________________
(decir la verdad)

9. I wonder if they know the difference. ______________________
(saber la diferencia)

10. He was probably able to study. ______________________
(poder estudiar)

Preguntas Personales

1. ¿Por qué son útiles los exámenes psicológicos?

____

2. ¿Cuándo es necesario un examen psicológico?

____

3. ¿En qué situaciones no dirías la verdad?

____

4. Recibiste un telegrama. ¿Qué piensas si eres optimista (pesimista)?

____

5. ¿Qué problemas tiene una persona antipática?

____

Composición

You have been assigned to construct a personality test that will determine a person's ability to get along with others. Make up five questions for the test:

1. ______________________
2. ______________________
3. ______________________
4. ______________________
5. ______________________

Diálogo

You have gone to the guidance counselor for advice. Here are his answers. Complete the dialog.

CÁPSULA CULTURAL

Su personalidad y los signos del zodíaco

Cada día, todos los periódicos españoles y latinoamericanos publican una sección dedicada exclusivamente al horóscopo. Algunos lectores consideran esta columna más importante que las noticias diarias y comienzan su lectura con esta parte. Según ellos, todos nacimos bajo un signo del zodíaco y esos signos pueden revelar el carácter de cada persona.

La astrología esta basada en la creencia de que el movimiento y las posiciones de los planetas y las estrellas influyen las vidas de los individuos. El zodíaco está dividido en doce porciones o constelaciones, cada una con su propio signo.

¿Quiere descubrir su verdadera personalidad? (o por lo menos divertirse). Busque su signo en la tabla siguiente: (Y recuerde, dicen que las estrellas no mienten).

el lector reader

según according to

la creencia belief

influir *to influence*

verdadera *true*

por lo menos *at least*

SIGNO	FECHA DE NACIMIENTO	CUALIDAD	DEFECTO
aries	21 marzo – 20 abril	valiente	impulsivo
tauro	21 abril – 21 mayo	paciente	obstinado
géminis	22 mayo – 21 junio	generoso	hablador
cáncer	22 junio – 22 julio	sensitivo	emocional
leo	23 julio – 23 agosto	simpático	intolerante
virgo	24 agosto – 23 septiembre	exacto	crítico
libra	24 septiembre – 23 octubre	fiel	indeciso
escorpión	24 octubre – 22 noviembre	vigoroso	extremista
sagitario	23 noviembre – 21 diciembre	sincero	impaciente
capricornio	22 diciembre – 20 enero	ambicioso	pesimista
acuario	21 enero – 18 febrero	independiente	desorganizado
piscis	19 febrero – 20 marzo	imaginativo	tímido

Para pensar

1. ¿Por qué es importante para alguna gente la sección del horóscopo?
2. ¿En qué está basada la astrología?
3. ¿Cómo está dividido el zodíaco?
4. ¿Cómo es tu personalidad, según la tabla?
5. ¿Por qué alguna gente quiere creer en cosas fantásticas?

20

Hacemos un viaje

Past Participles; Present Perfect Tense

1 Vocabulario

ACTIVIDAD A

Work with a partner. One tells what a person does; the other tells who that person is.

EXAMPLE: **ayudar a los pasajeros en el avión**
La *azafata ayuda* a los pasajeros en el avión.

1. llevar el equipaje de los pasajeros ______________________
2. volar el avión ______________________
3. examinar los documentos y el equipaje ______________________
4. visitar países durante las vacaciones ______________________
5. viajar en avión, autobús o tren ______________________

ACTIVIDAD B

Now describe various objects and name them.

EXAMPLE: **una lista de salidas y llegadas**
***Un horario* es una lista de salidas y llegadas**

1. identificación oficial para entrar a un país
____
2. documento necesario para subir a un avión, un tren o un autobús
____
3. lugar donde se pone la ropa y otros artículos en un viaje
____
4. un medio de transporte en el mar
____
5. lugar adonde llegan y de donde salen los autobuses y los trenes.
____

Cruzando la frontera

Let's read a one-act play about a family's problems while traveling. Pay attention to the verbs in bold type.

Personajes: Mario Fuentes, un turista de unos 40 años de edad
Matilde, su esposa, más o menos de la misma edad
Minerva, la hija mayor, de 13 años
Maruja, la hija menor, de 8 años

Escena: En la frontera, la familia Fuentes espera su turno para pasar la aduana. Han llegado en carro y **han descargado** todo su equipaje.

la frontera *border*

MATILDE: ¿Mario, **has traído** todos los documentos que vamos a necesitar?

MARIO: Creo que sí. **He traído** los pasaportes, las visas y los certificados de salud y de vacunación.

MATILDE: Bien. **Hemos viajado** mucho hoy y estoy muy cansada. No quiero problemas.

MARIO: No te preocupes, mi vida. Todo está en orden. Allí viene el inspector.

preocuparse *to worry*

ADUANERO: Buenas tardes, señores. ¿Tienen Uds. algo que declarar?

MARIO: No señor, absolutamente nada.

ADUANERO: ¿**No han comprado** comida, cigarrillos, licores, joyas u otros artículos de oro o de plata?

MARIO: **No hemos comprado** ni cigarrillos ni licor. Yo no fumo ni bebo.

MATILDE: Bueno, **hemos traído** unas pocas cosas para nuestro uso personal y regalos para unos pocos amigos. Las únicas «joyas» que tenemos son nuestras hijas.

ADUANERO: Veo nueve maletas. Parece que tienen muchos amigos. ¿Quiere Ud. abrir esa maleta verde, por favor?

MATILDE: (a Mario) No recuerdo ninguna maleta verde.

MARIO: (a Matilde) Ni yo tampoco.

ni yo tampoco *neither do I*

ADUANERO: (abriendo la maleta) ¡Ajá! Uds. no fuman ni beben y **han comprado** sólo unas pocas cosas de uso personal. ¿Eh? ¿Cómo explican Uds. esto? Tres cartones de cigarrillos, tres botellas de coñac, dos de vino, dos relojes de oro . . .

M. Y M.: ¿Ay, Dios mío!

MINERVA: Pero, papá, esa maleta no es nuestra. Miren la etiqueta con el nombre y la dirección adentro: Héctor González.

MARUJA: Yo vi la maleta en el pasillo del hotel y la puse en el carro. Pensé que era nuestra.

MARIO: Señor, mi hija dice la verdad. Ud. puede verificarlo.

ADUANERO: Está bien. Uds. pueden cruzar la frontera. Nosotros se la devolveremos al señor González. Pero de ahora en adelante tengan cuidado con sus «joyas».

de ahora en adelante *from now on*

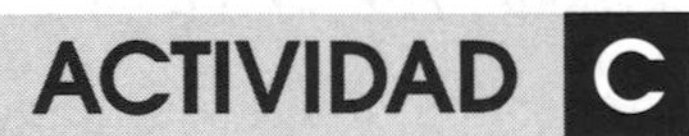

Conteste las siguientes preguntas con frases completas.

1. ¿Qué espera la familia Fuentes?

____

2. ¿Quiénes son los miembros de la familia?

____

3. ¿Qué documentos ha traído el marido?

____

4. ¿Qué pregunta el aduanero?

____

5. ¿Qué artículos declara Mario?

____

6. ¿Qué dice la mujer que tienen en las maletas?

____

7. ¿Qué hay dentro de la maleta verde?

____

8. ¿Quién puso la maleta en el carro? ¿Por qué?

____

9. ¿Dónde encontró la chica la maleta?

____

10. ¿Qué va a hacer el aduanero con la maleta?

____

2

Look at the following sentences.

El museo estaba *cerrado.* *The museum was closed.*

El dinero está *escondido.* *The money is hidden.*

Mi hermano está *aburrido.* *My brother is bored.*

What are **cerrado**, **escondido**, and **aburrido** in these sentences? ____________. These adjectives are derived from the verbs **cerrar** (to close), **esconder** (to hide), and **aburrir** (to bore), and they are called past participles. Can you figure out how these past participles were formed? ______________________________

RULE: To form the past participle remove the infinitive endings **-ar**, **-er**, **-ir** and replace them with the corresponding endings **-ado**, **-ido**, and **-ido**.

You have been using many past participles as adjectives. Here are some that you know. From which infinitives were they derived?

PAST PARTICIPLE		INFINITIVE
sentado	*seated*	______________
preocupado	*worried*	______________
vestido	*dressed*	______________
dormido	*asleep*	______________

Now let's try the opposite. Here are some infinitives you know. What are their past participles?

INFINITIVE		PAST PARTICIPLE
apagar	*to turn off*	____________
encender	*to turn on*	____________
casar(se)	*to marry, get married*	____________
cansar(se)	*to tire, get tired*	____________
perder	*to lose*	____________

Remember that past participles used as adjectives agree in gender and number with the noun they accompany.

***María* y *Juan* están *sentados* en la sala.**	*María and Juan are seated in the living room.*
***Rosa* está *sentada* en el comedor.**	*Rosa is seated in the dining room.*

Complete the sentences, using the past participle of one of the following verbs.

descansar	**dormir**	**apagar**
aburrir	**preocupar**	**encender**
cansar		

EXAMPLE: **Manuel durmió la siesta y ahora está *descansado*.**

1. Los muchachos corrieron diez millas y están ____________.
2. María no tiene nada que hacer y está ____________.
3. Mis padres oyeron malas noticias y están ____________.
4. Es muy tarde y el bebé está ____________.
5. Es de noche y las luces están ____________.
6. Es de mañana y la luz está ____________.

3 The past participle is used to form the present perfect tense. In Spanish, the present perfect consists of two words: the present tense form of the verb **haber** (*to have*) and a past participle. Let's start by learning the present tense of **haber**:

PRESENT TENSE	
yo	**he**
tú	**has**
Ud., él, ella	**ha**
nosotros, -as	**hemos**
Uds., ellos, ellas	**han**

NOTE: Do not confuse the verb **haber** with the verb **tener**. **Haber** is the only verb that can be used with a past participle to form the present perfect.

PRESENT PERFECT	
yo	**he estudiado**
tú	**has estudiado**
Ud., él, ella	**ha estudiado**
nosotros, -as	**hemos estudiado**
Uds., ellos, ellas	**han estudiado**

Note that the past participle does not change in the present perfect tense; it always ends in **o**. Look at these examples.

Esta semana *he ido* dos veces al cine. — *This week I have gone twice to the movies.*

¿Me *ha llamado* alguien hoy? — *Has anybody called me today?*

In Spanish, the present perfect is generally used to describe an action that happened in the past but is connected to the present.

ACTIVIDAD E

You are having a picnic in the park. How has each of these people contributed?

EXAMPLE: **Ramón / comprar el pan** — **Ramón *ha comprado* el pan.**

1. Julio y Jaime / preparar la ensalada ______________________

2. yo / encender el fuego ______________________

3. Uds. / cocinar las hamburguesas ______________________________

4. Nora / buscar dónde comprar sodas ______________________________

5. tú / sacar fotos ______________________________

6. Ud. / decidir dónde hacer el picnic ______________________________

7. Mario y yo / lavar las frutas ______________________________

8. Rosa y Josefina / organizar los juegos ______________________________

ACTIVIDAD F

Answer the following questions. Work with a partner.

1. ¿Has estudiado mucho últimamente?

____

2. ¿Adónde has ido recientemente?

____

3. ¿Cuántos exámenes has tenido este semestre?

____

4. ¿Con quién has salido este mes?

____

5. ¿Qué notas has sacado este año?

____

4

Now look at these examples:

¿*Has hablado* con Juan?	*Have you spoken with Juan?*
No, no *he hablado* con él.	*No, I haven't spoken with him.*

Where does **no** stand in the second Spanish sentence? ____________________ .

RULE: The two words forming the present perfect cannot be separated in Spanish; **no** stands before the conjugated form of **haber**.

What happens if you use an object pronoun?

¿*Has comido* paella alguna vez?	*Have you ever eaten paella?*
Sí, *la he* comido.	*Yes, I have eaten it.*
No, *no la he comido.*	*No, I haven't eaten it.*

RULE: The object pronoun comes before the conjugated form of **haber**. In negative sentences, **no** comes before the object pronoun.

ACTIVIDAD G

Answer the following questions negatively. Work with a partner.

1. ¿Han terminado las clases?

____

2. ¿Has estado en el Perú?

____

3. ¿Has montado a caballo alguna vez?

____

4. ¿Has visitado la Casa Blanca?

____

5. ¿Ha llegado la profesora a clase?

____

ACTIVIDAD H

Answer these questions, using an object pronoun in your response. Work with a partner.

EXAMPLE: ¿Has escuchado las noticias?
Sí, *las he escuchado.*

1. ¿Has buscado trabajo? ______________________________

2. ¿Ha preparado ella la comida? ______________________________

3. ¿Ha enseñado la profesora las lecciones? ______________________________

4. ¿Han aprendido los alumnos español? ______________________________

5. ¿Has escuchado muchos discos? ______________________________

The past participles of **-ER** and **-IR** verbs with stems ending in a vowel have an accent mark.

STEM	ENDING	PAST PARTICIPLE
ca	**er**	**ca*í*do** *fallen*
cre	**er**	**cre*í*do** *believed*
le	**er**	**le*í*do** *read*
o	**ír**	**o*í*do** *heard*
tra	**er**	**tra*í*do** *brought*

A few verbs have irregular past participles, and you will have to memorize them.

INFINITIVE	PAST PARTICIPLE
abrir	***abierto*** *open(ed)*
cubrir	***cubierto*** *covered*
decir	***dicho*** *said*
escribir	***escrito*** *written*
hacer	***hecho*** *done*
morir	***muerto*** *died*
poner	***puesto*** *put*
romper	***roto*** *broken*
ver	***visto*** *seen*
volver	***vuelto*** *returned*

Remember that compounds of the following verbs also have irregular past participles.

INFINITIVE	PAST PARTICIPLE
describir	***descrito*** *described*
descubrir	***descubierto*** *discovered*
devolver	***devuelto*** *returned*

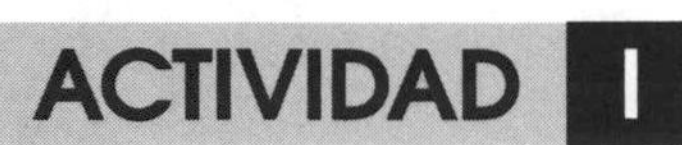

It's Sunday and you have slept till noon. Write what the other members of your family have done while you slept.

1. mi papá / leer el periódico ______________________________

2. mi mamá / poner la mesa ______________________________

3. mis hermanos / hacer las tareas ________________

4. mis hermanas / escribir cartas ________________

5. mi gato / descubrir un ratón ________________

6. mi perro / romper un florero ________________

7. mi tía / volver del supermercado ________________

8. tú / ver un programa de televisión ________________

ACTIVIDAD J

What have these people done for your birthday party?

1. mi padre / traer los refrescos

____

2. mis amigos / decir «¡Feliz cumpleaños!»

____

3. mi mamá / hacer una torta

____

4. mis hermanas / cubrir la torta con chocolate

____

5. tú / escribir las invitaciones

____

6. yo / abrir los regalos

____

ACTIVIDAD K

Describe what you and your friend Carlos have done before leaving for Spain. Use the following expressions.

sacar el pasaporte	pedir la visa
hacer las reservaciones	ir a la agencia de viajes

escribir a los hoteles	cambiar dólares por euros
leer las guías turísticas	oír casetes en español
ver al cónsul español	hacer las maletas
decir adiós a los amigos	devolver libros a la biblioteca

EXAMPLE: **Carlos y yo *hemos hecho* las reservaciones.**

1. ______________________________

2. ______________________________

3. ______________________________

4. ______________________________

5. ______________________________

6. ______________________________

7. ______________________________

8. ______________________________

9. ______________________________

10. ______________________________

5

Now look at these sentences.

¿Has hablado con Darío?	*Have you spoken with Dario?*
Sí, *acabo de hablar* con él.	*Yes, I have just spoken with him.*
¿Dónde está Consuelo?	*Where is Consuelo?*
Ella *acaba de salir*.	*She has just gone out.*

If you want to express in Spanish the idea that something has just taken place, use the following construction.

present tense of **acabar** + **de** + infinitive

El avión acaba de aterrizar.	*The plane has just landed.*
Acabo de levantarme.	*I have just gotten up.*
Acabamos de llegar.	*We have just arrived.*

Acabar is a regular **-AR** verb that by itself means *to finish*:

¿Cuándo vas a acabar las tareas? *When are you going to finish your homework?*

ACTIVIDAD L

You want to go out, but all your friends have called saying they are too tired from having done various physical activities.

EXAMPLE: Pedro / jugar al fútbol **Pedro *acaba de jugar* al fútbol.**

1. Roberto y Raúl / correr cinco millas ______________________
2. tú / limpiar tu cuarto ______________________
3. Uds. / estudiar para un examen difícil ______________________
4. Rosario / trabajar en el jardín ______________________
5. José / lavar el carro ______________________

Preguntas Personales

1. ¿Has viajado a otro país? ¿Adónde?

____

2. ¿Qué documentos necesitas generalmente si vas salir de los Estados Unidos?

____

3. ¿Qué necesitas para viajar a Puerto Rico?

____

4. ¿Qué tienes que obtener para hacer un viaje a Europa?

____

5. ¿Prefieres viajar por autobús, por barco, o por avión?

____

6. ¿Cuáles son los medios de transporte más comunes? ¿Cuál prefieres? ¿Por qué?

____

Información Personal

List some things you haven't done up to now but would like to do. You may use some of the suggested activities.

visitar	viajar
aprender	ir
comprar	hacer
ver	decir

EXAMPLE: **No *he visto* una ópera.**

____

____

____

____

____

____

Composición

The customs officials have been stopping all suspicious-looking luggage. They have asked you to fill out a form describing your recent activities before they allow you to cross the border. Tell where you have been, for how long, your reasons for going there, the nature of your work; list the merchandise you have purchased abroad and any other pertinent information that will convince the customs officials that you are an honest citizen.

____

____

____

____

____

____

____

Diálogo

You have come back from a trip to South America and the customs official is asking the usual questions. Complete the dialog.

CÁPSULA CULTURAL

Un viaje por el Camino Real

El Camino Real es un sendero que cubre una distancia de 600 millas, desde San Diego a Sonoma. Fue establecido por frailes españoles, entre ellos el padre Junípero Serra, mientras exploraba y establecía comunidades en los nuevos territorios.

El Camino Real, actualmente *U.S. Highway 101*, comenzó como un sendero que conectaba las 21 misiones de los franciscanos. Cada misión estaba localizada a un día de viaje a caballo.

Una de las misiones más famosas es San Juan Capistrano, una hora al sur de Los Ángeles. Construida en 1776, esta «joya de las misiones» es el edificio más viejo de California. San Juan Capistrano es conocida por sus golondrinas. Cada 19 de marzo, miles de golondrinas vuelven de pasar el invierno en el sur para anidar en los arcos de la misión. Los pájaros no siempre llegan exactamente el 19 a causa de las condiciones del tiempo, pero siempre vuelven.

Junípero Serra murió en 1784, a la edad de 71 años. Su cuarto todavía esta allí, amueblado con un catre de madera, una sola frazada, una mesa, una silla, un cofre, un candelero y una calabaza para agua.

Su lema era: «siempre adelante, nunca atrás».

el sendero *trail*

el fraile *friar*
entre *among*

actualmente *currently*

la golondrina *swallow*

anidar *to nest*

amueblado *furnished*
el catre *cot*
la frazada *blanket*
el cofre *chest, trunk*
la calabaza *gourd*
el lema *motto*

Para pensar

1. ¿Qué sabemos de la exploración de California?
2. ¿Qué es El Camino Real? ¿Para qué servía al principio? ¿Cómo se llama ahora?
3. ¿Qué pasa todos los años en la misión de San Juan Capistrano?
4. ¿Quién fue Junípero Serra? Considerando el cuarto donde vivía Junípero, ¿qué tipo de persona era él?
5. ¿Cómo afectaron los exploradores españoles la historia de los Estados Unidos? ¿Qué efectos han tenido en nuestra historia y en nuestra lengua?

21

La ecología

Present Subjunctive

1 Vocabulario

¡Planeta en peligro!

Cada año, **es probable que** la raza humana **destruya** un área de selva de casi la mitad del tamaño de Texas. El recurso natural más grande del mundo está quemándose literalmente; y más de 320 millas cuadradas de selva irremplazable son quemadas o cortadas cada día. Hace sólo veinte años, las selvas cubrían 14 por ciento del planeta. Hoy día, las selvas cubren menos del seis por ciento.

quemarse *to burn*

cubrir *to cover*

A este paso, **es posible que** esta parte importantísima del planeta **sea** totalmente destruida en unos cuarenta años. Con él se perderán tesoros todavía no descubiertos y recursos irremplazables obtenibles sólo dentro de estos ecosistemas únicos. ¿**Duda que sean** importantes para nuestro mundo estos frágiles ecosistemas?

Considere estos datos:

datos *facts*

- Más de la mitad de las especies vivientes están allí. Dos acres y medio de la selva amazónica contienen 750 tipos de árboles— más variedades que en toda Norte América.
- En Perú hay una reserva forestal donde habitan más especies de pájaros que en todos los Estados Unidos.
- La selva amazónica produce veinte por ciento del oxígeno del mundo.

- El Río Amazonas contiene dos terceras partes del agua dulce del mundo.
- Veinticinco por ciento de todos los productos farmacéuticos tienen su origen en plantas de la selva. Todavía se están descubriendo nuevas plantas y los científicos esperan nos den muchas de las medicinas del futuro.

agua dulce *fresh water*

A este paso, **es probable que** la contaminación del aire, de los ríos y del océano **continúe** por el mundo entero. Muchos temen que las emisiones de los coches y de las fábricas **sean** un riesgo a la zona ozono y que **causen** un aumento de la temperatura global.

Además, la población creciente contribuye a la erosión de nuestras costas y la contaminación de la tierra con químicos, plásticos y basura. ¿Crees que **haya** soluciones a estos problemas? Sabemos por ejemplo, que cada tonelada de papel reciclado salva diecisiete árboles de la destrucción. ¿Qué más podemos hacer para evitar la destrucción de nuestro planeta? ¿Tienes algunas sugerencias?

creciente *growing*

ACTIVIDAD A

Answer the following questions based on the reading.

1. ¿Qué cantidad de la selva es destruida cada año? ¿Cada día?

____

____

2. Si el nivel de destrucción continúa así, ¿cuánto tiempo durará la selva?

____

____

3. Si la selva desaparece, ¿qué pasará a muchas especies de animales y plantas?

____

____

4. ¿Qué porcentaje del oxígeno del mundo se produce en la selva amazónica?

____

____

5. ¿Por qué son importantes las plantas de la selva?

____

____

6. Además de en la selva, ¿dónde más hay destrucción de nuestro ambiente?

____

____

7. ¿Cuáles son las causas de los diferentes tipos de contaminación?

____

____

8. ¿Qué problemas causa la sobrepoblación?

____

____

9. ¿Cuales son algunas cosas que debemos hacer para conservar nuestros recursos?

____

____

10. ¿Qué puedes hacer tú personalmente para proteger al planeta?

____

____

ACTIVIDAD B

Work with a partner. One student poses a question dealing with an ecological problem. The other student answers with a possible solution.

EXAMPLE: Problema: ¿Qué podemos hacer para evitar la contaminación del aire?
Solución: **Podemos usar más el transporte público y menos el automóvil.**

1. Problema: deforestación

   Solución: ____

2. Problema: extinción de especies animales y vegetales

   Solución: ______________________________

3. Problema: acumulación de basura

   Solución: ______________________________

4. Problema: emisiones de los automóviles

   Solución: ______________________________

5. Problema: humo de las fábricas

   Solución: ______________________________

6. Problema: derrames del petróleo

   Solución: ______________________________

7. Problema: el nivel del ruido

   Solución: ______________________________

8. Problema: erosión de la tierra

   Solución: ______________________________

9. Problema: contaminación con químicos y plásticos

   Solución: ______________________________

10. Problema: consumo excesivo de energía

    Solución: ______________________________

2

When you read about our endangered planet, do you remember seeing the following statements?

Es probable* que la raza humana *destruya	*It's probable that the human race will destroy*
***Es posible* que esta fuente *sea* destruida**	*It's possible that this source may be destroyed*
Los científicos *esperan* que nos *den*	*Scientists hope that we get*
Dejamos que* esta destrucción *continúe	*We allow this destruction to continue*

***Temen* que *sean* un riesgo a la zona de ozono**	*They fear that they will be a risk to the ozone layer*

Destruya, **sea**, **esperen**, **continúe** are all verbs in the SUBJUNCTIVE. Up to now, we have been using verbs in the various tenses of the indicative mood.

Yo sé que ellos *están* aquí ahora.	*I know that they are here now.*
Es cierto que él *hablará*.	*It is true that he will speak.*
Ella dijo que Juan vino a casa.	*She said Juan came home.*

The indicative mood is based on knowledge or certainty. It is used to express what is actually happening, happened, or will happen.

There are times, however, when something is hoped for, feared, or desired. It is a possibility, but not an actual fact. At these times Spanish uses the SUBJUNCTIVE mood.

Yo espero que ellos *estén* aquí.	*I hope that they are here.*
Es dudoso que él *hable*.	*It's doubtful that he will speak.*

In the above examples the verbs **estén, hable,** and **venga** are all in the **subjunctive**. To learn this new concept, we must do **three** things:

- Learn how to form the subjunctive in Spanish.
- Learn when to use the subjunctive.
- Learn how to express the meaning of the subjunctive.

3 Formation of the present subjunctive

To form the present subjunctive drop the **-o** of the **yo**-form of the present indicative and add the "opposite" endings (**-AR** verbs add endings beginning with **-e**; **-ER** and **-IR** verbs add endings beginning with **-a**).

	habl*ar* (**habl~~o~~**)	**com*er*** (**com~~o~~**)	**viv*ir*** (**viv~~o~~**)
yo	**habl*e***	**coma**	**viv*a***
tú	**habl*es***	**comas**	**viv*as***
Ud., él, ella	**habl*e***	**coma**	**viv*a***
nosotros, -as	**habl*emos***	**comamos**	**viv*amos***
Uds., ellos, ellas	**habl*en***	**coman**	**viv*an***

NOTE: 1. The reason we use the **yo**-form minus the **-o** rather than the infinitive is that the **yo**-form is often irregular, and this irregularity is carried over into the subjunctive.

	pon*er* (pon*go*)	**pod*er* (p*ue*do)**	**sal*ir* (sal*go*)**
yo	**pon*g*a**	**p*ue*da**	**salga**
tú	**pon*g*as**	**p*ue*das**	**salgas**
Ud., él, ella	**pon*g*a**	**p*ue*da**	**salga**
nosotros, -as	**pon*g*amos**	**podamos**	**salgamos**
Uds., él, ella	**pon*g*an**	**p*ue*dan**	**salgan**

2. Does all this sound familiar? It should, because these are the same rules we used to form the informal commands.

¡*Venga* (Ud.) ahora! *Come now!*

¡*Escriba* (Ud.) la carta! *Write the letter.*

¡*Traigan* (Uds.) el dinero! *Bring the money.*

¡*Hable* (Ud.) despacio! *Speak slowly.*

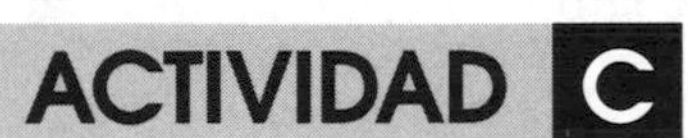

The following verbs are all in the present indicative. Change them to the present subjunctive.

EXAMPLE: ellos vienen **ellos *vengan***

1. yo gano yo ______________________
2. ellos salen ellos ______________________
3. Pepe trabaja Pepe ______________________
4. nosotros hacemos nosotros ______________________
5. yo tengo yo ______________________
6. ellos reciben ellos ______________________
7. María piensa María ______________________
8. ellos piden ellos ______________________

9. yo conozco yo ____________

10. ellas ven ellas ____________

4 There are a few common verbs that are irregular because they do not follow the above rules.

d*ar*	**dé, des, dé, demos, den**
est*ar*	**esté, estés, esté, estemos, estén**
ir	**vaya, vayas, vaya, vayamos, vayan**
sab*er*	**sepa, sepas, sepa, sepamos, sepan**
ser	**sea, seas, sea, seamos, sean**

ACTIVIDAD D

Give the proper form of the subjunctive, according to the subject.

1. yo ____________ (ser)
2. él ____________ (saber)
3. nosotros ____________ (dar)
4. ellos ____________ (estar)
5. tú ____________ (ir)

ACTIVIDAD E

Complete the following sentences using the subjunctive, when necessary:

1. Es dudoso que ellos ____________ a tiempo.
   (regresar)

2. Es importante que nosotros ____________ la tienda.
   (abrir)

3. Es probable que Lupe ____________ la comida.
   (traer)

4. Es necesario que Uds. ____________ temprano.
   (venir)

5. Es imposible que ella _______________ mañana.
(ir)

6. Es importante que tú _______________ bueno.
(ser)

7. Es una lástima que ellos no me _______________ la información.
(dar)

8. Es evidente que Manuel no _______________ en casa.
(estar)

9. Es necesario que tú _______________ la verdad.
(saber)

10. Es mejor que Uds. _______________ conmigo.
(salir)

5

Compare the following sets of sentences.

Es importante *estudiar*.	*It's important to study.*
Es importante que Juan *estudie*.	*It's important that Juan study.*
Es mejor no *hablar*.	*It's better not to talk.*
Es mejor que Ud. no *hable*.	*It's better that you don't talk.*

NOTE: In order to use the subjunctive you must have **two** separate clauses with **two** definite subjects indicated. A general statement not referring to anyone in particular uses an infinitive.

As was stated in the introduction of the topic, the subjunctive is used when something is impossible, doubtful, uncertain, etc. Therefore, the subjunctive is used after expressions of emotions (fear, hope, anger, happiness), wishing or wanting, doubt, denial, uncertainty and the like.

RULE The subjunctive is used **after** the following impersonal expressions:

es posible (imposible) *it's possible (impossible)*

es probable *it's probable*

es preciso (necesario) *it's necessary*

es dudoso *it's doubtful*

es importante *it's important*

es una lástima *it's a pity*

es mejor *it's better*

NOTE: **1.** There are other expressions: **es ridículo** (it's ridiculous), **es necesario** (it's necessary), **es raro** (it's rare), etc., but the ones above are the most common.

2. The following impersonal expressions of certainty are followed by the indicative, not the subjunctive:

es seguro	*it is sure*	**es evidente**	*it is clear*
es cierto	*it is certain*	**es verdad**	*it is true*

***Es evidente que* el alumno no *sabe* la respuesta.** — *It's evident that the student doesn't know the answer.*

RULE The subjunctive is used after certain verbs. The most common verbs requiring the subjunctive are:

querer, desear	*to want, to wish*	**temer**	*to fear*
pedir	*to ask*	**tener miedo de**	*to be afraid*
mandar	*to command*	**dudar**	*to doubt*
hacer	*to make*	**preferir**	*to prefer*
dejar	*to allow*	**permitir**	*to permit*
esperar	*to hope*	**prohibir**	*to forbid*
alegrarse	*to be glad*		

Dudamos que el carpintero termine el trabajo. — *We doubt that the carpenter will finish the work.*

Yo prefiero que tú vayas solo. — *I prefer that you go alone.*

NOTE: As with the impersonal expressions there must be TWO clauses and TWO different subjects for the subjunctive to be used.

Él quiere hablar. — *He wants to speak.*

Él quiere que yo hable. — *He wants me to speak.*

In addition to the above verbs, negative and interrogative verbs of thinking and believing are followed by the subjunctive since there is doubt and uncertainty in the mind of the speaker.

Creo que ella sale mañana. — *I think she's leaving tomorrow.*

But:

No creo que ella salga mañana. — *I don't think she's leaving tomorrow.*

¿Cree Ud. que ella salga mañana? — *Do you think she's leaving tomorrow?*

ACTIVIDAD F

Work with a partner. One student recites the indicative sentences. The partner, using the clues, changes the sentences to the subjunctive.

1. El médico viene hoy. Yo quiero que ______________________________.
2. Salgo mañana. Ella duda que ______________________________.
3. Aprendemos la lengua. Es importante que ______________________________.
4. El niño tiene un resfriado. Es una lástima que ______________________________.
5. Ellas traen la comida. El jefe manda que ______________________________.
6. Él es inteligente. ¿Crees que ______________________________?
7. Ellos vuelven al país. El capitán prohíbe que ______________________________.
8. Ud. piensa en su hijo. Me alegro de que ______________________________.
9. El chico no estudia. Tengo miedo de que ______________________________.
10. Sabemos la lección. Es necesario que ______________________________.

There are many ways of translating the subjunctive into English. Here are some examples:

Él manda que ella *hable*.	*He orders her to speak.*
Pedimos que Ud. *estudie*.	*We ask you to study.* *We ask that you study.*
Es una lástima que tú *vayas*.	*It's a shame that you're going.* *It's a shame for you to go.*
Es importante que Ud. *sepa* la verdad.	*It's important for you to know the truth.* *It's important that you know the truth.*
Tengo miedo de que no *venga*.	*I'm afraid he's not coming.* *I'm afraid he won't come.*

As can be seen, no matter how the thought is interpreted and expressed in English, Spanish follows set patterns and set rules. If you follow them, you will always be correct.

Preguntas Personales

1. ¿Qué cosas reciclas para proteger el ambiente?

___

2. ¿Cómo puedes ahorrar electricidad?

___

3. ¿Qué harías para proteger el hábitat de los animales en peligro?

___

4. ¿Menciona algunas cosas que haces para reducir la cantidad de agua que usas (cuando te bañas, cuando lavas el carro, etc.)?

___

5. ¿Qué se puede hacer para conservar gasolina?

___

Composición

You're writing an article for the local paper. Explain how citizens can do their part for a cleaner and healthier environment and show how each individual <u>does</u> make a difference.

___

___

___

___

___

___

___

___

___

___

Diálogo

Complete el siguiente diálogo sobre la ecología.

CÁPSULA CULTURAL

El ecoturismo

Los gobiernos de varios países hispanoamericanos están estimulando la conservación de sus recursos naturales por medio de un turismo sensitivo al ambiente. Están demostrando que pueden traer beneficios económicos a sus respectivos países y mejorar la calidad de la vida, a la vez que protegen su patrimonio ambiental.

Uno de estos países es Costa Rica. Mientras que muchos países explotan sus recursos naturales sin ningún control, Costa Rica está aumentando sus bosques y parques. Su sistema de parques nacionales, uno de los más comprensivos y extensos del mundo, protege una gran variedad de ecosistemas. Más de 10 por ciento del país ha sido declarado reserva forestal. Volcanes, selvas, playas y ríos están protegidos para siempre. Por esta razón, Costa Rica es conocida como "el santuario de los animales salvajes de las Américas".

Otro país, Venezuela, le provee al viajero la mejor oportunidad en Sud América de inspeccionar los animales salvajes en su estado natural. Un ranchero venezolano, dueño de la hacienda «Hato Piñero», ha prohibido la caza en su propiedad y la convirtió en un refugio de animales. Ahora los turistas pueden tener la experiencia maravillosa de ver jaguares, pumas, anacondas, halcones, ocelotes, monos, osos hormigueros, murciélagos, zorros y capibaras viviendo en su estado natural.

el beneficio *benefit*
el patrimonio *heritage*
comprensivo *comprehensive*
la hacienda *farm*
la caza *hunting*
el mono *monkey*
el oso hormiguero *anteater*
el zorro *fox*

Para pensar

1. ¿Qué es el ecoturismo?
2. ¿Qué ha hecho Costa Rica para conservar su ambiente?
3. ¿Qué es el «Hato Piñero»? ¿Qué tiene de especial?
4. Nombre y describa algunos animales salvajes.
5. ¿Cuáles son las ventajas del ecoturismo? ¿Cuáles son algunos de sus peligros?

Repaso V

(Lecciones 19–21)

LECCIÓN 19

a. The conditional of regular verbs is formed by adding the conditional endings to the infinitive.

	estudi*ar*	**aprend*er***	**escrib*ir***
yo	**estudiar*ía***	**aprender*ía***	**escribir*ía***
tú	**estudiar*ías***	**aprender*ías***	**escribir*ías***
Ud./él/ella	**estudiar*ía***	**aprender*ía***	**escribir*ía***
nosotros, -as	**estudiar*íamos***	**aprender*íamos***	**escribir*íamos***
Uds./ellos/ellas	**estudiar*ían***	**aprender*ían***	**escribir*ían***

b. In Spanish, the conditional tense is sometimes used to express wonder or probability in the past.

¿Quién *llamaría* a esta hora? — *I wonder who was calling at that hour.*

***Sería* Carlos.** — *It was probably Carlos.*

c. **Poder**, **querer**, and **saber** drop the **e** of the infinitive before adding the regular endings of the conditional tense.

Yo *podría* visitarte. — *I would be able to visit you.*

Ella *querría* ir conmigo. — *She would like to go with me.*

***Sabríamos* los resultados del examen.** — *We would know the test results.*

d. **Poner, tener, salir**, and **venir** change the **e** and then the **i** of the infinitive to **d** before adding the regular endings of the conditional tense.

Tú *pondrías* los libros en la mesa. — *You would put the books on the table.*

Él *tendría* que estudiar.	*He would have to study.*
Uds. *saldrían* para Europa.	*You would leave for Europe.*
Ellas *vendrían* temprano.	*They would come early.*

e. **Decir** and **hacer** have irregular stems in the conditional tense forms.

Ud. me *dir*ía la verdad.	*You would tell me the truth.*
Ellos *har*ían las tareas.	*They would to their homeworks.*

LECCIÓN 20

a. In Spanish, past participles are formed by dropping the **-ar, -er**, and **-ir** ending of the infinitive and adding **-ado, -ido**, and **-ido,** respectively.

sentar: ***sentado*** *seated*

perder: ***perdido*** *lost*

vestir: ***vestido*** *dressed*

Many past participles can be used as adjectives, agreeing in gender and number with the noun they accompany.

Nosotros* estamos *cansados.	*We are tired.*
***La niña* está *vestida* de blanco.**	*The girl is dressed in white.*

b. The past participle is used to form the present-perfect tense. The present perfect consists of the present-tense form of **haber** (to have) and a past participle.

	haber	PAST PARTICIPLE
yo	**he**	**viajado**
tú	**has**	**viajado**
Ud., él, ella	**ha**	**viajado**
nosotros, -as	**hemos**	**viajado**
Uds., ellos, ellas	**han**	**viajado**

In the present perfect tense, the past participle always ends in **o**.

c. The present perfect in Spanish describes an action that happened in the past but is connected to the present.

El correo *ha llegado*. *The mail has arrived.*

d. In Spanish, contrary to English, the two words forming the present perfect cannot be separated.

Juan no me *ha llamado* todavía. *Juan hasn't called me yet.*

e. The past participles of **-ER** and **-IR** verbs with stems ending in a vowel have an accent mark.

leer: ***leído***

oír: ***oído***

The following verbs have irregular past participles.

abrir: ***abierto*** *opened*	**morir:** ***muerto*** *dead*
cubrir: ***cubierto*** *covered*	**poner:** ***puesto*** *put*
decir: ***dicho*** *said*	**romper:** ***roto*** *broken*
escribir: ***escrito*** *written*	**ver:** ***visto*** *seen*
hacer: ***hecho*** *done, made*	**volver:** ***vuelto*** *returned*

f. In Spanish, the present tense of **acabar** + **de** + *infinitive* expresses the idea that something has just taken place.

***Acabo de terminar* las tareas.** *I have just finished my homework.*

Acabar is a regular **-AR** verb that by itself means to *finish*.

El electricista *acabó* el trabajo. *The electrician finished the job.*

LECCIÓN 21

The subjunctive mood expresses a possibility rather than an actual fact.

The Subjunctive With Regular Verbs

The present subjunctive is formed by dropping the **o** of the **yo** ending of the present indicative and adding **-e**, **-es**, **-e**, **-emos**, and **-en** to **-AR** verbs and **-a**, **-as**, **-a**, **-amos**, and **-an** to **-ER** and **-IR** verbs.

	habl*ar*	**com*er***	**viv*ir***
yo	**habl*e***	**com*a***	**viv*a***
tú	**habl*es***	**com*as***	**viv*as***
Ud., él, ella	**habl*e***	**com*a***	**viv*a***
nosotros, -as	**habl*emos***	**com*amos***	**viv*amos***
Uds., ellos, ellas	**habl*en***	**com*an***	**viv*an***

The Subjunctive With Irregular Verbs

	d*ar*	**est*ar***	**ir**	**sab*er***	**s*er***
yo	**d*é***	**est*é***	***vay*a**	***sep*a**	**sea**
tú	**des**	**est*és***	***vay*as**	***sep*as**	**seas**
Ud., él, ella	**d*é***	**est*é***	***vay*a**	***sep*a**	**sea**
nosotros, -as	**demos**	**estemos**	***vay*amos**	***sep*amos**	**seamos**
Uds., ellos, ellas	**den**	**est*én***	***vay*an**	***sep*an**	**sean**

Uses of the Subjunctive

a. The subjunctive is used after the following impersonal expressions.

es posible (imposible) que *it's possible (impossible) that*

es probable que *it's probable that*

es preciso (necesario) que *it's precise (necessary) that*

es dudoso que *it's doubtful that*

es importante que *it's important that*

es una lástima que *it's a shame that*

es mejor que *it's better that*

b. The subjunctive is used after the following verbs.

alegrarse *to be happy* **desear** *to wish*

dejar *to allot, let* **dudar** *to doubt*

esperar	*to hope*	**permitir**	*to allow*
hacer	*to make*	**preferir**	*to prefer*
mandar	*to order*	**prohibir**	*to prohibit*
no creer	*to not believe*	**querer**	*to want*
pedir	*to ask for*	**temer** **tener miedo de**	*to fear, to be afraid of*

NOTE: To use the subjunctive there must be **two** different clauses separated by **que** and each clause has a different subject.

Yo dudo **que él** sepa. — *I doubt that he knows.*

Es importante **que nosotros** vayamos. — *It's important that we go.*

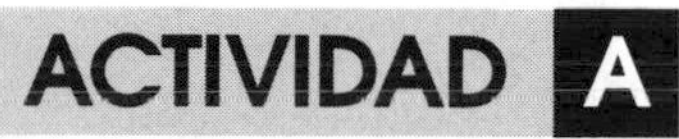

Tell all of the things you would do if you became rich.

EXAMPLE:

______________ **Yo *compraría* un carro nuevo.**
(comprar)

1. ______________________________
(tener)

2. ______________________________
(ir)

3. ______________________ (hacer)

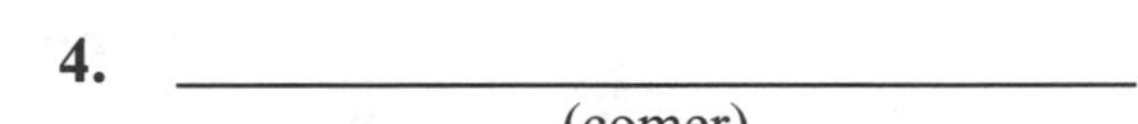

4. ______________________ (comer)

5. ______________________ (descansar)

6. ______________________ (vivir)

7. ______________________ (ayudar)

8. ______________________ (salir con)

ACTIVIDAD B

What have all these people done? Use a form of the verb **haber** + past participle.

1. El niño ______________________ el regalo.
   (abrir)

2. Mi papá ______________________ el auto.
   (cubrir)

3. Yo ______________________ una carta a mi amiga.
   (escribir)

4. Nosotros ______________________ la tarea de español.
(hacer)

5. Tú ______________________ los platos.
(romper)

6. Yo no ______________________ la película.
(ver)

7. Mamá ______________________ la mesa.
(poner)

ACTIVIDAD C

Complete the sentences with the correct form of the verb in parentheses.

1. Yo dudo que ellos ______________________ mañana.
(venir)

2. Temo que ______________________ hoy.
(llover)

3. Yo prohibo que tú ______________________ con ese muchacho.
(jugar)

4. Me alegro de que ellas ______________________ ahora.
(trabajar)

5. Es cierto que mis padres no ______________________.
(saber)

6. Ella prefiere que nosotros ______________________ más tarde.
(ir)

7. El policía no cree que yo ______________________ verdad.
(decir)

8. Es una lástima que Uds. no ______________________ dinero.
(tener)

9. ¡Yo mando que tú ______________________ de esta casa!
(salir)

10. Es preciso que nosotros ______________________ aquí.
(estar)

ACTIVIDAD D

Complete the following Spanish crossword puzzle about personality traits.

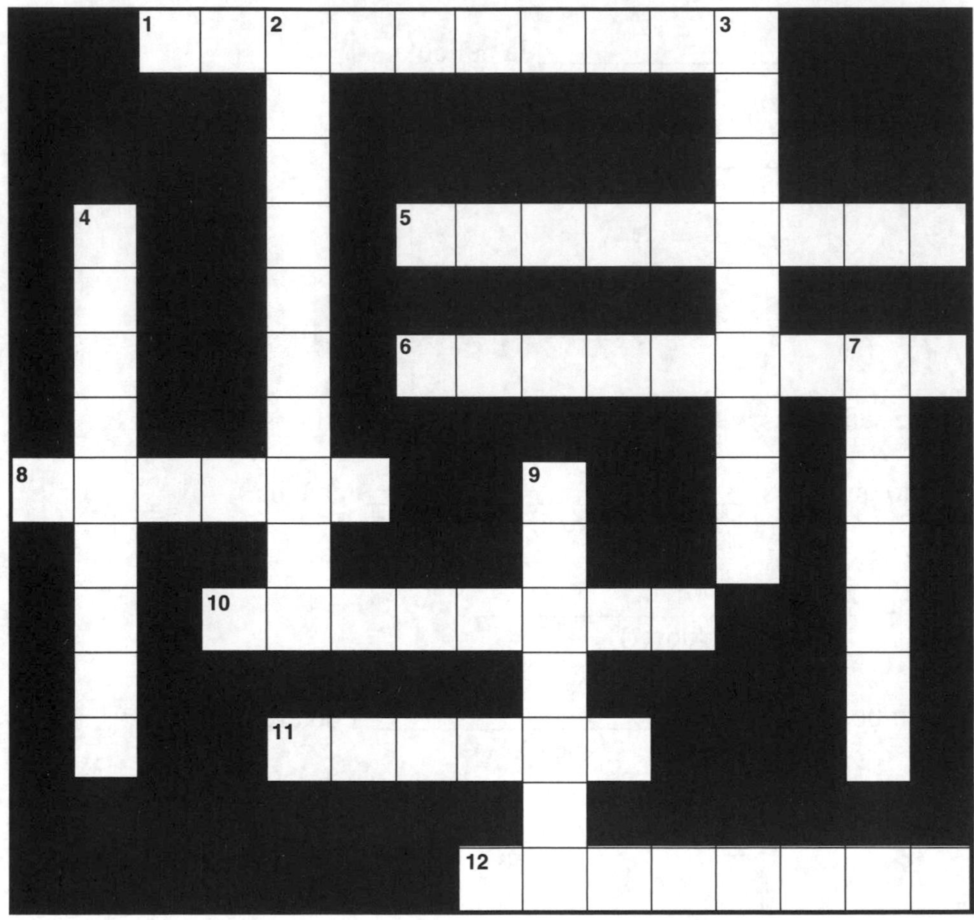

HORIZONTALES

1. disagreeable, not nice
5. pessimist, pessimistic
6. envious
8. shy
10. funny
11. jealous
12. patient

VERTICALES

2. hard working
3. optimist
4. liar, lying
7. honest, sincere
9. egoist, egotistical

ACTIVIDAD E

Work with a partner. Study the illustration and spot the things that are harming our environment. One student identifies the problem, the other gives the solutions.

ACTIVIDAD F

Las siete diferencias

Work with a partner. Compare the following two scenes and find out 7 differences between them.

Picture Story

Nuestro  está en peligro. Estamos destruyendo los , los 

y los .

Hay mucha contaminación:  y producen  y contribuyen a la  ácida y a la destrucción del ozono. Cortamos los  y las que se usan para producir medicinas. Además estamos contribuyendo a la eliminación de varias especies de .

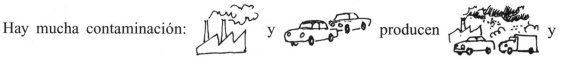

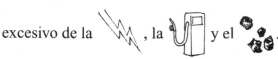

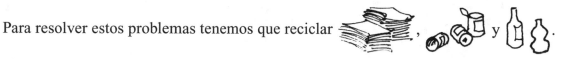

Para resolver estos problemas tenemos que reciclar , y .
Debemos utilizar la energía del , el y el  y reducir el uso excesivo de la , la y el .

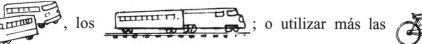

También debemos caminar y usar los medios de transportación pública, como los , los ; o utilizar más las . Así podremos salvar nuestro  para las generaciones del futuro.

Appendix

Cosas de la lengua

1 «¡Zas! ¡Cataplúm!»: Onomatopeia in Spanish

Sounds are universal. People the world over hear bells ringing, dogs barking, children crying and so on. Each language, however, attempts to reproduce these sounds in its own individual way. The technical term for naming a sound with a word that is pronounced like the sound is *onomatopoeia*.

For example, if we see the English words "knock, knock," we recognize it as the sound of someone knocking at the door. In Spanish, however, the equivalent sound is "**pam, pam, pam**" or "**toc, toc.**" "Cock a doodle doo" is immediately recognizable by English speakers as the crowing of a rooster. In Spanish, the same sound is represented by the words "**qui qui ri quí**," which sounds "kee kee ree kee."

Here are some sounds made by other animals. Match the Spanish sounds with the English ones.

SPANISH	ENGLISH
pío, pío	bow wow
jau, jau	neigh
cuá, cuá	peep, peep
miau	meow
jiii	quack, quack

Here are some more everyday sounds. Match the Spanish and the English.

SPANISH	ENGLISH
bum	choo, choo
rataplán	whack
chuu, chuu, chuu	crash
cras	rat-a-tat
zas	boom

Finally, here are some sounds in Spanish with a description of the sounds on the right. Match the two columns.

SPANISH	ENGLISH
buaaa	person sneezing
din don	doorbell ringing
achiiis	engine revving up
room, room	bell chiming
glu, glu, glu	baby crying
riiin riiin	person out of breath
uf, uf	gurgling sound

2 Compound Words (Word Building)

There are many words in Spanish that are combinations of other words in the language, forming compound words. If you know the meanings of the simple words, you can usually figure out the meaning of the more complex ones. Here are a few common examples:

abre (*open*) + **latas** (*cans*) = **abrelatas** (*can opener*)

ante (*before*) + **ojos** (*eyes*) = **anteojos** (*eyeglasses*)

saca (*take out*) + **puntas** (*points*) = **sacapuntas** (*pencil sharpener*)

para (*for*) + **aguas** (*water*) = **paraguas** (*umbrella*)

guarda (*keep*) + **ropa** (*clothing*) = **guardarropa** (*wardrobe*)

Now try these: they're a bit more difficult. Match the compound words with their English equivalents.

lava (*washes*) + **manos** (*hands*) = **lavamanos**	seesaw
monda (*cleans*) + **dientes** (*teeth*) = **mondadientes**	pastime
cuenta (*counts*) + **gotas** (*drops*) = **cuentagotas**	wash basin
pasa (*passes*) + **tiempo** (*time*) = **pasatiempo**	toothpick
sube (*goes up*) + **baja** (*goes down*) = **subibaja**	eyedropper

Finally, figure out the meanings of these words.

rompe (*breaks*) + **cabezas** (*heads*) = **rompecabezas**

rasca (*scratches*) + **cielo** (*sky*) = **rascacielo**

para (*for*) + **choques** (*crashes*) = **parachoques**

espanta (*frightens*) + **pájaros** (*birds*) = **espantapájaros**

3 **«Tiene un tornillo flojo»:** Idiomatic Expressions

In every language there are expressions called idioms, whose meanings make perfect sense to the native speaker, but not necessarily to the non native, especially if these expressions are translated word for word. In English, for example, we say things like, "it's raining cats and dogs," "he hit the ceiling," "that was the last straw," and so on. If we translated the words of these expressions into Spanish, they would make absolutely no sense to the Spanish speaker.

And yet, idioms are an essential part in speaking or understanding any language. What we must do then, is to find equivalent expressions in both Spanish and English. Here are some Spanish idioms (**modismos**) with their literal translations and their English equivalents.

Cuesta un ojo de la cara. (*It costs an eye of the face.*) It costs an arm and a leg. It costs a fortune.

Tiene el corazón hecho pedazos. (*He has his heart made pieces.*) His heart is broken.

Le toma el pelo. (*He's taking your hair.*) He's kidding you. He's pulling your leg.

Sólo hay cuatro gatos aquí. (*There are only four cats here.*) There's hardly anyone here. There's hardly a soul.

Here are some idioms with their English translations. Match them with their English equivalents.

1. **Es la gota que rebosa la copa.** (*It's the drop that makes the glass overflow.*)

2. **Es echar agua al mar.** (It's throwing water into the ocean.)

3. **No es cosa del otro mundo.** (It's not anything from another world.)

4. **Estoy entre dos aguas.** (I'm between two waters.)

5. **Son como dos gotas de agua.** (They're like two drops of water.)

   a. I'm undecided. I don't know what to do.
   b. It's nothing to write home about. It's nothing special.
   c. They're like two peas in a pod. They're very similar.
   d. It's pointless. It makes no sense.
   e. That's the straw that broke the camel's back.

4 **«En boca cerrada no entran moscas»:** Spanish proverbs

One of the best ways to understand the language and culture of a people is through its common sayings. Each language has its own proverbs, little sayings of folk wisdom that develop over the years. In some cases, the way a proverb is expressed is unique to that particular culture. But in many cases, since proverbs are an outgrowth of experiences common to all cultures, these sayings, called **refranes** in Spanish, are almost identical from one language to another.

A **refrán** is a saying, often in the form of a rhyme, that is usually short and sweet, clever or funny, and contains useful knowledge that can be applied to real-life situations.

Here are a few common proverbs, together with a translation and their English equivalent.

SPANISH PROVERB	LITERAL TRANSLATION	EQUIVALENT ENGLISH PROVERB
Antes que te cases mira lo que haces.	Before you get married, look at what you're doing.	Look before you leap.
El consejo de mujer es poco y quien no lo toma es loco.	Advice from a woman is little and those who don't take it are crazy.	Always listen to what a woman tells you.

Al cabo de cien años todos seremos calvos.	In a 100 years, we'll all be bald.	Don't worry about life's small problems.
Si quieres vivir sano acuéstate y levántate temprano.	If you want to be healthy get up early and go to bed early.	Early to bed and early to rise makes a man healthy, wealthy, and wise.
Al mal tiempo buena cara.	To bad weather, good face.	Keep your chin up.

Now, here are some Spanish proverbs and their English translations. Match them with the appropriate English proverbs that follow.

1. Aunque la mona se vista de seda, mona se queda. (*Even though a monkey dresses in silk, it still is a monkey.*) ______

2. El gato escalfado del agua fría huye. (*The scalded cat runs away from cold water.*) ______

3. No hay que ahogarse en un vaso de agua. (*You shouldn't drown in a glass of water.*) ______

4. A lo hecho, pecho (*to what's done, chest*) ______

5. De tal palo, tal astilla (*from such a stick, such a splinter*) ______

a. Don't cry over spilled milk.
b. You can't make a silk purse out of a sow's ear.
c. A chip off the old block. Like father, like son.
d. Once bitten, twice shy.
e. Don't make a mountain out of a molehill.

5 Suffixes: Changing the meanings of words

Some Spanish nouns may add endings that change the original meaning. They are called suffixes.

One common suffix is **-ito** or **-ita,** which indicates "little, small" or a feeling of affection. Thus, **mi casa** simply means *my house*. But **mi casita** is my "home, sweet, home." Similarly, **mi hermanito** is "my little brother." These endings can also be added to proper nouns: **Juan** becomes **Juanito**, **Ana** becomes **Anita**, **Jorge** becomes **Jorgito,** and so on.

Just as the ending **-ito/-ita** has an agreeable meaning, the ending **-illo/-illa** has a disagreeable one. **Un hombrecito** is a mature, well-mannered boy, "just like a grown-up." However **un hombrecillo** expresses contempt: a pipsqueak, a small insignificant man. Unlike **-ito** and **-illo**, the ending **-ón** enlarges a noun. **Un hombrón** is a hulk of a man.

Some endings are used so often that they become part of the word itself. The word with its ending then takes on a new meaning. Here are some examples:

el gatito (*kitten*), from **el gato**

el perrito (*puppy*), from **el perro**

el sillón (*armchair*), from **la silla**

la señorita (*miss*) from **la señora**

There are many suffixes in the Spanish language, such as

-ero/-era	**la carta** (*letter*)	**el cartero** (*postman, lettercarrier*)
-ura	**alto** (*tall*)	**altura** (*height*)
	largo (*long*)	**largura** (*length*)
-dad	**oscuro** (*dark*)	**oscuridad** (*darkness*)
	cruel (*cruel*)	**crueldad** (*cruelty*)
-ez/-eza	**rápido** (*fast*)	**rapidez** (*speed*)
	pobre (*poor*)	**pobreza** (*poverty*)

By learning the above suffixes, one can often figure out the meanings of many different words that belong to the same family.

la mesa (*table*)

la mesera ____________________

el mesero ____________________

la mesita ____________________

enfermo (*sick*)

la enfermera ____________________

la enfermedad ____________________

la cocina (*kitchen*)

cocinar ______________________

el cocinero ______________________

la cocinera ______________________

invitar (*to invite*)

el invitado ______________________

la invitación ______________________

escribir (*to write*)

el escritorio ______________________

el escritor ______________________

Spanish-English Vocabulary

The Spanish-English Vocabulary is intended to be complete for the contexts of this book.

Nouns are listed in the singular. Adjectives are listed in the masculine form. The following abbreviations are used:

m. = masculine	*sing.* = singular	*adj.* = adjective
f. = feminine	*pl.* = plural	*irr.* = irregular
m. & *f.* = masculine and feminine	*sing.* & *pl.* = singular and plural	

Verbs with spelling changes, stem-changing verbs, and irregular verbs are identified by the type of change as follows: **poder (ue)**; **tener (*irr.*).**

a to, at
abajo below
abeja *f.* bee
abierto open
abogado(-a) lawyer; **abogado defensor** defense lawyer
abrigo *m.* coat
abrir to open
aburrido bored, boring
acabar to finish; **acabar de** to have just
aceite *m.* oil
acelerador *m.* accelerator, gas pedal
acera *f.* sidewalk
acercarse (qu) to approach, come near
acompañar to accompany, go with
acordarse de (ue) to remember
acostar (ue) to put to bed; **acostarse** to lie down, go to bed
activo active
acto *m.* act
actuar to act
acuerdo *m.* agreement; **estar de acuerdo** to agree; **de acuerdo** agreed; yes, of course
adelante forward; **de ahora en adelante** from now on
adelanto *m.* advance
además (de) besides
adentro inside
adivino(-a) fortune teller
adivinar to guess, foretell
¿adónde? where (to)?
aduana *f.* customs
aduanero(-a) customs official
aeromozo(-a) flight attendant
aeropuerto *m.* airport
afeitarse to shave
aficionado(-a) fan
afortunadamente fortunately, luckily
afuera outside; **comer afuera** to eat out
agresivo aggressive
agua *f.* **(el agua)** water
aguacate *m.* avocado
aguafiestas *m.* & *f.* partypooper, spoilsport
agüero *m.* omen
ahí there; **por ahí** that way, over there
ahora now; **ahora mismo** right now
aire acondicionado *m.* air conditioning
ahorrar to save
ajo *m.* garlic
alegre happy
alegremente happily
alemán(-ana) German
alfabeto *m.* alphabet
alfombra *f.* rug
algo something
algodón *m.* cotton

alguien somebody
alguno some, any
aliento *m.* breath
aliviar to relieve
alivio *m.* relief
allá there, over there
allí there
almacén *m.* store; warehouse; department store
almacenaje *m.* storage
almorzar (ue, c) to eat (have) lunch
almuerzo *m.* lunch
alrededor de around
alto tall, high
alunizar (c) to land on the moon
amable kind, nice
amanecer *m.* dawn
amarillento yellowish
amarillo yellow
ambicioso ambitious
amigo(-a) friend
amiguito(-a) little friend, pal
amor *m.* love; **amorcito** my love, my darling
ampliar to enlarge
amuleto *m.* charm
ancho wide
andar (*irr.*) to go about, walk
anillo *m.* ring
año *m.* year
anoche last night
anteayer the day before yesterday
antena *f.* antenna
antes (de) before
antiguo old, ancient
antipático unpleasant
anunciar to announce
anuncio *m.* announcement, sign; **anuncio clasificado** classified ad; **anuncio comercial** ad
apagar (gu) to turn off
aplauso *m.* applause, clapping
aprender to learn
aquel, aquella that
aquellos, aquellas those
aquí here; **por aquí** this way
araña *f.* spider
árbitro *m.* umpire
árbol *m.* tree
ardilla *f.* squirrel
arena *f.* sand
arete *m.* earring
armonía *f.* harmony
arrancar (qu) to start (auto)
arreglar to fix, repair
arrogante arrogant, haughty
arroz *m.* rice; **arroz con leche** rice pudding
artículo *m.* article; **artículo de fondo** editorial
ascensor *m.* elevator
asegurado insured
asegurar to insure; to assure
asesino(-a) murderer
así so, thus
asiento *m.* chair, seat; **tomar asiento** to take a seat, sit down
asistir to attend
asociación *f.* society
aspirina *f.* aspirin
astro *m.* star
astrología f. astrology
astronauta *m. & f.* astronaut
astronave *f.* spaceship
asunto *m.* matter, affair
atención *f.* attention; **prestar atención** to pay attention
atento attentive, polite
aterrizar (c) to land
atractivo attractive
atrapar to trap; to catch
atrás back, backwards
atropellar to run over
aún even
aunque even though
auto *m.*, **automóvil** *m.* car
auxilio *m.* help
avalúo *m.* appraisal
avanzar (c) to advance
avenida *f.* avenue
avión *m.* plane
ayer yesterday; **anteayer** the day before yesterday
ayuda *f.* help
ayudante *m. & f.* helper, assistant
ayudar to help
azafata *f.* flight attendant
azul blue

bailar to dance
baile *m.* dance
bajar to go (come) down
bajo short; under, underneath
balón *m.* large ball
baloncesto *m.* basketball
ballena *f.* whale
banco *m.* bank
banda *f.* band
bandera *f.* flag
bañar to bathe; **bañarse** to take a bath
baño *m.* bathroom; **traje de baño** *m.* bathing suit
barba *f.* beard
barbacoa *f.* barbecue
barco *m.* boat; **barco de vela** sailboat
barrio *m.* neighborhood
basado based
básquetbol *m.* basketball
bastante enough
basura *f.* garbage
bata *f.* robe, housecoat
bate *m.* bat
bateador(-ora) batter
batear to bat
batería *f.* battery
bautizo *m.* baptism
batir to beat, break a record
bebé *m. & f.* baby
béisbol *m.* baseball
beso *m.* kiss
biblioteca *f.* library
bien well; **está bien** it's all right; O.K.
bienvenido welcome
bigote *m.* mustache
blanco white
blando soft
blusa *f.* blouse
bobo silly, foolish
boca *f.* mouth
boda *f.* marriage, wedding
bola *f.* ball
bolera *f.* bowling alley
boleto *m.* ticket
bolo: jugar (ue, gu) a los bolos to bowl
bolsillo *m.* pocket
bolso *m.* purse
bombero(-a) firefighter
bondadoso generous
bonito pretty, good-looking
bota *f.* boot

botar to throw away
botella *f.* bottle
botón *m.* button
boxeo *m.* boxing
brazalete *m.* bracelet
brazo *m.* arm; **brazo gitano** sponge cake roll with rum cream filling
brillante shiny, brilliant
brillar to shine
brisa *f.* breeze
broche *m.* brooch, pin
bronceador *m.* tanning lotion
bruja *f.* witch
brujo *m.* wizard, sorcerer
buenaventura *f.* fortune, good luck; **decir** (*irr.*) **la buenaventura** to tell one's fortune
bueno good
bufanda *f.* scarf
buscar (qu) to look for
buscado looked for, searched
butaca *f.* armchair, easy chair
buzón *m.* mailbox

caballero *m.* gentleman
caballo *m.* horse; **montar a caballo** to go horseback riding
cabeza *f.* head
cabina telefónica *f.* phone booth
cada each, every
cadena *f.* chain
caer(se) (*irr.*) to fall (down)
café *m.* coffee; café
caída *f.* fall
caja *f.* box; **caja fuerte** safe
cajero(-a) cashier
calamar *m.* squid
calavera *f.* skull
caldo *m.* broth; **caldo gallego** soup with white beans, turnips, and potatoes
caliente hot
calle *f.* street
cama *f.* bed
camarón *m.* shrimp
cambiar to change, exchange
caminata *f.* hike, long walk; **dar** (*irr.*) **una caminata** to go hiking
caminar to walk
camión *m.* truck
camisa *f.* shirt; **camisa de dormir** nightgown
camiseta *f.* t-shirt
campamento *m.* camp
campeón(-ona) champion
campo *m.* country, field
canción *f.* song
canguro *m.* kangaroo
canjear to exchange
cansado tired
cantante *m.* & *f.* singer
cantar to sing
capital *f.* capital
capítulo *m.* chapter
capó *m.* hood
cápsula *f.* capsule
cara *f.* face
cárcel *f.* jail
carga *f.* freight
cariñoso caring
carne *f.* meat
carnicería *f.* butchershop
carnicero(-era) butcher
caro expensive
carrera *f.* race
carretera *f.* highway
carro *m.* car
carta *f.* letter
cartelera *f.* billboard
cartera *f.* purse
cartón *m.* carton, cardboard
casa *f.* house; **a casa** home; **en casa** at home
casado married
casarse to get married
casco *m.* helmet
casi almost
caso *m.* case
castillo *m.* castle
catarro *m.* cold
causa: a causa de because of
cavar to dig
celda *f.* cell
celoso jealous
cenar to have dinner
centro *m.* center, middle; downtown
cepillar(se) to brush
cepillo *m.* brush; **cepillo de dientes** toothbrush
cerca (de) near
cerrado closed
cerrar (ie) to close, shut
certificado *m.* certificate
cerveza *f.* beer
cesta *f.* basket
chaleco *m.* vest
chica *f.* girl
chico *m.* boy
chile *m.* red pepper; **chile con carne** spiced chopped meat with chili sauce
chiste *m.* joke
chocar (qu) to crash
chofer *m.* driver
chupar to suck; **chuparse el dedo** to suck one's finger
ciclismo *m.* cycling
ciclista *m.* & *f.* cyclist
cielo *m.* sky, heaven; **mi cielo** my love, sweetheart
ciencia *f.* science; **ciencia ficción** science fiction
científico(-a) scientist
ciento (one) hundred; **por ciento** percent
cierto certain, sure; **es cierto** it's true
ciervo *m.* deer
cigarrillo *m.* cigarette
cine *m.* movies
cintura *f.* waist; lower back
cinturón *m.* belt
cita *f.* date, appointment
ciudad *f.* city
ciudadano(-ana) citizen
claro light; clear; of course!; **claro que no** of course not; **claro que sí** of course!
clase *f.* class, kind
clave *f.* key (to code)
clima *m.* climate, weather
cobrar to charge
cocina *f.* kitchen
cocinar to cook
cocodrilo *m.* crocodile
coche *m.* car; carriage
codo *m.* elbow
coger (j) to grasp, grab, catch, take
cohete *m.* rocket
cola *f.* tail, line
colchón flotante de aire *m.* air mattress

colección *f.* collection
colocar (qu) to place, put
collar *m.* necklace
combatir to combat, fight
comedor *m.* dining room
comenzar (ie, c) to begin
comer to eat
cometa *m.* comet
cometer to commit
cómico funny, amusing, comical
comida *f.* food, meal
como as, like **¿cómo?** how?, what?
cómoda *f.* dresser
cómodo comfortable
comportamiento *m.* behavior
cómplice *m.* & *f.* accomplice
compra *f.* purchase; **de compras** shopping
comprador(-ora) buyer
comprar to buy
comprender to understand
comprensivo understanding
comprobar (ue) to check, verify
compromiso *m.* commitment; engagement
computadora *f.* computer
común common
comunidad *f.* community
con with
concierto *m.* concert; **sala de conciertos** *f.* concert hall
concursante *m.* & *f.* contestant
concurso *m.* contest
concha *f.* (sea)shell
conejo *m.* rabbit
confianza *f.* confidence, trust
congelador *m.* freezer
conjunto *m.* set
conmigo with me
conocer to know, be acquainted with
conocido(-ida) acquaintance
conseguir (i, g) to obtain
consejero(-era) counselor, adviser
consejo *m.* advice
considerar to consider
consistir (en) to consist of
consultorio *m.* doctor's office
contado: al/de contado cash down, for cash
contaminación contamination
contar (ue) to tell; to count
contento happy, satisfied
conteo count; **conteo regresivo** countdown
contestar to answer
contigo with you (*fam.*)
continuación *f.* continuation; **a continuación** next, as follows
continuo continuous
contra against
contrario opposite; **al contrario, por el contrario** on the contrary
contrato *m.* contract
convencer to convince
convertir (*irr.*) **en** to turn into
copa *f.* glass, goblet
coro *m.* choir
corregir (i, j) to correct
correo *m.* mail; post office
correr to run
cortar to cut
cortés courteous, polite
corto short
cortina *f.* curtain
cosa *f.* thing; **eso es otra cosa** that's something else
costar (ue) to cost; **costar un ojo de la cara** to cost a fortune
creencia *f.* belief
creer to believe
crema *f.* cream
criminal *m.* & *f.* criminal
cristal *m.* glass, crystal
crucero *m.* cruise, crossing; **hacer un crucero** to take a cruise
crueldad *f.* cruelty
cruzar (c) to cross
cuadro *m.* picture, painting; square; **a cuadros** plaid
cuadrado square
¿cuál? which (one)?, what?
cualidad *f.* quality, characteristic
cualquier any
¿cuándo? when?
¿cuánto? how much?; **¿cuántos?** how many?
cuarto *m.* room; *adj.* fourth
cubierta *m.* hood
cubierto covered
cubo *m.* pail
cubrir to cover
cuello *m.* neck; collar
cuenta *f.* bill; account
cuerpo *m.* body
cuidado *m.* care; **tener** (*irr.*) **cuidado** to be careful
cuidadoso careful
culebra *f.* snake
cumpleaños *m.* birthday
cura *m.* priest
curita *f.* bandage
curso *m.* course; session

dama *f.* lady
daño *m.* damage
dar (*irr.*) to give; **dar un paseo** to take a walk; **me da pena** it makes me sad
de of, from
debajo (de) underneath, under, below; **por debajo de** underneath
deber must
débil weak
decidir to decide
décimo tenth
decir (*irr.*) to say; **querer decir** to mean
declaración *f.* declaration, statement
declarar to declare; to testify
decorar to decorate
dedo *m.* finger
defectuoso defective
defender (ie) to defend
defensa *f.* defense; **defensa propia** self-defense
defensivo defensive; **a la defensiva** defensively
dejar to leave; to let, allow; **dejar de** to stop, give up
delante (de) in front (of)
delfín *m.* dolphin
delincuencia *f.* delinquency
demás: los demás the others, the rest
demasiado too much
demostrar (ue) to demonstrate
dentro de inside, in
dependiente *m.* & *f.* clerk
deporte *m.* sport

deportista *m. & f.* sportsman, sportswoman
deportivo sports (*adj.*)
derecho *m.* right (*law*)
derramar to spill
desarrollar(se) to develop
desarrollo *m.* development
desayuno *m.* breakfast
descansar to rest
descargar (gu) to unload
desconocido unknown; **lo desconocido** the unknown
describir to describe
descubrir to discover
desde since; from
desempacar to unpack
deseo *m.* desire, wish; **tener deseos de** to feel like
desesperado desperate
desierto empty, deserted
desodorante *m.* deodorant
desorden *m.* disorder
despacho *m.* office
despacio slowly
despedida *f.* farewell
despedir (i) to dismiss, fire
despegar (gu) to take off
despertar(se) (ie) to wake up
después later, afterwards; **después de** after
desvestirse (i) to undress
detalle *m.* detail
detrás (de) in back of, behind
devolver (ue) to return (an object)
día *m.* day; **al día siguiente** the following day; **del día** of the day; **hoy día** nowadays; **todos los días** every day
diamante *m.* diamond
diario *m.* newspaper, daily
diente *m.* tooth; **cepillo de dientes** toothbrush; **pasta de dientes** toothpaste
difícil difficult
dinámico dynamic
dinero *m.* money
dirección *m.* address
director(-ora) manager; principal
dirigir (j) to direct
disco *m.* record
discutir to discuss, argue
diseñar to design
distancia *f.* distance
divertido entertaining, enjoyable, amusing
divertir (ie) to amuse; **divertirse** to have fun (a good time)
divino divine, heavenly
dólar *m.* dollar
doler (ue) to hurt
dolor *m.* pain; **dolor de cabeza** headache
donde where; at (someone's place); **¿dónde?** where?
dormido asleep
dormir (ue) to sleep; **dormirse** to fall asleep
dormitorio *m.* bedroom
duda *f.* doubt
duende *m.* leprechaun, goblin
dueño(-a) owner
dulce *m.* sweet, candy; *adj.* sweet, gentle
durar to last

echar to throw, toss
edad *f.* age
edificio *m.* building
efectivo *m.* cash
egoísta selfish
ejemplo *m.* example; **por ejemplo** for example
ejercicio *m.* exercise
electricista *m. & f.* electrician
elegir (i, j) to elect
empanada *f.* meat pie
embarcar (qu) to sail away, embark
embargo: sin embargo however, nonetheless
empacar to pack
empezar (ie, c) to begin
empleado(-ada) employee
en in, on
enamorado in love
encabezamiento *m.* heading
encaje *m.* lace
encantador charming
encantar to enchant, charm; **me encanta** I love it
encender (ie) to light; to turn on
encontrar (ue) to find; **encontrarse** to find oneself; to meet (each other)
enchilada *f.* stuffed and rolled tortilla with chili sauce
endurecimiento *m.* hardening
enemigo(-a) *f.* enemy
enfermedad *f.* illness
enfermero(-a) nurse
enfermo sick
enojarse to get angry
enorme enormous, huge
ensalada *f.* salad; **ensalada mixta** mixed salad
ensayar to try
enseñar to teach
entender (ie) to understand
enterarse to find out
entero whole
entonces then
entrada *f.* entrance; ticket
entrar to enter, go in
entre among, between
entrenador(-ora) trainer
entrenar to train
entrevista *f.* interview
enviar to send; **enviar de regreso** to return, send back
envidia *f.* envy
envidioso envious
equipaje *m.* luggage
equipo *m.* set, equipment; team
equivalente equivalent
equivocado mistaken, wrong
equivocarse (qu) to make a mistake
error *m.* mistake, error
escalera *f.* stairs; ladder
escaparse to get away, run away
escenario *m.* stage
escoger (j) to choose
esconder to hide
escondido hidden
escritorio *m.* desk
escribir to write
escritor(-ora) writer
escuchar to listen to
escuela de automovilismo *f.* driving school
esa(-e, -o) that; **ésa, ése** that one; **en eso** just then
esas, esos those
escoba *f.* broom
esfuerzo *m.* effort
esgrima *f.* fencing
esmeralda *f.* emerald

espada *f.* sword
espalda *f.* back
espacial space
español Spanish
especial special; **en especial** especially
especialidad *f.* specialty
especializarse to specialize
especie *f.* species
espectáculo *m.* spectacle, show
espejo *m.* mirror; **espejo retrovisor** rear-view mirror
esperar to wait (for)
espíritu *m.* spirit
esposa *f.* wife
esqueleto *m.* skeleton
esquí *m.* ski; skiing
esquiar to ski
esquina *f.* corner
establecer to establish
estación *f.* station
estacionado parked
estacionamiento *m.* parking
estadio *m.* stadium
estado *m.* state; **Estados Unidos** United States
estampilla *f.* stamp
estante *m.* shelf; **estante para libros** bookshelf
estar (*irr.*) to be
esta(-e, -o) this; **ésta(-e)** this one
estas(-os) these; **éstas(-os)** these ones
estómago *m.* stomach, abdomen
estornudar to sneeze
estrecho narrow
estrella *f.* star
estricto strict, severe
estudiar to study
estudioso studious
estufa *f.* stove
estupendo great, marvelous
estupidez *f.* stupidity
estúpido stupid
eternidad *f.* eternity
etiqueta *f.* label, tag
evitar to avoid
exactamente exactly
examen *m.* exam, test
examinar to examine
exhibición *m.* exhibit
exhibirse to show oneself
existir to exist
éxito *m.* success; **tener** (*irr.*) **éxito** to be successful
explicar (qu) to explain
extranjero foreign; **al extranjero** abroad
extraño strange

fabada *f.* thick bean soup with sausages
fácil easy
falda *f.* skirt
fama *f.* fame
familia *f.* family
fantasía *f.* fantasy
fantasma *m.* ghost
farmacéutico(-ica) pharmacist
farmacia *f.* pharmacy, drugstore
faro *m.* headlight
favor *m.* favor; **por favor** please
fecha *f.* date
felicitaciones congratulations
feo ugly
feroz fierce, savage
fiebre *f.* fever
fiesta *f.* party, celebration; **día de fiesta** *m.* holiday; **fiesta infantil** children's party
filmación *f.* filming
fin *m.* end; **por fin** finally
final *m.* end; **al final** in the end; **al final de** at the end of
financiamiento *m.* financing
firmar to sign
fiscal *m.* & *f.* prosecutor; district attorney
flaco skinny, thin
flan *m.* caramel custard
flor *f.* flower
florero *m.* vase
flota *f.* fleet
foca *f.* seal
foto *f.* picture; **sacar (qu) fotos** to take pictures
fotógrafo(-a) photographer
fracaso *m.* failure
francés(-esa) French
frase *f.* sentence
frecuentemente frequently, often
freno *m.* brake
frente *m.* front; **frente a** opposite, in front of
frijol *m.* bean
frío cold
frito fried
frontera *f.* border, frontier
fruta *f.* fruit
fuego *m.* fire
fuerte strong
fuerza *f.* strength
fugitivo *m.* fugitive
fumar to smoke
función *f.* show, performance
funcionar to work
fútbol *m.* soccer; **fútbol americano** football

gafas *f. pl.* glasses; **gafas de sol** sunglasses
ganador(-ora) winner
ganga *f.* bargain
ganar to win; to earn
garganta *f.* throat
gastar to spend
gato *m.* cat
gaviota *f.* seagull
gazpacho *m.* cold, fresh vegetable soup
general general; **por lo general** in general
generalmente generally
generoso generous
gente *f.* people
gerente *m.* & *f.* manager
giro postal postal money order
gitano(-a) Gypsy
globo *m.* balloon
golpe *m.* blow
goma *f.* rubber
gordo fat
gordura *f.* fat, fatness
gorra *f.* cap
grabar to record
gracias thanks; **dar** (*irr.*) **las gracias** to thank
gracioso funny
grado *m.* degree; stage
graduarse to graduate
grande large, big; great
gratuitamente free (of charge)
gripe *f.* flu
gritar to yell, scream, cry out
grito *m.* scream, cry
grupo *m.* group
guacamole *m.* avocado dip

guante *m.* glove
guapo handsome
guardafango *m.* fender
guardar to keep
guía *m. & f.* guide, *f.* guidebook
guiar to guide; to drive
gusano *m.* worm
gustar to like
gusto *m.* taste

haber (*inf.*) to have
había there was, there were
hábil skillful
habitación *f.* room
hábito *m.* habit
habla *f.* speech
hace ago; **hace poco** a little while ago
hacer (*irr.*) to do, make; **hacer calor** to be hot; **hacer caso de** to pay attention to; **hacer pedazos** to break into pieces; **hacer sol** to be sunny; **hacer un viaje** to take a trip; **hacerse** to become
hacia towards
hada *f.* (**el hada**) fairy
hasta until, up to; as far as
hay there is, there are; **hay que** it is necessary, one must
helado *m.* ice cream
herencia *f.* inheritance
hermana *f.* sister
hermano *m.* brother
hierba *f.* grass
hielo *m.* ice; **patinar en el hielo** to ice skate
hija *f.* daughter
hijo *m.* son; *pl.* sons, children
hipnotismo *m.* hypnotism
hipnotista *m. & f.* hypnotist
hogar *m.* home
hoja *f.* leaf
hombre *m.* man
hombro *m.* shoulder
honesto honest
horario *m.* schedule
hormiga *f.* ant
horno *m.* oven
hoy today; **hoy día** nowadays; **de hoy en ocho días** a week from today; **de hoy en quince días** two weeks from today
huella *f.* track, footprint; **huella digital** fingerprint
huevo *m.* egg

idear to devise, think of
idioma *m.* language
iglesia *f.* church
ignorancia *f.* ignorance
igual equal, the same, similar
ilimitado unlimited
impedir to impede, prevent
impermeable *m.* raincoat
importar to matter; **¿qué importa?** what difference does it make?
impuesto *m.* tax
impulsivo impulsive
incendio *m.* fire
inclinarse to bend over, bend down
increíble unbelievable
indicar (qu) to indicate, point out
individuo *m.* individual
inesperado unexpected
influencia *f.* influence
ingeniero(-era) engineer
inglés(-esa) English
ingrediente *m.* ingredient
iniciar to start, initiate
inseguridad *f.* insecurity
invierno *m.* winter
ir (*irr.*) to go; **irle bien (a una persona)** to go well; **irse** to go away, leave; **le va bien** it fits you well; **¡qué va!** no way!, nonsense!; **vamos a** let's
isla *f.* island
izquierdo left

jabón *m.* soap
jamás never, not ever
jarabe *m.* syrup; **jarabe para la tos** cough syrup
jardín *m.* garden
jirafa *f.* giraffe
jonrón *m.* homerun
joven *m. & f.* young man, young woman; *adj.* young
joya *f.* jewel
joyería *f.* jewelry store
juego *m.* game; set
juez *m. & f.* judge
jugador(-ora) player
jugar (ue, gu) to play
jugo *m.* juice
juguete *m.* toy
juntos together
jurar to swear
justamente precisely, exactly
justo just, fair
juvenil juvenile

lado *m.* side; **al lado** next to, beside; **al otro lado** on the other side; **de al lado** next
ladrar to bark
ladrillo *m.* brick
ladrón *m.* thief
lago *m.* lake
lámpara *f.* lamp
lana *f.* wool
largo long
lavadora *f.* washer
lavaplatos *m.* dishwasher
lavar to wash; **lavarse** to get washed, wash oneself
leche *f.* milk
legumbre *f.* vegetable
lejos far (away); **a lo lejos** in the distance
lengua *f.* tongue; language
lentamente slowly
leopardo *m.* leopard
letra *f.* letter; lyrics
letrero *m.* sign
levantar to lift, raise; **levantarse** to get up
libra *f.* pound
libre free
librero *m.* bookcase
libreta *f.* notebook
licor *m.* liquor
líder *m.* leader
liebre *f.* hare
liga *f.* league
ligero light
limpiar to clean
listo ready
llamada *f.* call
llamar to call; **llamarse** to be named, to be called
llanta *f.* tire
llegar (gu) to arrive
llevar to wear; to carry, take; **llevarse** to take away; **llevarse bien** to get along

llover (ue) to rain
local *m.* place, quarters
loción *f.* lotion
loco crazy
lucha *f.* fight; **lucha libre** wrestling
luego soon, then, later; **hasta luego** see you later
lugar *m.* place; **tener** (*irr.*) **lugar** to take place
lujoso luxurious
luna *f.* moon
luz *f.* light

madera *f.* wood
maestro(-a) teacher; master; **maestro de ceremonias** TV host, master of ceremonies
magia *f.* magic
magnífico magnificent, wonderful
mago *m.* magician
maíz *m.* corn
mal badly, poorly
maleducado ill-mannered, rude
maleta *f.* suitcase
maletero *m.* trunk
maletín *m.* briefcase; small bag
malo bad
manchado stained
manejar to drive
manera *f.* manner
manga *f.* sleeve
maniquí *m.* mannequin
mano *f.* hand
manta *f.* blanket
manzana *f.* apple
mañana tomorrow; **pasado mañana** the day after tomorrow
mapa *m.* map
máquina *f.* machine
mar *m.* ocean, sea
marca *f.* brand
marido *m.* husband
mariposa *f.* butterfly
mariscos *m. pl.* shellfish; **zarzuela de mariscos** *f.* shellfish stew
martes Tuesday
más more, most
matar to kill
matemáticas *f. pl.* mathematics
matrimonio *m.* married couple, husband and wife, marriage
mayonesa *f.* mayonnaise
mayor greater, greatest; older, oldest
medianoche *f.* midnight
medio half
medio *m.* means
medir (i) to measure
mejor better, best
mejorarse to get better
memoria *f.* memory; **aprender de memoria** to learn by heart; **saber** (*irr.*) **de memoria** to know by heart
mencionar to mention, name
menor least, slightest; younger, youngest
menos less
mensual monthly
mentir (ie) to lie
mentira *f.* lie
mentiroso(-a) liar
mes *m.* month; **al mes** per month
mesero *m.* waiter
mesita *f.* small table; **mesita de café** coffee table; **mesita de noche** night table
meter to place, to put in
método *m.* method
metro *m.* subway
mexicano Mexican
mi my
miedo *m.* fear; **tener** (*irr.*) **miedo** to be afraid
miembro *m.* & *f.* member
mientras while
mil a thousand
milla *f.* mile
millón *m.* a million
mirar to look at; **mirarse** to look at oneself
mismo same; **lo mismo** the same thing; **ahora mismo** right now; **sí mismo** himself, herself; **ti mismo** yourself
moda *f.* fashion, style; **de moda** in fashion
mojado wet
moneda *f.* coin
monje *m.* monk
mono *m.* monkey
monopatín *m.* skateboard
montaña *f.* mountain
montar to mount; **montar a caballo** to ride a horse; **montar en bicicleta** to ride a bicycle
morder (ue) to bite
morir (ue) to die
mosca *f.* fly
mostrar (ue) to show
moto *f.* (from **motocicleta**) motorcycle
motor *m.* engine, motor
mover(se) (ue) to move
movimiento *m.* movement
mucho much, a lot; **muchos** many
mudanza *f.* moving
mueble *m.* piece of furniture; *pl.* furniture
mueblería *f.* furniture store
muerto *m.* dead man
mujer *f.* woman
multa *f.* ticket, fine; **poner** (*irr.*) **una multa** to issue a ticket
mundial world
murciélago *m.* bat (animal)
mundo *m.* world; **por todo el mundo** everywhere; **todo el mundo** everybody
muy very

nacer to be born
nada nothing
nadar to swim
nadie nobody
naranja *f.* orange
natación *f.* swimming
natilla *f.* soft custard
nave *f.* ship, vessel; **nave espacial** spaceship
navegar to sail
Navidad *f.* Christmas
necesitar to need
negro black; **de negro** in black
nervioso nervous
nevar (ie) to snow
nevera *f.* ice box, refrigerator
ni neither, nor
ninguno no, not any
niño(-a) child; **de niño** as a child
nivel *m.* level

noche *f.* night; **esta noche** tonight; **por la noche** at night
norteamericano North American
nota *f.* note; grade
noticia *f.* news item; **noticias** news
novela *f.* novel; **novela policíaca** detective story
noveno ninth
novia *f.* bride
nube *f.* cloud
nuestro our
nuevo new
número *m.* number
nunca never, not ever

obedecer to obey
objeto *m.* object
obstante: no obstante nevertheless
obtener to obtain
octavo eighth
ocupado busy
ocurrir to happen
oficina *f.* office
ofrecer to offer
oído *m.* ear
oír (*irr.*) to hear
ojo *m.* eye
ola *f.* wave
onza *f.* ounce
opuesto opposite; opposed
órbita *f.* orbit
orden *m.* order
ordinario ordinary, common
oreja *f.* ear
orilla *f.* shore, bank
oro *m.* gold
oscuro dark
oso *m.* bear
otro other

paciencia *f.* patience
paella *f.* yellow rice with saffron, meat, seafood, and vegetables
pagar (gu) to pay
página *f.* page
pago *m.* payment
país *m.* country
pájaro *m.* bird
pala *f.* shovel
palabra *f.* word
palmera *f.* palm tree
pan *m.* bread
panadero(-era) baker
pantalones *m. pl.* pants
pantera *f.* panther
pantufla *f.* slipper
pañuelo *m.* handkerchief; **pañuelo de papel** tissue
papa *f.* potato
papagayo *m.* cockatoo
papel *m.* paper; **papel higiénico** toilet paper
para for, (in order) to
parabrisas *m.* windshield
parachoques *m.* bumper
parada *f.* stop; **parada de autobús** bus stop
paraguas *m. sing. & pl.* umbrella
paraíso *m.* paradise, heaven
parar to stop
parecer to seem; **al parecer** apparently; **¿qué le parece?** what do you think?
parecido similar
pareja *f.* couple, pair
parte *f.* part; **en cualquier parte** anywhere; **en todas partes** everywhere
partida *f.* certificate; **partida de matrimonio** marriage certificate; **partida de nacimiento** birth certificate
partido *m.* game, match
pasado *m.* past; **el lunes (mes, verano, año) pasado** last Monday (month, summer, year)
pasaje *m.* ticket, pass
pasajero(-era) passenger
pasaporte *m.* passport
pasar to pass; to spend (time); to happen; **¿qué pasa?** what's going on?, what's up?; **pase por aquí** come this way
paseo *m.* stroll, walk; **dar** (*irr.*) **un paseo** to take a walk
pasillo *m.* corridor, lobby, hall
pasta *f.* paste; **pasta de dientes** toothpaste
pastel *m.* cake, pastry
pastilla *f.* tablet; **pastilla para la tos** cough drop
pata *f.* animal leg or foot
patata *f.* potato
patín *m.* skate
patinaje *m.* skating
patinar to skate
patrulla *f.* police squad car
pavo *m.* turkey
payaso(-a) clown
paz *f.* peace
peatón *m.* pedestrian
pedir (i) to order, ask for, request; **pedir prestado** to borrow
peinar to comb; **peinarse** to comb one's hair
peine *m.* comb
pelear to fight
película *f.* film
peligroso dangerous
pelo *m.* hair
pelota *f.* ball
peluquero(-era) hairdresser
pena *f.* sorrow; **¡qué pena!** what a shame!
pensar (ie) to think
pequeño small, little
perder (ie) to lose
periódico *m.* newspaper
periodista *m. & f.* reporter, journalist
perito *m.* expert
perla *f.* pearl
permiso *m.* permission; permit
permitir to permit
pero but
perro *m.* dog
perseguir (i, g) to pursue
pesa *f.* weight; **levantar pesas** to lift weights
pesadilla *f.* nightmare
pesado heavy
pesar to weigh
pescado *m.* fish
pescar (qu) to fish, go fishing
peso *m.* weight
picante hot (spicy)
pie *m.* foot; **pie cuadrado** square foot
piedra *f.* stone
piel *f.* skin; leather
pijama *m.* pajama
píldora *f.* pill
piloto *m.* pilot

pingüino *m.* penguin
piraña *f.* piranha
pirata *m.* pirate
piscina *f.* swimming pool
piso *m.* floor
pistola *f.* pistol
placa *f.* license plate
planear to plan
planeta *m.* planet
planta *f.* plant
plata *f.* silver
plato *m.* dish, plate
playa *f.* beach
plaza *f.* public square
plazo *m.* installment
poción *f.* potion
poco little
poder (ue) (*irr.*) to be able, can
poder *m.* power
poema *m.* poem
policía *m.* & *f.* police officer; *f.* police force
pollo *m.* chicken
ponche *m.* punch
poner (*irr.*) to put; **ponerse** to put on
por for, by, through, along; **¿por qué?** why?
porque because
poseer to possess
posible possible; **todo lo posible** everything possible
postre *m.* dessert
precio *m.* price
precioso lovely, beautiful
preferido favorite
preferir (ie) to prefer
pregunta *f.* question; **hacer** (*irr.*) **una pregunta** to ask a question
preguntar to ask
premio *m.* prize
prenda *f.* article of clothing
prendedor *m.* pin, brooch
preocupado worried
preocuparse to worry
preparar to prepare
prestado: pedir prestado to borrow
prestar to lend; **prestar atención** to pay attention
primerísimo foremost
primero first
primo(-a) cousin
principio *m.* beginning; **al principio** at the beginning
principiante *m.* & *f.* beginner
probar (ue) to try; **probarse** to try on
problema *m.* problem
programa *m.* program
programador(-ora) computer programmer
promesa *f.* promise
pronto quickly, soon; **por lo pronto** meanwhile
propiedad *f.* property
proprietario(-a) owner
propio own
proponer (*irr.*) to propose
propósito *m.* purpose; **a propósito** by the way
proteger (j) to protect
próximo next
psiquiatra *m.* & *f.* psychiatrist
publicar (qu) to publish
puerta *f.* door
pues well, then
puesto *m.* job, position
pulsera *f.* bracelet; **reloj de pulsera** *m.* wristwatch
punto *m.* point; period; **en punto** on the dot

que that; **más que** more than; **¿qué?** what?
quedar to remain; to be (located); **quedarse** to stay, remain; **quedarse con** to keep
querer (ie) (*irr.*) to want, wish for; **querer decir** to mean
querido dear
¿quién? who?; **¿a quién?** whom?; **¿de quién?** whose?
quinto fifth
quiropráctica *f.* chiropractic
quitarse to take off
quizás perhaps, maybe

rana *f.* frog
rápido fast
raqueta *f.* racket
rascacielos *m. sing. & pl.* skyscraper
ratón *m.* mouse
raya *f.* stripe; **a rayas** striped
razón *f.* reason; **tener** (*irr.*) **razón** to be right; **no tener razón** to be wrong
reaccionar to react
realizar (c) to realize, fulfill
realmente really
receta *f.* prescription
recibir to receive; to go and meet
reciclamiento *m.* recycling
recientemente recently
recoger (j) to pick up; to gather
reconocer to recognize
recordar (ue) to remember
recostado leaning on; **estar** (*irr.*) **recostado** to be lying down
red *f.* net
refinado refined
reflejar to reflect
refresco *m.* soft drink; **refrescos** refreshments
refrigerador *m.* refrigerator
refrito refried
regalar to give (away)
regalo *m.* present, gift
regla *f.* rule; ruler
regresar to return
reír(se) (í) to laugh
relajarse to relax
reloj *m.* watch; **reloj de pulsera** wristwatch
remar to row
remitir to send
rendido exhausted
repente: de repente suddenly
repetir (i) to repeat
reservado reserved
resolver (ue) to resolve, solve
respetar to respect
respuesta *f.* answer, response
restar to subtract
restaurante *m.* restaurant
resultado *m.* result
retraso *m.* delay
revelar to reveal
revisar to check, go through
revista *f.* magazine
rey *m.* king
ridículo ridiculous
rincón *m.* corner
río *m.* river
robar to steal

robo *m.* theft
roca *f.* stone, rock
rodear to surround
rodilla *f.* knee
rojo red
romper to break
ropa *f.* clothes
rubí *m.* ruby
rubio blond
rueda *f.* wheel

sábado Saturday
saber (*irr.*) to know
sacar (qu) to take out, remove; to get (grade); **sacar fotos** to take pictures
saco *m.* coat, jacket; **saco de sport** sport jacket
sal *f.* salt
sala *f.* living room; **sala de conciertos** concert hail
salir to go out, leave
salsa *f.* sauce
saltamontes *m. sing. & pl.* grasshopper
saltar to jump
salud *f.* health
saludar to greet, say hello
salvaje savage, wild
salvavidas *m. & f., sing. & pl.* lifeguard
satélite *m.* satellite
secadora *f.* dryer
sección *f.* section
seda *f.* silk
seguir (i) to follow; to continue
según according to
segundo *m.* second; *adj.* second
seguro sure, certain
sello *m.* stamp
semáforo *m.* traffic light
semana *f.* week; **la semana pasada** last week; **la semana que viene** next week
señal *f.* signal, sign
sentado seated
sentar (ie) to seat; **sentarse** to sit down
sentido *m.* sense
sentimiento *m.* feeling
sentir(se) (ie) to feel; **lo siento** I'm sorry
séptimo seventh
sepultado buried
ser (*irr.*) to be; *m.* being
seriamente seriously
serie *f.* series
serio serious, reserved
serpiente *f.* snake, serpent
servir (i) to serve; to be useful; **¿en qué puedo servirle?** what can I do for you?
sexto sixth
si if
siempre always
siglo *m.* century
significar (qu) to mean
siguiente following
silla *f.* chair; **silla de playa** beach chair
sillón *m.* armchair
simpático nice, pleasant
sin without
sincero sincere
siquiera: ni siquiera not even
sirena *f.* siren
sitio *m.* place, spot
sobre on, on top of, over; about; *m.* envelope
sobrenatural supernatural
socorro *m.* help
sofa *m.* sofa, couch
sofisticado sophisticated
sol *m.* sun; **tomar el sol** to sunbathe
solamente only
soldado *m.* soldier
solo only, just
sólo alone
soltero single
sombra *f.* shadow
sombrero *m.* hat
sombrilla *f.* umbrella, sunshade
sonar (ue) to sound, ring; **sonarse las narices** to blow one's nose
sonido *m.* sound
sonreir (í) to smile
soñar (ue) con to dream of
sopa *f.* soup
sorprender to surprise
sortija *f.* ring
su his, her, its, your, their
subir to climb, to go (come) up
subterráneo *m.* subway
sucio dirty
sudadera *f.* warm-up suit
suegra *f.* mother-in-law
sueldo *m.* salary
sueño *m.* sleep; dream; **tener** (*irr.*) **sueño** to be sleepy
suerte *f.* luck; **tener suerte** to be lucky
suéter *m.* sweater
suficiente enough
sumar to add (up)
supuesto: por supuesto of course, naturally
suspiro *m.* sigh; **echar un suspiro** to sigh

tabla *f.* board
tacaño stingy
talla *f.* size
también also
tampoco neither; **ni yo tampoco** neither do I
tanque *m.* tank
tanto so much; **tanto como** as much as
tarde *f.* afternoon late; **más tarde** later; **por la tarde** in the afternoon
tarea *f.* homework
tarjeta *f.* card; **tarjeta** postal postcard
tela *f.* fabric, material
telaraña *f.* spider's web, cobweb
teléfono *m.* telephone; **hablar por teléfono** to be on the phone; **llamar por teléfono** to telephone
televidente *m. & f.* TV viewer
televisor *m.* TV set
temor *m.* fear, dread
temprano early
tener (irr.) to have; **tener * años** to be * years old; **tener cuidado** to be careful; **tener miedo** to be afraid; **tener sueño** to be sleepy
teniente *m. & f.* lieutenant
tercero third
terciopelo *m.* velvet
terco stubborn
terminar to finish, end
termómetro *m.* thermometer

ternera *f.* veal
terrestre terrestrial, earthly
tesoro *m.* treasure
testigo *m.* & *f.* witness
tiburón *m.* shark
tiempo *m.* time; weather
tienda *f.* store
tierno tender
tierra *f.* earth; land
tímido shy
tinta *f.* ink
típico typical, traditional
tipo *m.* type
tirar to throw
títere *m.* puppet
toalla *f.* towel
tocar (qu) to touch; to knock; to play (musical instrument); **tocar a la puerta** to knock on the door; **tocar madera** to knock on wood
todavía yet
todo all, everything; **todos** everybody
tomar to take; to drink; **tomar asiento** to take a seat; **tomar el sol** to sunbathe
tontería *f.* silly thing, foolishness; **tonterías** nonsense
tonto foolish, silly
toro *m.* bull
torta *f.* cake
tortilla *f.* cornmeal pancake; omelette
tortuga *f.* turtle
tos *f.* cough
toser to cough
trabajo *m.* work
traer (*irr.*) to bring
traje *m.* suit; **traje de baño** bathing suit
tránsito *m.* traffic
transporte *m.* transportation
tratar to treat, to deal with; **tratar de** to try to
trato *m.* deal
través: a través through
travieso mischievous
trébol *m.* clover
triste sad
truco *m.* trick
tubo *m.* tube

últimamente lately
último last
único original, unique, only
universitario university (*adj.*)
usar to use; to wear
uso *m.* use; **de uso** used
utilizar (c) to use

vacaciones *f. pl.* vacation, holidays
vacío empty
vacunación *f.* vaccination
valer to be worth; **más vale** (it's) better
valiente brave
valor *m.* value
vara *f.* stick
variedades *f. pl.* variety show
varios several, some
vaso *m.* glass
vecino(-a) neighbor
vegetal *m.* vegetable
vela *f.* sail
veloz fast, quick
venda *f.* bandage
vendado bandaged; blind-folded
vendar to bandage
vendedor(-ora) salesperson
vender to sell
venir (*irr.*) to come; **el mes que viene** next month
venta *f.* sale
ventaja *f.* advantage; **llevar ventaja a** to have the advantage over
ventana *f.* window
ventanilla *f.* small window, car window
ver to see
verano *m.* summer
veras: de veras really, truly
verdad *f.* truth; **¿verdad?** isn't that so?
verde green
vestido *m.* dress
vestir (i) to dress; **vestirse** to get dressed
veterinario(-a) veterinarian
vez *f.* time; **en vez de** instead of; **otra vez** again; **por primera vez** for the first time; **tal vez** perhaps
viajar to travel
viaje *m.* trip; **viaje espacial** space voyage; **hacer** (*irr.*) **un viaje** to take a trip
víctima *f.* victim
vida *f.* life; **mi vida** my love (term of endearment)
viejo old
viernes Friday
visa *f.* visa
visita *f.* visitor; visit
visitar to visit
vitamina *f.* vitamin
viviente living
vivir to live
volante *m.* steering wheel
volar (ue) to fly
voleibol *m.* volleyball
volver (ue) to return, to go (come) back
vuelo *m.* flight
vuelta *f.* turn; **vuelta ciclista** long-distance cycle race

ya already
yodo *m.* iodine

zapatero(-era) shoemaker
zapatilla *f.* slipper
zapato *m.* shoe

English-Spanish Vocabulary

The English-Spanish Vocabulary includes only those words that occur in the English-to-Spanish exercises.

about sobre, acerca de
address dirección *f.*
advice consejo *m.*
afterwards después
ago hace
airplane avión *m.*
airport aeropuerto *m.*
all todo, todos
also también
always siempre
answer contestar
any cualquier; alguno; **not any** ninguno; **anymore** más
anything algo; **not anything** nada
appetizer entrada *f.*
armchair butaca *f.*, sillón *m.*
arrive llegar (gu)
ask preguntar; **ask for** pedir (i)
asleep dormido; **to fall asleep** dormirse (ue)
aspirin aspirina *f.*

baby bebé *m. & f.*
bad malo
baker panadero(-era)
barbecue barbacoa *f.*
baseball béisbol *m.*
bath baño *m.*; **to take a bath** bañarse
bathroom cuarto de baño *m.*
bathing suit traje de baño *m.*
be estar (*irr.*); ser (*irr.*)
beach playa *f.*
bear oso *m.*
beautiful bonito, precioso
because porque
bed cama *f.*; **to go to bed** acostarse (ue)
belt cinturón *m.*
best (el / la) mejor
bicycle bicicleta *f.*
body cuerpo *m.*
bookcase librero *m.*
bookshelf estante para libros *m.*
boot bota *f.*
brake freno *m.*
breakfast desayuno *m.*
bring traer (*irr.*)
brother hermano *m.*
brush cepillo *m.*; cepillarse
building edificio *m.*
bus autobús *m.*
but pero
butcher carnicero *m.*
buy comprar

cafeteria cafetería *f.*
call llamar
can poder (ue) (*irr.*)
candidate candidato(-a)
careful cuidadoso; **to be careful** tener (*irr.*) cuidado
carefully cuidadosamente
chain cadena *f.*
chair silla *f.*
champion campeón(-ona)
choose escoger (j)
city ciudad *f.*
close cerrar (ie)
clothes ropa *f.*
coat abrigo *m.*
cold frío; **to be cold** hacer (*irr.*) frío
comb peine *m.*; **to comb one's hair** peinarse
come venir (*irr.*); **come back** volver (ue), regresar
comfortable cómodo
comfortably cómodamente
concert concierto *m.*
correct corregir (i, j)
cost costar (ue)
cough tos *f.*; toser
country país *m.*
crazily locamente
criminal criminal *m. & f.*
crocodile cocodrilo *m.*
cruise crucero *m.*; **to take a cruise** hacer (*irr.*) un crucero
curtain cortina *f.*

dangerous peligroso
day día *m.*
deodorant desodorante *m.*
dessert postre *m.*
dining room comedor *m.*
dish plato *m.*
dog perro *m.*
door puerta *f.*
downtown centro *m.*
dress vestido; **to get dressed** vestirse (i)
dresser cómoda *f.*
dressing gown bata *f.*
driver chofer *m.*
during durante

early temprano
earn ganar
earth tierra *f.*

easily fácilmente
eat comer; **eat out** comer afuera
elect elegir (i, j)
embrace abrazar (c)
employee empleado(-a)
English inglés *m.*
enough suficiente
enter entrar
envelope sobre *m.*
every cada; **every day** todos los días; **every morning** todas las mañanas
example ejemplo *m.*
exhibit exhibición *f.*
explain explicar (qu)

face cara *f.*
family familia *f.*
fast rápido, rápidamente
father padre *m.*, papá *m.*
favorite preferido
fender guardafango *m.*
film película *f.*
fingerprint huella digital *f.*
firefighter bombero(-era)
first primero
fish pescar (qu)
follow seguir (1, g)
food comida *f.*
football fútbol *m.*
freezer congelador *m.*
friend amigo(-a)
fun diversión *f.*; **to have fun** divertirse (ie)
furniture muebles *m. pl.*

game partido *m.*; juego *m.*
gas gasolina *f.*
get up levantarse
giraffe jirafa *f.*
give dar (*irr.*)
go ir (*irr.*); **to go away** irse
good bueno
grandparents abuelos *m. pl.*

hair pelo *m.*
hairdresser peluquero(-era)
hand mano *f.*
happy contento
hat sombrero *m.*
have haber (*irr.*); tener (*irr.*); **to have to** tener que
headlight faro *m.*, luz *f.*
helmet casco *m.*
here aquí
hike dar (*irr.*) una caminata
homework tarea *f.*
hood cubierta *f.*, capó *m.*
hour hora *f.*
house casa *f.*
how? ¿cómo?; **how old are you?** ¿cuántos años tienes?
hundred cien

idea idea *f.*
intelligently inteligentemente
invite invitar
island isla *f.*

jacket chaqueta *f.*; **sports jacket** saco de sport *m.*
jail cárcel *f.*
job puesto *m.*, trabajo *m.*
judge juez *m.* & *f.*

knock (on the door) tocar (qu) a la puerta
know saber (*irr.*); **(to be acquainted with)** conocer

land aterrizar (c)
large grande
last último; **last summer** el verano pasado
lawyer abogado(-a)
learn aprender
leave salir, irse (*irr.*)
lend prestar
leopard leopardo *m.*
license plate placa *f.*
lie mentira *f.*
light luz *f.*
like gustar
listen escuchar
little pequeño, chico; poco
live vivir
long largo
look (at) mirar; **to look for** buscar (qu)
lot: a lot mucho
lotion loción *f.*; **suntan lotion** loción bronceadora
lunch almuerzo *m.*; **to have lunch** almorzar (ue, c)
magazine revista *f.*
mailbox buzón *m.*
mail carrier cartero(-era)
many muchos; **how many?** ¿cuántos?
married casado
meal comida *f.*
meat carne *f.*
menu menú *m.*
mirror espejo *m.*; **rear-view mirror** espejo retrovisor
mistake error *m.*
Monday lunes
money dinero *m.*
moon luna *f.*
morning mañana *f.*
mother madre *f.*, mamá *f.*
movies cine *m.*
much mucho; **how much?** ¿cuánto?

name nombre *m.*; **what's your name?** ¿cómo te llamas?
near cerca (de)
need necesitar
neighborhood barrio *m.*
neither tampoco; **neither . . . nor** ni . . . ni
never nunca, jamás
new nuevo
newspaper periódico *m.* diario *m.*
night noche *f.*
nobody nadie
none ninguno
nothing nada
now ahora

obtain conseguir (i, g)
often a menudo; frecuentemente
oil aceite *m.*
old viejo; **older, oldest** mayor; **to be . . . years old** tener (*irr.*) . . . años; **how old are you?** ¿cuántos años tienes?
one un, uno
only sólo, solamente
open abrir
outing excursión *f.*

pail cubo *m.*
pajama pijama *m.*
palm tree palmera *f.*

pants pantalones *m. pl.*
parents padres *m. pl.*
party fiesta *f.*
people gente *f.*
perfectly perfectamente
photographer fotógrafo(-afa)
picture foto *f.*; **to take pictures** sacar (qu) fotos
pilot piloto *m. & f.*
place lugar; **to take place** tener (*irr.*) lugar
planet planeta *m.*
plate plato *m.*
play jugar (ue, gu)
player jugador(-ora)
political político
postcard tarjeta postal *f.*
prefer preferir (ie)
professional profesional
programmer programador (-ora)
protect proteger (j)
pursue perseguir (i, g)
put poner (*irr.*); **to put on** ponerse
pyramid pirámide *f.*

quickly rápidamente; pronto
quietly en silencio, sin hacer ruido

rain llover (ue)
raincoat impermeable *m.*, gabardina *f.*
ready listo; **to be ready** estar (*irr.*) listo
really realmente
reporter periodista *m. & f.*
ring anillo *m.*, sortija *f.*
river río *m.*
robbery robo *m.*
room cuarto *m.*
row remar
rubber goma *f.*
rug alfombra *f.*
rule regla *f.*
ruler regla *f.*
run correr; **to run away** escaparse

sailboat barco de vela *m.*
sand arena *f.*
sandcastle castillo de arena *m.*
say decir (*irr.*)
scream gritar
sea mar *m.*
seashell concha *f.*
see ver
seriously seriamente
serve servir (i)
shark tiburón *m.*
shine brillar
shirt camisa *f.*
shoe zapato *m.*
shoemaker zapatero(-era)
shovel pala *f.*
sister hermana *f.*
sit (down) sentarse (ie)
ski esquiar
sleep dormir (ue)
slipper pantufla *f.*, zapatilla *f.*
snake culebra *f.*, serpiente *f.*
soap jabón *m.*
soccer fútbol *m.*
sock calcetín *m.*, media *f.*
somebody alguien
something algo
soon pronto
sorry perdón; **I'm sorry** lo siento
soup sopa *f.*
speak hablar
spider araña *f.*
squirrel ardilla *f.*
stamp estampilla *f.*, sello *m.*
star estrella *f.*
station estación *f.*; **police station** estación de policía
steering wheel volante *m.*
stop parar; parada *f.*
store tienda *f.*
story cuento *m.*, historia *f.*
stove estufa *f.*
strong fuerte
study estudiar
style moda; **in style** de moda
summer verano *m.*
sun sol *m.*
sunbathe tomar el sol
Sunday domingo
sunglasses gafas de sol *f. pl.*
sweater suéter *m.*
swim nadar
swimming pool piscina *f.*
syrup jarabe *m.*; **cough syrup** jarabe para la tos

table mesa *f.*; **coffee table** mesita de café; **night table** mesita de noche
take tomar; llevar; **to take away** llevarse; **to take off** quitarse
tank tanque *m.*
team equipo *m.*
tell decir (*irr.*); contar (ue)
thermometer termómetro *m.*
there ahí, allí
thief ladrón *m.*
thing cosa *f.*
tie corbata *f.*
tiger tigre *m.*
time tiempo *m.*; vez *f.*; **at what time?** ¿a qué hora?; **on time** a tiempo
tire llanta *f.*
tissue pañuelo de papel *m.*
today hoy
toilet paper papel higiénico *m.*
tomorrow mañana
too también
toothbrush cepillo de dientes *m.*
toothpaste pasta de dientes *f.*
towel toalla *f.*
train tren *m.*
travel viajar
tree árbol *m.*
trip viaje *m.*
trunk maletero *m.*
t-shirt camiseta *f.*
Tuesday martes
turkey pavo *m.*
turtle tortuga *f.*

umbrella paraguas *m. & f.*; sombrilla *f.*
underneath debajo de
understand comprender, entender (ie)
undress desvestirse (i)
use usar, utilizar

vacation vacaciones *f. pl.*
vase florero *m.*
very muy
vest chaleco *m.*
veterinarian veterinario(-a)
victim víctima *f.*
visit visitar

waiter mesero *m.*; camarero *m.*
wake up despertarse (ie)
wall pared *f.*
want querer (ie) (*irr.*)
wash lavar; **to wash oneself** lavarse
watch mirar
wear llevar, usar
weekend fin de semana *m.*
well bien
whale ballena *f.*
what? ¿qué?
wheel rueda *f.*
when cuando; **when?** ¿cuándo?
where? ¿dónde?; **where (to)?** ¿adónde?
which? ¿cuál? ¿qué?
who? ¿quién?
whole entero, todo
whom ¿a quién?
whose? ¿de quién?
why? ¿por qué?
window ventana *f.*
with con
word palabra *f.*
work funcionar; trabajar
write escribir

year año *m.*
yesterday ayer
young joven; **younger**, **youngest** menor, más pequeño; **young man** joven *m.*; **young woman** joven *f.*

zoo (parque) zoológico *m.*

Grammatical Index

Topical Index